MORE PRAISE FOR
RAISING BABY GREEN

"I urge parents, old and new, to read this book and to keep it on a visible bookshelf, so that these messages of simple change can be passed on until we've raised a generation of healthy children on a balanced and healthy planet."

Sara Snow, television host and green living expert;
host of "Get Fresh with Sara Snow" on *Discovery Health*

"This book will be the bible of the Green Baby Movement. It's written by the Web's number one pediatrician and one of the country's most effective champions for protecting kids and the rest of us from environmental contaminants."

Ken Cook, president, Environmental Working Group

"Alan Greene is a thoughtful pediatrician offering practical wisdom to parents. Even the small changes he recommends can make a big difference."

Rosalind Creasy, author, *The Complete Book of Edible Landscaping*

"In easy-to-understand terms, Dr. Greene explains what nature intended: healthy babies equal healthy lives. This is the child-raising map you're looking for!"

Steve Demos, founder and retired CEO, Silk Soymilk

"A wonderful guide to raising healthy babies and children. Brings together science, expert opinion, and experiential knowledge in an easy-to-follow book."

Philip Lee, M.D.; former U.S. Assistant Secretary of Health;
Chancellor of the University of California at San Francisco;
professor, Stanford University

"I wish I'd had this book when my daughter was born. Dr. Greene's ability to communicate how nutrition, organics, and the environment impact health puts him in a class all by himself."

Akasha Richmond, organic chef at the restaurant Akasha;
author, *Hollywood Dish*

"Loaded with illustrations and hundreds of product evaluations, this is a unique package for parents!"

Anthony Zolezzi, author, *Chemical-Free Kids*

"A tool kit and manifesto for moms and dads who want to tilt the odds in favor of five fingers, five toes, and a brain that can cope with what is coming next."

Charles Benbrook, Ph.D.; chief scientist,
The Organic Center

"Sixteen years ago, we lost our only child at age five to a nonhereditary cancer that we believe could have been prevented. Dr. Greene's book is more than a practical green guide; it is the only lifestyle that can assure the essential first steps to a lifetime of well-being."

Nancy and James Chuda, founders of (CHEC)
Healthy Child Healthy World and
The Colette Chuda Environmental Fund

"With this common-sense, science-backed book, difficult questions find thoughtful, experienced, truly intelligent answers. Our future depends upon parents making smarter decisions. Get this book to everyone you know with children."

Doug Greene, cofounder, New Hope Natural Media

"Simple tips in the right direction for a Healthy Child in a Healthy World— and it's easier than you think."

Christopher Gavigan, CEO, Healthy Child
Healthy World (formerly CHEC)

"The best green baby book I've ever read."

Christopher Moore, best-selling author, *Fluke*

"Dr. Alan Greene is a pioneer in teaching parents the connection between a healthy environment, organic products, and healthy, vibrant, happy babies."

Steven Hoffman, interim executive director,
The Organic Center; cofounder, *LOHAS Journal*
and the LOHAS conference

"An informed, practical, and hopeful guide to having a healthy baby. This book can make a difference not only in your baby's health but also in the health of your whole family, your community, and our beautiful earth."

Michael Lerner, Ph.D.; president, Commonweal;
and cofounder, The Collaborative on Health and
the Environment

Raising
Baby
Green

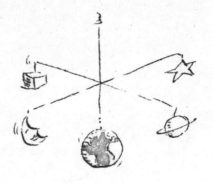

JB JOSSEY-BASS

Raising Baby Green

The Earth-Friendly Guide to
Pregnancy, Childbirth, and Baby Care

ALAN GREENE, M.D.

with JEANETTE PAVINI and THERESA FOY DiGERONIMO

ILLUSTRATIONS by VAL LAWTON

BICENTENNIAL
1807
WILEY
2007
BICENTENNIAL

John Wiley & Sons, Inc.

Published by Jossey-Bass
A Wiley Imprint
989 Market Street, San Francisco, CA 94103-1741   www.josseybass.com

Wiley Bicentennial logo: Richard J. Pacifico

Jossey-Bass books and products are available through most bookstores. To contact Jossey-Bass directly call our Customer Care Department within the U.S. at 800-956-7739, outside the U.S. at 317-572-3986, or fax 317-572-4002.

Jossey-Bass also publishes its books in a variety of electronic formats. Some content that appears in print may not be available in electronic books.

Library of Congress Cataloging-in-Publication Data
Raising baby green : the earth-friendly guide to pregnancy, childbirth, and baby care / Alan Greene . . . [et al.]. — 1st ed.
     p. cm.
   Includes bibliographical references and index.
   ISBN-13: 978-0-7879-9622-2 (pbk.)
   1. Pregnant women—Health and hygiene. 2. Pregnancy—Environmental aspects. 3. Pregnancy—Nutritional aspects. 4. Infants—Care—Environmental aspects. I. Greene, Alan R., date.
   RG525.R233 2007
   618.2—dc22   2007023342

Printed in the United States of America
FIRST EDITION
PB Printing   10   9   8   7   6   5   4   3   2   1

Contents

Acknowledgments

THIS BOOK HAS TRULY been a team effort, from start to finish. Cheryl Rinzler had the idea for the book in the first place. Cheryl and her husband, Alan Rinzler, of Jossey-Bass met with my wife, Cheryl, and me, and we all agreed we wanted to work on it together. Rinzler assembled the other key players, including the marvelous writer Theresa Foy DiGeronimo and our friend and consumer expert Jeanette Pavini.

Thanks to those who read our manuscript and made many helpful comments and criticisms, including Dr. Stacie Bering, Dr. Jon Bernstein, Cheryl Greene, Dr. John Greene, Gwen Greene, Dr. Howard Gruber, Chantal Guyette, and Cheryl Rinzler.

And special thanks to those who are making the green movement something we can write about. Basic science researchers, organic farmers, political leaders, visionaries, nonprofit groups, entrepreneurs, artisans, inventors, clothing designers, manufacturers, distributors, retailers, small companies, large corporations, physicians, nurses, doulas, lactation consultants, parents, grandparents, engineers, and grocers—all are working together to build a sustainable future for our children. I'm deeply grateful to my colleagues at the Environmental Working Group, the Environmental Media Association, Healthy Child Healthy World, and the Organic Center for getting the word out about the science and practice of sustainability.

Thanks to our publishers Jossey-Bass and John Wiley & Sons, including Debra Hunter, Paul Foster, Jennifer Wenzel, Mike Onorato, Seth Schwartz, Carol Hartland, Adrian Morgan, Jeff Puda, and Bev Butterfield.

I'd especially like to acknowledge Dr. Charles Benbrook, Dr. Jeff Bland, Michael Burbank, Domenica Catelli, Jim and Nancy Chuda, Theo Colburn, Ken Cook, Jesse Cool, Ann Cooper, Rosalind Creasy, Steve Demos, Katherine DiMatteo, Clark Driftmeier, Greg Engles, Ellen Feeney, Mark Fox, Michael Funk, Dr. Erica Frank, Christopher Gavigan, Anna Getty, Michelle Goolsby, Al Gore, Kim and Jason Graham-Nye, Cheryl Greene,

Doug Greene, Gary and Meg Hirshberg, Steven Hoffman, Jeffrey Hollander, Sonya Kugler, Sheryl Lamb, Dr. Phil Landrigan, Dr. Philip Lee, Dr. Michael Lerner, Debbie Levin, Susan Lintonsmith, Theresa Marquez, Bill McDonough, Melissa McGinnis, Blaine McPeak, Dr. Kathleen Merrigan, Bill and Sandra Nicholson, Dr. David Pimental, Nora Pouillon, Gil Pritchard, Donna Prizgintas, Dr. Stephan Rechtschaffen, Mark Retzloff, Akasha Richmond, Cindy Roberts, Walter Robb, Anthony and Sage Robbins, Peter Roy, Drake Sadler, Joseph Scalzo, Bob Scowcroft, Kelly Shea, Morris Shriftman, George Siemon, Niki Simoneaux, Dr. Shanna Swan, Alice Waters, James White, Dr. Andrew Weil, Caren Wilcox, Dr. Richard Wiles, Marci Zaroff, Anthony and Lisa Zolezzi, and too many other bold adventurers to name for their pioneering work and for teaching me so much about raising baby green.

ALAN GREENE

THANKS TO JOSH ZERKEL and Teresa Jung for help in research. I also want to thank the following people, and they know why! Sister Rita Marie, Rick, Nancy, John, Dee Dee, Dan, Ron, Tom, Theresa, Beau, June, Shirley, Andrew, Judy, Dianne, Candi, Sula, and Rita.

JEANETTE PAVINI

I WOULD LIKE TO acknowledge the help and direction I received from my lifelong friend Diane Korzinski, who was truly green long before I knew the value of the word. My daughter Colleen put in many long hours as my research assistant on this project and I would now like to thank her publicly for her help. And many thanks to all the various creative people who edited and contributed to the ideas in the book, including Cheryl Rinzler, Cheryl Greene, Alan Rinzler, and to the staff of Jossey-Bass, with whom I've worked these many years, particularly Jennifer Wenzel, Carol Hartland, Seth Schwartz, Karen Warner, Erik Thrasher, Paul Foster, Debra Hunter, and many others.

THERESA FOY DiGERONIMO

My wife, Cheryl Greene, and I dedicate this book to our children, Garrett, Kevin, Claire, and Austin; to our children's children; and to generations of children everywhere. May we leave the world for them an even better place than we found it.

—A. G.

To my father for showing me the meaning of integrity and to my mother for showing me the meaning of kindness. To Brandon, who has made parenting my greatest life lesson. To CBS 5 News for letting me tell stories that help consumers learn ways to save the environment. To Mark for making life so great. To Stacie for showing me what true courage is. To Mike, Ian, and Jim, my heroes, who have taught me to embrace every moment.

—J. P.

To my future grandchildren, who I hope one day will inherit a pure and sustainable planet.

—T.F.D.

The interior pages of this book are printed in a vegetable-based ink on 55-pound Cascades Rolland Enviro100 paper, which contains 100 percent recycled post-consumer fiber, is EcoLogo, processed chlorine free, and was manufactured using biogas energy.

Recycled post-consumer

Indicates that the product contains recycled materials that have been consumed and decontaminated to be reintroduced in the manufacturing process of a new product. The percentage under the sign indicates the proportion of recycled post-consumer fiber included.

Processed Chlorine Free

Certification mark of the Chlorine Free Product Association (CFPA), which identifies that no chlorine or chlorine compounds were used in the papermaking process.

EcoLogo

Certification mark of the Environmental Choice Program of Environment Canada, which identifies ecological products. Required criteria are green-house gas emissions, water and energy resources consumption, and use of recycled fiber.

Biogas

The paper manufacturing process uses the gas generated from the decomposition of waste buried in a landfill. This green energy helps to considerably reduce greenhouse gas emissions.

The cover stock for the book is New Leaf Kallima, 10 percent post-consumer fiber, with a minimum of 30 percent FSC (Forest Stewardship Council) certified virgin fiber and elemental chlorine free.

The binding is recyclable PUR (Poly Urethane Reactive).

Raising
Baby
Green

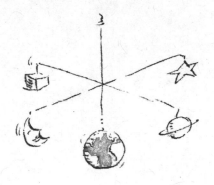

Introduction

WHY RAISE BABY GREEN?

HAVING A BABY CHANGES *everything*. Just thinking about welcoming a newborn changes your priorities and changes your awareness. A glass of wine, a daily prescription, or a cat's litter box each assumes new meaning.

Fortunately, nature has given us a powerful instinct to nurture and protect our children. For example, in many women the sense of smell is heightened during pregnancy, perhaps to make them more sensitive to what their baby needs and steer them away from what may be harmful. This awakened awareness could help shield the baby from malnutrition, spoiled food, and infection.

Today many parents are developing a heightened awareness of issues that could be important to their babies' futures. Whether it's when they first learn they're expecting, when they glimpse their baby on ultrasound, or when they first gaze into their baby's eyes, and she laughs out loud—somehow instinct and information combine as a catalyst for embracing a more eco-friendly lifestyle.

One of the goals of this book is to help you understand how the environment affects your baby and how raising your baby affects the environment. We're living at a time when environmentally conscious parenting is more possible than ever. We know so much more now about how to *raise* our babies in ways that can save energy, reduce greenhouse gases, and avoid toxic chemicals. Never before have we been better equipped to help babies thrive. Remember that every little thing we do can have an impact, so let's get started.

I have four children. My wife, Cheryl, and I have seen how this increased knowledge has inspired hundreds of new baby techniques and products. In my job as a pediatrician at Packard Children's Hospital at Stanford University School of Medicine over the last ten years, I've seen how clinical experience, science, research, and technology have increased the choices that doctors and parents can make, based on real knowledge about what's good for our babies and what isn't. But there's also an important new set of choices parents can make that can have a beneficial impact on the environment. What's good for our environment is also good for our babies.

This interest in making smart choices in technique, nutrition, and baby products has created a veritable "green baby movement." Parents with different backgrounds and diverse cultural, political, and religious beliefs understand the essential need to raise baby "green," and they want to know how. That's why I've been a champion and early pioneer in the green baby movement, joining with other pediatricians and professionals, experts, entrepreneurs, and devoted practitioners in the field of science, medicine, and agriculture, who want to provide healthier food, more effective medicine, and safer everyday products that have no known harm for babies. I'm one of many in this large, informal group spread across our country and beyond our borders in Canada, Europe, Australia, and elsewhere. We have been sharing ideas and information; organizing in person and over the Internet; going to meetings, trade shows, and conferences; and building Web sites (more than a million different people visit DrGreene.com each month).

Raising Baby Green is a result of this effort, a guide for parents to the techniques, foods, and new kinds of baby care products, equipment, furniture, and toys that are safer for babies and promote a sustainable environment.

As I tell my patients, family, and friends, "You can personally make a huge difference not only for your baby and your immediate environment but even on a much larger scale. You'd be surprised." In *Raising Baby Green* I'll show you the difference you can make on the planet every time you make a positive choice.

Let me give you one small example. When thinking about your new baby, you might dab a few sweet tears with a facial tissue. Or you might use a tissue to deal with a runny or stuffed-up nose that pregnancy can cause. But the tissue you reach for can make a difference! The Natural Resources Defense Council has calculated that if every household in the United States replaced just one box of conventional facial tissues (175 count) with 100% recycled ones, *together we could save 163,000 trees* for our children's world.[1] Many of these trees would be valuable virgin wood. Saving forests helps reduce global warming.

There are more benefits . . . Recycled tissues are made from previously used paper that would otherwise have gone into a landfill or burned in an incinerator. The people at Seventh Generation have calculated all of us switching just one box of facial tissues would save more than 453,000 cubic feet of landfill space (equal to a procession of 660 full garbage trucks) and avoid more than 10,600 pounds of pollution. (*www.seventhgen.com*). Along the way, it would also save more than 62 million gallons of water, a year's supply for 480 families of four.

And the benefits continue . . . The recycled tissues require considerably less energy to produce. Conventional tissues are often bleached with chlorine, which creates dangerous chemicals including dioxin, and other organochlorines. These accumulate in the environment, and in people and animals. If you make the smart choice and select tissues that have not been bleached with chlorine, you can help keep toxins out of your home and out of the larger environment.

All of this good from replacing just one box of facial tissues! Let's join together to make choices that are good for our babies and for the environment. Let's join the green baby movement.

What Is the Green Baby Movement?

In this book, *green* is a word representing a way of living in which we strive, with conscious awareness, to do things each day that in small, incremental steps improve the quality of our environment by preserving forests, cleaning air, husbanding soil, protecting wildlife, valuing dwindling resources, and at the same time maintaining our climate and sustaining our planet's crucial resources.

In this book, *sustainability* is a word that has been defined by the Brundtland Commission, led by the former Norwegian prime minister Gro Harlem Brundtland, as development that "meets the needs of the present without compromising the ability of future generations to meet their own needs." We wholeheartedly agree with this definition, which relates to the continuity of economic, social, institutional, and environmental aspects of human society, as well as the nonhuman environment.

So I have written this book to inspire, encourage, and guide you in this rewarding adventure of raising a "green" baby. I believe that we can travel this road together in ways that will protect and nurture our lives, our children's lives, and this increasingly fragile world we all share—and make "green" a tradition with an eternal life span.

The simple act of opening this book shows that you care about your baby and about the world around you.

This attitude *can* truly change the world.

Every Little Bit Helps

Raising your baby green doesn't require a revolution in your lifestyle or creature comforts. Do as much or as little as you want. For example, some mothers and fathers I know try to provide their baby with as much healthy, organic food as possible, avoiding artificial or overly processed foods. Others test their home drinking water and throw out all their toxic household cleaners (using services that can dispose of such liquids without polluting local waters). Others also watch out for safer baby toys, paints, floor coverings, cribs, and car seats. What you choose to do depends on the level of commitment you are able and ready to make.

I encourage you to take an approach that feels comfortable, that won't overwhelm or discourage you. You don't have to do each and every thing suggested in these pages to make a positive impact. Raising baby green is not an all-or-nothing proposition. It is a journey, one step at a time.

So pick the pieces of advice in this book that address your own concerns and needs. Try just one suggestion and see how you like the results. Then try another.

The guidelines in *Raising Baby Green* are meant to give you an easy, pleasant, doable, and practical approach based on the simple philosophy that we all should leave the campsite cleaner than it was when we arrived. I know that each of us can really make a difference, but I also know that none of us can do this alone.

This is a journey we all have to take together.

How I Became a Green Baby Pediatrician

As a medical doctor, I've always been interested in environmental issues and the way they affect one's health. But then I became a father. I found that each time I first looked into my newborn's eyes I was overwhelmed with a desire to make this world a better place for this child to live and grow. So for the last twenty years I have been on my own journey, learning about how to do that—about how to raise my children green.

The journey accelerated when a life-threatening illness in my family pushed us to re-evaluate ways to find good health. We made the choice to go organic and in so doing learned a lot more about the amazing personal benefits of good food.

Then, slowly, step-by-step, year after year, I began to recognize the many other ways that my daily choices affected my health and the health of my family. I remember the day I saw a trail of ants and grabbed a can of bug spray out of the kitchen cabinet. Suddenly I froze in my tracks as I made the connection between what I had already decided I didn't want on my foods and what I was now about to spray right in my own house.

On another day, as I was working in the garden, it suddenly struck me that the chemicals I was about to spread across my lawn to kill weeds and bugs were some of the very poisons I was trying to protect my family against. Not only that, but I was using a whole lot of water just to keep this little patch of grass going.

That was the day it occurred to me that the purity and preservation of the world's air and water and food was not something someone else would just take care of for me. I had to take responsibility for my own actions, in my own little world, because they could have a profound impact on this planet that my children would inherit. And, just as important, each time I made a decision to respect the environment in some small way, I was teaching this important lesson to my children as well. We're now in the process of shrinking our lawn and growing more of our own food—and using new technologies to decrease our water consumption.

How This Book Works

We know that many parents don't have a lot of time to sit around and study a book. As a father, husband, and pediatrician, I know how tired you can get and how you don't want to waste precious time ruminating over theories or big changes that require a lot of attention.

I have found that many parents of newborns focus on very basic needs, such as "What kind of diapers should we use?" or "What's the best kind of baby food for my baby?"

That's why this book has been designed so that you can read through it a little bit at a time or just skip to the issue at hand—to what you need to know about this very minute, without waiting! To find just what you need, look in the table of contents, which describes what's in every chapter, or look in the handy index at the end of the book.

I've organized the book so that there's a chapter for each "room" in your baby's life. For each room, I offer practical information based on the latest scientific research and progressive clinical practice.

This book has been prepared by a team of devoted and creative individuals, including researcher and writer Theresa Foy DiGeronimo; consumer expert Jeanette Pavini; my wife, Cheryl; and dedicated editor Alan Rinzler and his wife, Cheryl Rinzler, who had the original idea and title for this book and who contributed so many invaluable ideas and research every step of the way. I'm honored to be the leader of this team.

We're still learning more every day. With your help and input we can keep learning more about raising baby green, so e-mail me at RaisingBaby Green@DrGreene.com to send me your thoughts and let me know what new information or ideas you have.

Having a baby is a time of pivotal change. Your family is embarking on the journey of a lifetime together. Much will be spontaneous and unexpected, yet there is also something of a roadmap for this journey already written deep into your being. It's no accident that it occurs to so many parents who smoke that this is the time to stop. You want your body and your home to be welcoming and healthy environments. The future matters in a new and living way.

Wouldn't it be great if pregnancy also became the time, for instance, to stop overusing a bigger smokestack—fossil fuels—in our cars, our wall sockets, and in foods grown with oil-based pesticides and fertilizers. Let's let our children trigger deeper instincts, grander inspiration, and greater determination.

I know this will be a process of learning and growing for all of us far into the future, and I'm glad we can take this journey together.

Alan Greene, M.D., F.A.A.P.
Packard Children's Hospital
Stanford University School of Medicine, Palo Alto, California
DrGreene.com

THE
Womb

The first room your baby lives in is the pear-shaped organ called the uterus, which we know as the nurturing womb—that safe enclosure in the mother's body that separates the developing fetus from the outer world. In many ways, if you make the right choices, the womb can be the greenest room on the planet. The womb is a warm and comforting place where we have all been rocked, fed, and snuggled. It supplies with natural efficiency the food, water, oxygen, hormones, vitamins and minerals, and complex brew of neurological developmental messages needed by every baby to flourish in safety and good health.

The Greenest Room on the Planet

THE WOMB IS AN incredible piece of living engineering that provides an ideal environment for the amazing transformation that occurs during the forty weeks of gestation—a time when a baby's brain is developing faster than at any time later in life, at one point making one hundred thousand new neural connections an hour.

While growing and developing in this protected biosphere, your baby is intimately connected to the outside environment, including all the nutrients entering the womb, and the smells and sounds of the outer world, which have a lasting impact on her neurological, physical, mental, and anatomical development. These external influences provide you a once-in-a-lifetime opportunity to give your baby a strong and healthy foundation on which to grow. In fact, at no other time in your child's life will you have this degree of control over the way her environment influences her development.

The most direct way you can affect the health of your baby before he is even born is by making smart decisions about what you eat, drink, and absorb (through your lungs and skin), as well as what you introduce into the womb in the way of smells and sounds.

The swift passage of nutrients, protective proteins, and molecular messages through the umbilical cord from mother to baby offers the ideal opportunity to enrich your unborn baby's room in the womb and to contribute to the health of the planet your baby will inherit. You can do this each day through your own careful intake of organic foods and healthful beverages. Bring on the green!

The Umbilical Cord Connection

The umbilical cord is the living link through which a mother feeds her baby and removes its waste. The cord also becomes the conduit of an ongoing exchange, a silent conversation, in which hormones from the mother and the baby signal changes in each other's bodies.

The umbilical cord consists of three blood vessels—two umbilical arteries and one umbilical vein—embedded in slippery connective tissue called Wharton's jelly. The arteries spiral around the vein, giving the cord the toughness of a cable. At one end of the cord is the baby; at the other is the placenta.

The baby's heart pumps depleted blood out of its body through the umbilical arteries to the placenta, where the arteries divide into a network of tiny capillaries. The mother's blood in the placenta forms a free-flowing, living five-ounce lake about the size of a glass of red wine. This blood is refreshed completely three or four times each minute to supply the baby's needs. The replenished blood returns through the umbilical cord like a steady, unhindered river bringing the stuff of life to the fetus.

By the fourth month of pregnancy, seventy-five quarts of blood flow through this river every day, delivering oxygen-rich vital nutrients and removing waste. A typical blood cell will make a complete round trip every thirty seconds. By the time the baby is born, up to three hundred quarts of blood a day will flow through the umbilical cord.[1]

Three hundred quarts!

And you, the expectant mom, don't have to do anything out of the ordinary to make that happen as you prepare for the arrival of your little one. The human reproductive system is truly a remarkable thing.

However, this constant flow of blood that stimulates the baby to grow and develop also offers access to elements of our world that can harm a

Green Parent Report

Why Go Green During Pregnancy?

As a PEDIATRICIAN, I knew that the link between environmental dangers and the many cases of chronic illness in my patients was important, but the magnitude of the situation really hit home when I saw the preliminary results of an umbilical cord blood study conducted by the Environmental Working Group (EWG), in which I was fortunate to participate.

In this study, we examined the umbilical cord blood of ten babies born in August and September of 2004 in U.S. hospitals. We found a total of 287 different industrial chemicals circulating through the body of the newborns. These babies each carried an average of 200 chemicals, which included mercury, fire retardants, and pesticides. The report states, "Of the 287 chemicals we detected in umbilical-cord blood, we know that 180 cause cancer in humans or animals, 217 are toxic to the brain and nervous system, and 208 cause birth defects or abnormal development in animal tests." (See "The Womb" in the Green Information in the back of the book for a table of the chemicals.)

This small preliminary study suggests something very important: We are the environment; there is no separation. If a chemical is "out there" it may also be "in here," in the most protected inner sanctum of our bodies. And the presence of these chemicals in umbilical cord blood demands more research into what this means for babies. In the meantime, this report gives us further motivation to go green before your precious child is even born.

baby in the womb. Just as the umbilical cord can deliver high-quality nourishment and the fortifying hydration of healthy liquids, it also can transport unhealthy air, food, water, and fumes if those elements are coursing through the mother's body or in her environment.

That's why the decisions you make during your pregnancy about what to eat, drink, inhale, and put on your skin or hair can help ensure that this primal lake bathes your baby with enriching, beneficial nutrients.

How Do I Get Started?

The answer to this question demonstrates what's so wonderful about your decision to go green. Every small change, every step you take to follow even one of the suggestions in this chapter, can make a significant contribution to the health and well-being of your unborn child and our planet. Throughout this book you'll see many boxes that show the actual impact of specific small changes you can make easily and every day to preserve the health and safety of your baby, as well as sustain the earth for future generations.

Read through all the possible ways you can go green during your pregnancy and make whatever changes you're comfortable with, knowing that however big or small these changes may be, your child is indeed fortunate to have a parent like you who is going green right from the start.

In this chapter, you will learn what you need to know to make smart, green choices that will keep your body as healthy and nurturing as possible during your pregnancy. The following are the five main areas to think about:

1. Food
2. Drink
3. Exercise
4. Personal care products
5. Aromas

Eating for Two

I FREQUENTLY SEE moms-to-be quickly adjust their diets after getting the good news of the pregnancy. Without always knowing exactly how or why, most expectant moms instinctively understand that "eating for two" means they have an opportunity to be the direct source of healthy foods that supply all the nutrients, vitamins, and minerals a tiny fetus needs to thrive.

A case in point is the vital role that choline, a little-known nutrient, plays in protecting your baby's neural tube development in the earliest weeks of pregnancy, when the most rapid cell division occurs. Like the better known folate, it can reduce the risk of devastating brain and spinal chord defects. The March of Dimes recommends choline, along with protein, calcium, and folate for healthy pregnancies.

Choline remains important throughout your pregnancy as a critical building block of cells in your baby's rapidly growing brain. Getting plenty of choline appears to have a lasting effect on children's memory. Most women do not get an adequate supply from their prenatal vitamins. You can find lots of choline in eggs, cauliflower, asparagus, and spinach, as well as other vegetables, meats, fish, nuts, grains, herbs, and spices.

Choline is just one of the many vital nutrients you'll be supplying your baby through the foods you eat. And like choline, each has a significant role to play your baby's healthy development. The best way to make sure you're providing everything he needs is to enjoy a varied diet of your favorite fruits and vegetables, whole grains, legumes, healthy fats, and lean sources of protein and calcium—plus a vitamin supplement as a safety net.

Next we'll take a look at how your healthy food habits may influence your baby's own food tastes after birth.

"More broccoli please, Mom!"

Our taste preferences are formed by a complex mix of genetics and how we are raised. The great news is that we can start even before our babies are born to help them to learn to love great foods. The latest science is uncovering fascinating connections between what moms eat while pregnant

and what foods their babies enjoy after birth. Remarkable, but true. Babies have more taste buds before they are born than at any time later in life. Amniotic fluid is a flavored soup of what Mom has been eating, and babies in the womb taste, remember, and form preferences for some of these foods. I call this period "Taste Beginnings."

Consider a fascinating study involving carrot juice. As part of the study, one group of pregnant women drank ten ounces of carrot juice four times a week for three consecutive weeks. Another group of women in the study drank water. When their babies were old enough to start eating

Green Parent Alert

Preventing Allergies Even Before Birth

CHILDHOOD ASTHMA AND A number of food allergies are frequently diagnosed during early childhood. Often the key events that determine these allergies, it is thought, occur even earlier—in the womb. During this marvelous nine-month period, you might increase your child's chances of being allergy free by *increasing* your intake of foods

❖ Rich in omega-3 fatty acids, found, for example, in wild salmon or flaxseed

❖ Containing antioxidants—fruits, vegetables, and whole grains

❖ Containing cultures of beneficial bacteria (probiotics), as found in some yogurts

And by *decreasing* your exposure to

❖ Tobacco smoke

❖ Peanuts

❖ Acetaminophen

You might also reduce your child's allergy risk by making a visit to a farmyard! Studies have found that the children of women who were exposed prenatally to the microbial compounds in a farming environment were protected against the development of immune system changes that led to sensitization and asthma.[3]

cereal, it was time to look for a difference between the groups. An observer who didn't know to which group each baby belonged studied the babies as they ate cereal mixed with carrot juice. The babies who had missed this earlier experience protested and made unhappy faces when they first tasted the juice, whereas the others readily accepted and enjoyed the carrot juice in the cereal.[4] There was a dramatic difference between those who had sampled carrot juice in the amniotic fluid and those who had not.

The latest evidence from a 2006 study of identical and fraternal twins supports these findings and suggests that preferences for fruits, vegetables, and desserts are learned behaviors.[5] So as amazing as it seems, if you make it a priority to eat a diet that is loaded with whole grains, fruits, and vegetables, and short on sugary, fatty, and processed foods, you might actually influence your child's long-term taste preferences. What an opportunity to start training your child's taste buds to eat healthy nutritional food!

When a Peach Isn't Just a Peach

In our modern, industrialized world, achieving good nutrition can be a bit tricky. It's true that fruits and vegetables and lean, high-protein meats are preferable to doughnuts and greasy fast-food hamburgers, but the pollution of our food chain by environmental toxins has turned the simple decision to eat a peach into a reason for pause.

A peach is no longer just a peach.

A peach can be a delicious source of vitamins, minerals, and other nutrients that give our bodies good health, or it can be a tasteless repository of forty-two different types of toxic pesticides that are bad for our bodies and especially bad for a baby in the womb.[6]

Fortunately, by making informed choices and avoiding those foods known to contain high levels of such contaminants, you can easily reduce the harmful chemicals that can pass from mother to unborn child. Choosing foods grown locally, and in their natural growing season can greatly reduce pesticide levels. Choosing organically grown foods can virtually eliminate significant pesticide exposure.

Can You Be Vegetarian or Vegan?

Being a vegetarian or a vegan can be an option for a pregnant woman, if you make informed choices. Here are four things to keep in mind:

1. Being sure to get plenty of **Vitamin B$_{12}$**, typically found in animal foods (meat, dairy products, and eggs), is especially important for pregnant and nursing women (and for babies and children). Good sources of B$_{12}$ for vegetarians are dairy products and eggs. Vegans should be sure their diet includes foods that are fortified with B$_{12}$, like fortified breakfast cereals, fortified yeast extract, and fortified soy milk. Red Star Nutritional Yeast, Vegetarian Support Formula, for example, is one reliable vegan source of B$_{12}$. It tastes great as a seasoning sprinkled on soups, salads, and even popcorn. And don't forget, a prenatal vitamin is an important safety net for all women.

2. **Calcium** is also very important during pregnancy and nursing (and for moms, in the months just after nursing, to replenish the calcium in their own bones). If you're a vegetarian or vegan, add rich sources of calcium in your diet, such as tofu, tempeh, sesame seeds, greens

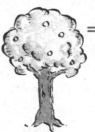

Going Green

Find a Farmer's Market Near You

SHOPPING AT A FARMER'S market is a great way to find fresh and often organic locally grown fruits and vegetables. You can also often find unusual and heirloom varieties that aren't sold in supermarkets. At many markets you can buy artisan baked goods, cheeses, and even meats and fish. What's more, you'll have a chance to meet the farmers face-to-face.

The U.S. Department of Agriculture (USDA) estimates that there are 4,385 farmer's markets now operating throughout the country, and this number is growing every year. More than 19,000 individual farmers are now selling their goods only through these markets, and a great majority are able to completely support their small farms through their sales.

Check the USDA's clickable map online to find a farmer's market near you:

www.ams.usda.gov/farmersmarkets/map.htm

(collard greens, turnip greens), and figs. (Check the label on your tofu. Tofu processed with calcium sulfate tends to have much higher levels of calcium than tofu processed with nigari.) You'll also get some calcium from kale, soybeans, bok choy, mustard greens, tahini, broccoli, almonds, and spinach. And you can find many calcium-fortified foods (soy milk, orange juice—even whole grain waffles), and of course, calcium supplements. *The lower animal protein intake of vegetarians does seem to reduce the body's calcium losses, but there is not enough evidence to say that vegans need less calcium when pregnant or nursing.* I recommend getting 1,000 milligrams every day (1,300 milligrams if you are under age nineteen).

3. **Variety** in your diet is especially important. I suggest that you eat a wide variety of fruits, vegetables, and whole grains to take advantage of all the unique phytonutrients in different foods. Phytonutrients are the thousands of different naturally occurring compounds in plants that have a positive effect on human health. While providing color, flavor, and disease-resistance in plants, they also benefit the humans who eat them. And don't rely too much on soy as your only major protein source. Soy contains natural phytoestrogens (plant estrogens). Although getting some can be very healthful, getting too much may not be. Use seeds, grains, and other legumes for balance.

4. Make a point of eating **organic foods**. Because vegetarians tend to eat larger amounts of fresh produce, choosing organic is even more important to reduce pesticide exposure.

What Exactly Is "Organic"?

The word *organic* extends a promise of a food that is natural, pure, and brimming with healthy nutrients. And the benefits extend well beyond the quality and taste of the food on our table. Conventional chemical agriculture depletes our dwindling oil reserves to an astonishing degree, while boosting greenhouse gases. The amount of oil used in agriculture, including that used to make chemical pesticides and chemical fertilizers, is about the same as the amount used in all of the automobiles in the country.[7] Organic farming is a method that honors our health and the health of the planet.

The criteria required in order to wear the organic label have been established and standardized by the United States Department of Agriculture (USDA).

Organic fruits and vegetables are grown in fertile soil teeming with life. Organic farmers follow earth-friendly cultivation practices, adopting techniques that utilize, as far as possible, renewable resources. This produce is grown and processed without any toxic pesticides, insecticides, herbicides, fungicides, chemical fertilizers, or genetically modified seeds (GMOs).

About 99.5 percent of U.S. farmland—almost 800 million acres—is still stuck in the heavily chemical agricultural system of the post–World War II twentieth century.[8] This system pollutes our air, water, soil, wildlife, and ourselves with chemical pesticides, while depleting our oil reserves at an alarming rate. Organic meats, eggs, and dairy come from animals that are kept according to strict standards, fed only organic foods, and raised without antibiotics, growth hormones, or cloning.

Organically raised animals are treated in a way that protects their natural development and behavior. For example, as recently as World War II, most American eggs came from local backyards and barnyard flocks. Today, more than 98 percent of the 345 million laying hens in the United States live out their lives in stacked rows of tiny wire cages. Their beaks are often trimmed to prevent them from harming themselves or others when jammed so closely together. In 2005, the United Egg Producers, in response to public concerns, recommended a gradual increase in cage space for each adult Leghorn, the most common breed, to 0.47 square feet. By

Green Parent Report

Choosing Organic

CHOOSING TO GO ORGANIC is a wonderful way to safeguard the health of your baby. In 2002, the USDA's National Organic Program created guidelines to help you find the purest foods possible.[9]

❖ A product labeled "100% organic" must contain only organic ingredients. You are most likely to find this designation on single-ingredient foods, such as fruits, vegetables, meat, eggs, cheese, and cartons of milk.

❖ The round green USDA seal indicates that at least 95 percent of the ingredients (by weight) are organic, and other ingredients, if any, are acceptable choices.

❖ Food packaging that says "Made with organic ingredients" must contain at least 70 percent organic ingredients (by weight). These products will not wear the USDA Organic seal, but they may list up to three organic ingredients on the front of the package.

❖ If a product has fewer than 70 percent organic ingredients, it cannot be called organic, but the organic ingredients can be listed as such on the nutrition facts panel.

comparison, an 8.5 x 11 sheet of notebook paper is 0.65 square feet—30 percent bigger than the new "humane" goal.[10]

Organic laying hens, however, are given room to walk around and lie down. Their beaks may not be trimmed. As another example, dairy cows get at least four hours of exercise a day, and during the growing season grazing animals must have access to pastures that are not treated with toxic herbicides or other chemicals. Such animals are fed organic feed that does not come from genetically modified seed. In short, the animals are raised in a healthier and more humane manner.

Sadly, conventionally farmed animals, which account for about 99 percent of all the meat and poultry in America, are not so carefully raised and slaughtered. They are often fattened up with hormones and routinely administered doses of antibiotics. The increased use of antibiotics results in the breeding of increasingly resistant bacteria. It's surprising to learn

Green Parent Report

What About Genetically Modified Food?

WHEN MY TWELVE-YEAR-OLD son was born, genetically modified organisms (GMOs) were not a part of the American diet. Today, about 30 percent of our cropland is growing GMOs. That's a fast change! Although 60 percent of Americans believe they have never eaten GM food, most Americans eat them every day, especially genetically modified corn, soy, canola, and/or cottonseed.[11] I'm concerned that these may be one of the reasons that food allergies have increased during this time. It will be years before some of the questions about the long-term safety of these new organisms are answered.

Until more is known about GMOs, do your best to eat fewer genetically modified foods during pregnancy and while nursing. This can be challenging, because in the United States GM foods are not labeled as such. Most soy, cotton, corn, canola, and papaya in the United States has been genetically modified, but you usually have no means of distinguishing modified from unmodified. Conventional meat, dairy, and eggs likely come from animals that have been treated with or fed GM products, but again, you may not know. But here's a helpful rule of thumb: you can reduce your intake of genetically modified food by eating fewer foods that contain corn syrup, high fructose corn syrup, vegetable oil (soy, corn, cottonseed, or canola), margarine, soy flour, soy protein, soy lecithin, textured vegetable protein, cornmeal, dextrose, maltodextrin, fructose, citric acid, or lactic acid. Or you could just stick to organic foods, which by law cannot be grown from genetically modified seed or fed GM foods.

that most of the antibiotic use in the United States occurs not in medical settings but rather on our feed lots as a growth promoter for livestock. European countries that have stopped this practice have seen a decrease in bacterial resistance.

Conventional cattle are often raised on "junk food," such as corn and other grains. (Cow's stomachs are designed to eat grasses and the like, so for them, corn is a fattening junk food.) These animals are fed grain that may be genetically modified and riddled with toxic pesticides. Corn and other grains make their stomachs more acidic, therefore more hospitable to dangerous *E. coli* bacteria.

The *E. coli* outbreaks of the last decade are a recent phenomenon. They often can be traced back to cattle raised on an unnatural diet in crowded, unhealthy conditions. From these cattle operations and dairies, the bacteria have spread to other crops.[12]

Eat Strategically to Save the Planet

More than four million acres of American farmland have already been dedicated to organic farming, helping our health and our future. That's four million acres farmed without the use of toxic pesticides or other toxic chemicals; four million acres nurtured with both ancient and modern techniques that are in balance with nature, helping to reduce the production of greenhouse gasses and reduce the threat of global warming.

Growing our foods organically has proven to be one of the hottest, fastest-growing movements of the twenty-first century. When Congress passed the Organic Foods Production Act in 1990, there were fewer than one million acres of organic farmland. In just twelve years, by 2002, that figure had doubled. Then the pace of progress picked up. Within just three more years, the amount of organic farmland doubled again. In 2005, we saw, for the first time, certified organic farmland in all fifty states. There has been exceptional progress, but we need to do more.

If organic cropland continues to double—*and it can!*—we can expect to see a revitalization and renewal of our streams and our soil as we build a smart, sustainable future. I can remember drinking stream water in our national parks when I was a child. I can remember catching and eating fish from our local streams. Today, all of the streams surveyed by the U.S. Geological Survey and more than 90 percent of fish tested in farming regions are polluted with pesticides.[13]

By eating strategically we can reclaim our streams, our food, and our future. Here's my take on the top five organic food choices a pregnant woman can make for the sake of her baby and the health of the planet:

- **Beef.** If you eat beef during pregnancy, I strongly suggest choosing organic beef. The meat from grass-fed, organically raised cattle tends to be leaner overall and has about five times the omega-3s of its conventional counterpart. In contrast, a 2007 study published in the Oxford journal *Human Reproduction* linked mothers who ate beef from conventionally raised cattle during pregnancy with lower sperm counts years later in their adult sons. The men in the study whose mothers ate conventional beef most frequently had sperm counts that averaged 24 percent lower than their counterparts, and they were three times more likely to be infertile. The authors of the study believe the added hormones were the culprit.[14]

- **Milk.** If you drink milk, opt for organic. Milk from organic, pasture-fed cows is produced without antibiotics, artificial hormones, and pesticides, and can also provide extra omega-3s and beta-carotene. I find that when women start making organic choices for themselves and for their families, they often intuitively start at the top of the food chain with organic milk. They understand that the foods they eat and the medicines they take will often get into their breast milk, so they easily make the connection that the medicines and foods given to dairy cows may affect their family's health. They prefer avoiding the routine use of antibiotics, artificial hormones, pesticides, and genetically modified feed. And I agree. Recent USDA monitoring data found that 27 percent of the conventional milk samples contained synthetic pyrethroid pesticides. By contrast, lower levels of the pesticide showed up in just 5 percent of the organic samples. There will be much more about milk in Chapter Four: "The Kitchen."

- **Potatoes.** When making the switch to organic vegetables, be sure to put potatoes on your shopping list. As the number one consumed vegetable in the United States, conventionally farmed white potatoes also have one of the highest levels of pesticide contamination. So by switching to organic, you can make a big difference in two important ways: by lowering your own exposure to chemical pesticides and by using your consumer clout to create a bigger market for the organic version of this

Green Baby Story

It's Never Too Late

WHEN I WAS A child growing up on a chicken farm in New Jersey in the 1930s, we never talked about "organic" or "natural" but we did feed our hens without adding anything artificial and let them run all over the range all day. We grew all of our own vegetables and some fruits, never using any chemicals but just natural fertilizer we got from the chickens. Sometimes we'd raise a pig to eat, and we'd buy parts of a healthy cow from a neighbor. I don't think I was ever in a food or supermarket during my childhood and teens, not until I got married.

Having a family of my own changed everything. I was a young mother with four children living in the suburbs and like all my neighbors, I bought modern processed foods—even TV dinners—from the supermarket. My husband and I wanted our kids to thrive, of course, but at that point we thought we were feeding them well and they seemed healthy enough.

But now everything's changed back. Our grandchildren are starting to have their own kids now. They're very concerned and advanced about feeding them properly, avoiding anything processed or fed with chemicals, hormones, or other unhealthy things. They've gone "green" they say, and they've taught me a lot, believe me, about how eating local organic foods—which was exactly what my parents were doing when I was a kid—cuts down on transportation costs and pollution to the environment. I've learned what *sustainability* means and how it can help us preserve our resources so these great-grandkids can inherit a world that can still support a broad variety of natural life.

So it's been full circle for me and my husband. We're back to where we started in eating natural, local, organic food, even though we spent our own child-rearing years being pretty unconscious about what was really good for us and the earth. But we're in our seventies now, so . . . thanks, all you green young people . . . it's never too late.

Evelyn Rossman
Montclair, New Jersey

popular veggie. And be sure to eat the peels! That way you'll get all the available nutrients, including high levels of potassium and Vitamin C.

- **Apples.** Among fruits, I would start with apples. Based on head-to-head, controlled studies, organic apples tend to have higher nutrient levels and taste better than the conventional variety.[15] And sadly, conventionally grown apples are one of the most pesticide-contaminated fruits tested by the USDA. They are a major source of exposure to organophosphate pesticide, a chemical linked to decreased intelligence and increased attention problems in kids[16] and hormone problems in adults.[17]

- **Soy.** Products made from organic whole soy beans can be very nutritious. Unfortunately only a tiny fraction of the nation's soy crop is presently organic. And to make matters worse, 87 percent of the conventionally grown soy in the United States is genetically modified—

Green Parent Alert

Small Amounts Can Be Harmful When Exposures Accumulate

THE GOVERNMENT ASSURES US that when evaluated separately, chemical fertilizers, herbicides, fungicides, insecticides, artificial additives, and preservatives each should be negligible threats. But what about the cumulative amount of additives one consumes on a daily diet of conventionally produced and processed foods?

The Environmental Protection Agency (EPA) acknowledges that there has been no way for researchers to measure cumulative effects. But data collected by Ana M. Soto and Carlos M. Sonnenschein of Tufts New England Medical Center show that *small amounts may be harmful when exposures are combined.*[18] So don't assume that apparently negligible amounts aren't adding up. Instead, avoid this potential danger and eat simple, delicious, whole foods, responsibly grown.

more than any other domestic crop. What's more, in recent years, soy has been the domestic crop most contaminated with organophosphate pesticides. Yet it's hard to avoid soy—it's found in virtually any processed food you eat these days, from soup (Campbell's) to nuts (Jiffy peanut butter). The only way out of this situation is to make sure that the processed foods you purchase are organic. That way you'll know that any soy you're eating wasn't genetically altered, and wasn't grown with any pesticides. So be sure to check the label before you buy.

How to Stay Safe from Some Basic Bacteria Risks

There are certain microscopic bacteria that can pose special health risks to pregnant women and to their babies. Although most people can safely eat food containing a type of bacteria called *Listeria*, pregnant women are ten times more likely to get sick if they eat those same foods. And if they do get sick, the infection can be devastating for the baby. The tricky thing about *Listeria* is that, unlike many bacteria, they can thrive at refrigerator temperatures. To be sure, while you're pregnant, avoid the following:

- Soft cheeses such as Brie, Camembert, feta, and Mexican queso fresco, or any cheeses with blue veins. Most hard cheeses are fine, as are pasteurized cream cheese, cottage cheese, cheese spreads, sliced cheese, and yogurt.

- Foods from deli counters (prepared salads, meats, and cheeses), unless they are heated to steaming right before you eat them.

- Hot dogs, packaged cold cuts, meat spreads, pate, smoked seafood, and leftovers, unless they are heated to steaming right before you eat them. Canned or shelf-stable products are generally fine.

- Raw or unpasteurized milk during pregnancy, including goat's milk, and foods that contain unpasteurized milk.

Raw and partially cooked eggs, meat, and poultry can harbor other unwanted visitors. In addition to *Listeria*, you want to be careful about *E. coli*, salmonella, and *Toxoplasma* by doing the following:

- If you eat ground beef, cook it until no pink is visible, and be sure pork and lamb are well done. If you celebrate with a turkey, or enjoy other poultry, cook thoroughly to 180° F (with a thermometer).

Try This Today

Start Buying Organic

LET'S ALL PULL TOGETHER to build the market for organic foods! If we each demand more organically grown foods on our store shelves, farmers and food companies will work together to supply them. And if organic food consumption rises from its current level of 3 percent to 10 percent of total food sales by the year 2010, the environmental impact will be enormous. We will have done the following:

❖ Eliminated pesticides from about *98 million servings* of drinking water per day across the U.S. population.

❖ Ensured that *20 million servings* of milk per day are produced without antibiotics and genetically modified growth hormones.

❖ Ensured that *53 million servings* of fruits and vegetables each day are free of pesticide residues. (This is enough to give 10 million kids five servings of fruit and vegetables each day.)

❖ Ensured that *915 million animals* are treated more humanely.

❖ Eliminated use of growth hormones, genetically engineered drugs and feeds, and *2.5 million pounds* of antibiotics used on livestock annually (more than twice the amount of antibiotics used to treat human infections).

❖ Captured an additional *6.5 billion pounds* of carbon in soil (the amount emitted per year by 2 million cars driven 12,000 miles).

❖ Eliminated *2.9 billion barrels* of imported oil annually (equal to 406,000 Olympic eight-lane competition pools).

❖ Restored *25,800 square miles* of degraded soils to rich, highly productive cropland (an amount of land equal to the size of West Virginia).

Source: Mission Organic (*www.MO2010.org*).

- Cook eggs until both the whites and the yolks are firm. Soft scrambled eggs aren't a pregnancy treat.

- Remember hidden sources of raw or partially cooked eggs, such as cookie dough, unpasteurized eggnog, and Hollandaise sauce.

- You've heard not to change kitty litter during pregnancy to avoid *Toxoplasma*. This is good advice, but you can also pick up *Taxoplasma* from unpasteurized milk and undercooked meats. So be sure your milk is pasteurized and your meats cooked to at least 150° F.

- Even if cooked food is safe, you may get these microbes on your hands or utensils while cooking. Wash before and after handling raw foods. And always wash cutting boards, kitchen surfaces, and utensils after use.

Cut Back on Processed Foods

Back in the 1950s, the TV dinner and packaged convenience foods became the harried housewife's best friend. The ease of use and low cost quickly made processed foods an American staple. Today, the average American consumes 150 pounds of processed food additives each year. This is not an astounding statistic, considering that during the twentieth century more than three thousand different additives found their way into our food.[19]

Many processed meats, such as most hot dogs and packaged bologna, salami, and many *other sandwich meats, are preserved with food additives called nitrates and nitrites* (on food labels the additive may be listed as sodium nitrate or sodium nitrite).

The link between these nitrates and cancer has been studied for years, but the effects on the growing fetus are still largely unknown. As I've said before about genetically modified foods, until we know more, it's better to be on the safe side. Because nitrates are present in large amounts and are water-soluble, they get into the bloodstream very easily and pass directly to your unborn child. Instead, choose a healthier alternative such as a hot organic chicken breast or a sandwich made with canned salmon.

The packaging of processed foods can also be a health issue. A 2007 study by the Environmental Working Group found a highly toxic chemical called *bisphenol A* (BPA) in the linings of more than half the cans of food tested. In this study, the highest levels of BPA were found in canned pastas and soups. That's another reason I strongly recommend eating more fresh foods and fewer canned foods during pregnancy. We'll talk more about BPA later in this chapter in our discussion of water bottles.[20]

Evidence That Green Parenting Really Works

Can simple changes make a positive difference? Absolutely. The power of a simple dietary change was shown in a study recently published in the National Institutes of Health (NIH) journal *Environmental Health Perspectives.*[21] The researchers conducted this study using typical suburban children. They collected morning and evening urine samples daily from each child. Pesticide breakdown products appeared routinely in the urine samples.

Then the researchers made a simple change: the kids began eating organic versions of whatever they were eating before. For example, if they typically ate an apple for lunch, now they ate an organic apple. The kids didn't have to learn to like any new foods—they made the switch only if there was a simple organic substitution available nearby for what the kids were already eating.

Within twenty-four hours, the concentration of pesticide breakdown products in the urine plummeted! The children continued eating this way for five days, with clean urine samples morning and night.

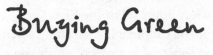

Produce Report Card

Do you want to reduce pesticides on your plate? It can help to know which conventionally grown fruits and vegetables tend to have the highest and lowest levels of pesticides. This table is based on the results of nearly forty-three thousand tests for pesticides on produce collected by the USDA and the FDA between 2000 and 2004. Items are ranked from worst (highest pesticide load) to best (lowest pesticide load).

Source: Environmental Working Group at *www.foodnews.org.*

Rank	Fruit or Vegetable	Score	Rank	Fruit or Vegetable	Score
1	Peaches	100	23	Mushrooms	37
2	Apples	89	24	Cantaloupe	34
3	Sweet bell peppers	86	25	Honeydew melon	31
4	Celery	85	26	Tomatoes	30
5	Nectarines	84	27	Sweet potatoes	30
6	Strawberries	82	28	Watermelon	28
7	Cherries	75	29	Winter squash	27
8	Pears	65	30	Cauliflower	27
9	Grapes, imported	65	31	Blueberries	24
10	Spinach	60	32	Papaya	21
11	Lettuce	59	33	Broccoli	18
12	Potatoes	58	34	Cabbage	17
13	Carrots	57	35	Bananas	16
14	Green beans	53	36	Kiwi	14
15	Hot peppers	53	37	Sweet peas, frozen	11
16	Cucumbers	52	38	Asparagus	11
17	Raspberries	47	39	Mango	9
18	Plums	45	40	Pineapples	7
19	Grapes, domestic	43	41	Sweet corn, frozen	2
20	Oranges	42	42	Avocado	1
21	Grapefruit	40	43	Onions	1
22	Tangerine	38			

Then the kids went back to their previous diets. Immediately the children's urine samples indicated an exposure to organophosphate pesticides from their diets, often above the safety limits set by the EPA.

This study suggests that even if you eat organic foods only when convenient and only to replace the conventional versions of foods you are already accustomed to eating, you could immediately reduce the pesticide levels in your body. It's not necessary for you to eat differently. You can eat the same foods. Just opt for organic.

More Options for Fresher Produce

Organic food products are no longer specialty items sold only in hard-to-find "health food" stores. Today they are sold in most supermarkets nationwide. But whether or not you're able to find organic fruits and vegetables, follow these guidelines:

- Try to eat produce that is grown locally. Imported produce often contains higher pesticide levels than food grown in the United States. There are exceptions, where certain countries actually have more stringent rules, but unless you know the regulations of the particular country, it's safer to reduce imported produce.

- Buy produce in its peak season. Skip summer fruits in February! This helps in two ways. First, the food is more likely to be grown in the United States. Second, the timing can further cut down on your intake of pesticides. As produce reaches the end of its growing season, farmers often use more chemicals to keep them growing, keep them from rotting, and keep them from being consumed by insects and other pests.

- Wash all fresh fruits and vegetables in water. This will remove some (but not all) of the pesticide residues on the surface. You can go a step further by spraying and rubbing the produce with distilled white vinegar, followed by a cold-water rinse. This will remove most wax, soil, and surface residues.

- Grow your own. Whether you have a yard with room for a farmer's yield of fruits and vegetables or only a windowsill with a few pots for fresh herbs, what you grow yourself is bound to be fresh and tasty—

and you'll know exactly how the produce was raised. You can even start with organic seeds or seedlings.

- Choose produce known to be less contaminated. Either choose organic or use the Buying Green box on page 29.

What About Seafood?

For an expectant mom, trying to eat seafood as safely as possible is difficult because the USDA has no classification yet for organic seafood. Therefore, seafood is a double-edged sword. On the one edge, some varieties of fish offer high levels of the fatty acids that help a baby's brain grow well. The omega-3 oils in Pacific salmon, for example, offer powerful benefits to both you and your baby. A 2007 study even suggested that women who regularly eat fish during pregnancy have smarter babies.[22] But on the other edge of that sword, a number of species—including tuna, swordfish, Atlantic salmon, and Chilean sea bass—can contain high levels of polychlorinated biphenyls (PCBs), mercury, and other contaminants.

In the future I would like to see strict government regulations to control the industrial emissions that cause pollution of our rivers, lakes, and oceans. But for now, the fact is that there is a big difference between the benefits and risks of different types of seafood. So I recommend that you choose those with the greatest health benefits, the least contaminants, and the most positive impact on the environment.

reen Parent Alert

Are Wild-Caught Fish Always Healthier?

WILD-CAUGHT FISH ARE harvested from their natural habitat. They may have a more varied diet, less disease, and lower levels of contaminants than farmed fish—or not, depending on the species and location of the fish. And, despite labels you may see on their packaging, they may not really be wild-caught. Fortunately, the Marine Stewardship Council at *www.msc.org* provides a certification program. For products from a wild-capture fishery to be eligible to display the MSC logo, the fishery must undergo a certification by an accredited certification body (and the supply chain must undergo a chain of custody certification) to ensure sustainability, traceability, and prevent mislabeling. You can obtain further information by visiting the MSC's Web site at *www.msc.org*.

Focus on healthier, eco-friendly seafood that is high in omega-3s and low in contaminants for you and your baby. Here are some great choices:

- ❖ Wild Alaskan or Pacific salmon
- ❖ Canned wild pink or sockeye salmon
- ❖ Sardines
- ❖ Farmed oysters
- ❖ Atlantic mackerel (not king mackerel), Atlantic herring, and anchovies
- ❖ Blue crab, flounder, and haddock (very low in contaminants)
- ❖ Farmed trout (both healthy and ecologically sound, unlike farmed shrimp)
- ❖ Farmed abalone
- ❖ Farmed catfish

- ❖ Farmed (not wild) caviar
- ❖ Farmed clams
- ❖ Dungeness crab
- ❖ Snow crab
- ❖ Stone crab
- ❖ Mahi mahi
- ❖ Farmed mussels
- ❖ Bay scallops
- ❖ Farmed scallops
- ❖ Northern shrimp, Oregon shrimp, spot prawns
- ❖ Farmed striped bass
- ❖ Farmed sturgeon

The high levels of mercury found in some fish is especially troubling for the unborn baby. Mercury damages a fetus's immune system and kidneys, and interferes with normal brain development. For this reason, despite the value of seafood, the Food and Drug Administration (FDA) and the EPA have recommended that pregnant women avoid shark, swordfish, king mackerel, and tilefish entirely. I agree with this, but would recommend that you also avoid canned tuna, sea bass, Gulf Coast oysters, marlin, halibut, pike, walleye, grouper, orange roughy, rock cod, and largemouth bass while pregnant. And of course, look for local advisories about the safety of fish caught by family and friends in local lakes, rivers, and coastal areas.

Should you eat wild or farmed fish? This is not always an easy choice. Farm-raised fish are fish raised in inland ponds, a room of tanks, or even a net enclosure in a bay, ocean, or lake. Some farmed fish are great for you; some are poor choices, especially during pregnancy. Farm-raised salmon, for example, contains significantly higher concentrations of PCBs, dioxin, and other cancer-causing contaminants than salmon caught in the wild, according to a study of commercial fish sold in North America, South America, and Europe.[23] It also tends to contain lower levels of beneficial omega-3s.

Concerns About Shrimp and Tuna

Shrimp and prawns account for 31 percent of all seafood sales. Although shrimp is low in mercury, it is often not sustainably harvested or raised. In fact, shrimp trawling can be one of the most harmful fishing practices, due to high by-catch (meaning that other species are killed inadvertently along with the shrimp harvest). Shrimp aquaculture can also destroy coastal wetlands and mangrove forests. The often indiscriminate use, or misuse, of antibiotics, pesticides, and other water and shrimp feed additives is another reason to avoid most farmed shrimp. If you want shrimp, northern shrimp, Oregon shrimp, and spot prawns may be your best bets. Or you might also enjoy bay scallops or farmed scallops.

Tuna too should move to your "avoid" list. Despite FDA recommendation that women can safely eat up to six ounces of albacore (white) tuna, weekly,[24] an EPA analysis shows that if women follow this advice, more than 90 percent of all women (and their babies) would be exposed to mercury above the government's safe dose at least once during the pregnancy.[25]

Try This Today

Save the Fish

SEAFOOD CAN BE HIGHLY nutritious, but the fishing methods used worldwide are endangering this valuable food source. According to the journal *Nature*, 90 percent of large predatory fish, such as tuna, swordfish, and sharks, have already disappeared from the world's oceans.[26] The *New York Times* reports this dire warning: "If fishing around the world continues at its present pace, more and more species will vanish, marine ecosystems will unravel and there will be 'global collapse' of all species currently fished, possibly as soon as mid-century."[27]

But there is hope. Environmental Defense has published a research-based 2007 plan to replenish our oceans: *Sustaining America's Fisheries and Fishing Communities: An Evaluation of Incentive-Based Management.* Let's all keep an eye on which fishing methods are most disruptive, which fish are most endangered, and which fishing locations are most ecologically threatened—and on which seafood choices are healthiest for us and for our planet. You can make seafood choices that help you, your family, and the oceans. As conditions evolve, please visit these two sites for up-to-date information that will help explain this global problem and your role in its solution:

❖ Monterey Bay Aquarium Guide: *www.mbayaq.org/cr/seafoodwatch.asp*

❖ Environmental Defense Guide: *www.oceansalive.org*

Drinking for Two

AH, WATER—THE ELIXIR of life. It keeps our bodies hydrated and healthy—supporting our digestion, oxygenation, and cell efficiency. No wonder so many people are walking around clutching water bottles. Drinking plenty of water is an important part of a healthy lifestyle.

As a pregnant woman, you especially need to stay hydrated. The water you drink carries nutrients through your blood to the baby, and initially it also supplies the liquid needed for the amniotic fluid in the womb. *Remember that your placenta is providing approximately one cup of water needed each hour to replenish the amniotic fluid in the womb.* And for your own sake, water helps flush out the body systems and dilute your urine, which helps you prevent the urinary tract infections so common later in pregnancy. In addition, oddly enough, the more water you drink, the less likely you are to retain water and end up with swollen ankles.

So listen to your body and drink whenever you begin to feel thirsty, and even before you feel thirsty. By the time you feel thirsty you may already be behind on your optimal fluid intake. But drink green. Some sources of fluids contain impurities that pregnant women should avoid, so before you quench that thirst, take some time to consider what you're drinking. Check the labels on bottled water and filter your tap water:

- When drinking bottled water, two good choices are those labeled "purified water" or "sterile water." **Purified water** can come from any source, but must be treated to meet the U.S. Pharmacopeia (USP) definition of "purified," meaning that it is free of all chemicals; it may also be free of microbes if it is further treated by distillation or reverse osmosis. **Sterile water** can come from any source, but must be treated to meet the USP standards and therefore be free from all microbes.

- Bottled water may be treated using a number of different techniques, including filtration, ozonation (disinfecting water using ozone) or ultraviolet (UV) light treatment. The water bottle label should state the source and treatment method.[28] If you want more detailed information on any contaminants that may remain in your bottled water, contact the bottler and ask if and how the water is tested for contaminants and ask for the latest testing results.

- Your home tap water can also be filtered with a number of in-home systems, including distillation, reverse osmosis, and micron filtration. See Chapter Four and the "The Kitchen" in the Green Information section at the back of the book for more details.

Green Parent Alert

The Biggest Problem with Bottled Water May Be the Bottle

OK. YOU'RE HAVING A baby, and you want to carry your own really good water that you've checked out and love a lot. It comes in a plastic bottle, however, and the plastic composition of polycarbonate water bottles includes bisphenol-A (BPA), a potent chemical that mimics the estrogen hormone in the body, risking impairment of the reproductive tissues and organs in both males and females—especially before they are born. BPA has been found in the blood of pregnant women, within the placenta, and in umbilical cord blood.[29]

Studies have recorded the leaching of this chemical from the polycarbonate bottle into the water when the bottle is frozen, heated, at room temperature, damaged, worn, reused, and so on.[30] The bottom line is that there are questions about the safety of any kind of polycarbonate plastic container under any condition. PVC and styrene plastics are also known to leach harmful chemicals.

My advice is to minimize eating or drinking from plastics with the recycling numbers 3, 6, or 7 whenever possible. If you use plastic bottles, opt for those with the symbols 1, 2, 4, or 5. This is consistent with the recommendations of the Mount Sinai Medical Center and the Food and Health Program of the Institute for Agriculture and Trade Policy. Or better yet, trade in your plastic bottle for a lightweight stainless steel water bottle—they're easy to carry, durable, and can be washed either by hand or in a dishwasher.

The Caffeine Question

Coffee, tea, cola, and chocolate—for some, these are gifts from the gods, enriching each day with joy for the taste buds and a reprieve from fatigue. But to the unborn baby, they could become the bearers of a potentially harmful caffeine overload. If your fetus could talk, he would certainly ask you to be careful about too many caffeinated products.

Caffeine easily passes through the placenta into the amniotic fluid and umbilical cord blood and into the unborn baby. There the developing fetus sustains higher levels of caffeine than his mother because of an immature metabolism.

And it's not just that morning cup of java that gives the fetus a jolt. Caffeine is a stimulant present in many foods and beverages and in some medications. It enters the mother's central nervous system quickly, and slightly increases both blood pressure and heart rate (also affecting fetal heart rate and movement patterns). Although the negative effects of daily moderate intake of one eight-ounce cup of brewed coffee (typically less than 150 milligrams) on a pregnancy are debatable, there is strong evidence that larger daily amounts of caffeine (more than 150 milligrams) during pregnancy may increase the risks of miscarriage, preterm delivery, and low birth weight. For example, one study found that pregnant women who consumed large quantities of caffeine (five or more cups of coffee a day) were twice as likely to miscarry as those who consumed less.[31]

As much as you might enjoy that morning cup of coffee, it's quite clear that this is one opportunity you have each day to reduce your baby's exposure to potentially harmful products. You might even choose pregnancy as a time to cleanse your body of caffeine. But if you do, don't try to stop your caffeine intake all at once, cold turkey. Your body will miss its daily dose and may complain with a headache when it's suddenly gone. Other symptoms of abrupt withdrawal can include drowsiness, irritability, and even nausea and vomiting. So I suggest that you cut down a little each day until you and your unborn baby are slowly weaned at least down below 150 milligrams of caffeine per day. (A detailed analysis of caffeine's reported effects on pregnancy outcome can be found at *www.motherisk.org*.)

What About Decaf Coffee?

One way to reduce caffeine is to drink decaffeinated coffee, but be aware that a five-ounce cup of decaf usually still contains from two to five milligrams of caffeine, and sometimes even more. Because many decaffeinated coffees are made from beans processed using methylene chloride (a dangerous chemical also used in paint strippers), it's greener to choose a decaf bearing the "Swiss Water Process" logo. That's your guarantee that the decaf you're drinking was brewed with coffee beans that were decaffeinated using a certified organic chemical-free process. Lots of retailers sell coffees decaffeinated using the Swiss Water Process, including Starbucks (Komodo Dragon Blend), Seattle's Best Coffee (Organic Twilight), and Sam's Clubs (Marques de Paiva Gourmet Coffees). Check *www.swiss water.com* for other retailers in your area.

A cautionary note: you might come across other decaffeinated coffees described as "water processed" or "European processed," but be sure to ask if they have the Swiss Water Process logo. If not, the beans may have been processed using something called the indirect method, which still uses the same harsh chemicals in combination with a water bath.

What About Alcoholic Beverages?

Many couples enjoy relaxing together with a glass of wine, hanging out at a barbecue with a bottle of beer, or socializing with a round of margaritas. So it's not unusual for moms-to-be to ask me how much alcohol they can safely drink while pregnant. The answer is direct and nonnegotiable: *none*.

Sorry, but no level of alcohol has been proven safe for an unborn child—and that means beer, wine, wine coolers, and hard liquor. All alcohol passes quickly through the placenta to the fetus, and the unborn baby's immature metabolism breaks it down more slowly than an adult's. This can cause a variety of mild to severe birth defects. In fact, alcohol is now recognized as the most destructive environmental agent influencing fetal development. It is the most common cause of mental retardation and is directly responsible for 10 to 20 percent of the cases of mental retardation in the 50 to 80 IQ range, and it is the root cause of cerebral palsy in one in six cases. Fetal alcohol syndrome, one of the most severe outcomes of alcohol consumption during pregnancy, can be devastating. Many fetal alcohol syndrome babies are born to alcoholic mothers, but milder features are found in babies born to women who have as little as two drinks per day. These features include a lower IQ, poor growth and development, hyperactivity, and a small head.

Making wise choices to keep your baby healthy in the womb must include eliminating alcohol from your diet. Alcohol exposure is most damaging when the synapses (connections) of the brain are being formed—during the last trimester of pregnancy. Evidence published in *Science* suggests that when the developing baby is exposed to alcohol for even a few hours, a number of brain cells and synapses are permanently destroyed.[32]

Health Drinks

Health drinks are a very popular and efficient way to take in important nutrients, vitamin C, and antioxidants, and to provide fiber in the diet. These combination drinks, often with such names as Cider Vinegar and Honey, Wheat Orange, and Papaya Blend, are mixed and sipped on the go, helping busy people get their minimum daily five servings of fruits and vegetables.

Most health drinks made from fresh produce are good for pregnant women—especially if the produce is organic. But there are two reasons to be cautious about health drinks:

1. **They may be too much of a good thing.** The prenatal vitamin supplements often prescribed to expectant moms are packed with 100 percent of recommended daily allowances. The vitamin intake from a balanced daily diet added to the vitamin supplement pushes those levels to the upper limit. Adding a nutrient-packed health drink to the mix can easily push the daily dose of vitamins over the limits of safety. This is especially true with vitamin A.

   At proper levels, vitamin A is important for your baby's brain and eye development. But too much (more than the USDA recommended daily maximum of 3,000 mcg or 10,000 International Units) can cause brain development to be slowed and can lead to neural tube defects. In this case, vitamin A overload is definitely too much of a good thing.

2. **They may not be healthy.** Not all products with the words "healthy" or "fruit" or even "vegetable" in their names are actually good for you.

Green Parent Report

Choose Your Caffeinated Beverages Wisely

THIS CHART WILL HELP you make smart choices to reduce your daily intake of caffeine each day.[33] If you must have your daily shot, strive to keep it under 150 milligrams. (Caffeine content of beverages varies due to brewing method, plant variety, and brand.)

Item	Caffeine (milligrams)
Cappuccino mocha, 16 oz.	120–130
Cappuccino, per 16 oz.	116
Iced tea, 12 oz.	67–76
Coffee, brewed by drip method, 5 oz.	60–180
Latte, 12 oz.	58
Espresso, 2 oz.	40–170
Coffee, instant, 5 oz.	30–120
Some dark carbonated beverages, 12 oz.	30–46
Baking chocolate, 1 oz.	26
Brewed teas, 5 oz.	20–90
Semi-sweet chocolate, 1 oz.	5–35
Chocolate syrup, 2 tbls.	4
Cocoa beverages, 5 oz.	2–20
Chocolate milk, 8 oz.	2–7
Decaffeinated coffee, 5 oz.	2–5
Milk chocolate, 1 oz.	1–15
Citrus flavored carbonated beverages, 12 oz.	0–65
Decaffeinated or herbal teas, 5 oz.	0–1
Decaffeinated carbonated beverage, 12 oz.	0

Fruity soft drinks, flavored ice teas, sugary fruit juices, fruity wine coolers, and energy and sport drinks as well as fruit "flavored" drinks may *not* be healthy drinks. They often contain excess sugar, calories, caffeine, and artificial sweeteners and flavorings that easily cross the placenta.

Exercising for Two

EXERCISE IS A GREEN approach to health care. Yes, a green pregnancy means making the most of what you take *into* your body, through what you eat, drink, and breathe, and also absorb through your skin, hair, and nails. But how you *move* your body is another powerful green way to make a difference.

There are many benefits of exercise during pregnancy, including improved physical conditioning, strength, flexibility, and stamina. It builds endurance for labor and delivery and a quicker postnatal recovery. By exercising regularly, you may be able to reduce some of the common discomforts of pregnancy such as backache, swelling, and constipation. Most of all, you feel great about yourself when you exercise.

How Exercise Can Help More Than Medication

Let's take a look at the effects of exercise versus medications for two of the most important complications of pregnancy.

Gestational diabetes. As many as one in eight women will develop gestational diabetes sometime during their pregnancies, increasing health risks for themselves and their babies. Researchers at the University of Southern California School of Medicine studied a group of women who had already developed gestational diabetes and who had fasting blood glucose levels high enough to require insulin.[34]

Half of the women in the study received the recommended insulin. The other half got personal trainers instead. The trainers supervised the women while they did simple twenty-minute stints on exercise bikes. The results were startling: moderate aerobic exercise was equally effective to insulin! Blood glucose levels were statistically the same in both groups.

If exercise can be a prescription-strength way to control gestational diabetes that has already developed, how much better to be active throughout pregnancy and perhaps prevent the problem in the first place.[35]

Insulin costs in the United States are staggering. The state Medicaid programs alone pay $500 million a year just for the drug.[36] The indirect costs of diabetes are huge. Exercise is a green approach to health care.

Preeclampsia is complication of a pregnancy in which blood pressure increases and blood flow to the baby decreases. The only effective treatment for preeclampsia is to deliver the baby, so it contributes to the growing epidemic (and resource cost) of preterm deliveries. Again, regular brisk walking or other moderate physical activity begun during pregnancy significantly lowers the risk of preeclampsia. The benefit is even greater if the exercise is begun before pregnancy.[37] As thankful as I am for neonatal intensive care units, they also represent one of the most intense uses of resources in health care. A walk in the park is a much greener way to deal with preeclampsia, when possible.

Prenatal Yoga

Yoga is one of the oldest physical practices in existence. Yoga balances mind and body, work and relaxation. Through movement, posture, relaxation, meditation, and intentional breathing, yoga aims to bring a healthy, lively, flexible approach to life. With its emphasis on harmony and balance, it is a beautiful metaphor for raising baby green.

Two recent studies compared an hour of prenatal yoga daily to an hour of brisk walking daily. One of the studies looked just at women with uncomplicated pregnancies. In this study, those who were randomly assigned to the yoga group were significantly more likely to have an ideal weight baby, significantly less likely to have preterm labor, and significantly less likely to develop hypertension than the women who exercised an hour a day by walking.[38]

The other similar study looked at women with complicated pregnancies, who had already been diagnosed with abnormal blood flow through the umbilical and uterine arteries. These women were at increased risk of delivering babies that were too small. Again, those randomly assigned to the yoga group were significantly more likely to have a normal weight baby than those who walked for the same amount of time.[39]

If you are interested in a home guide to yoga before and after having a baby, I like Anna Getty's *Guide to Prenatal and Postnatal Yoga*, a DVD boxed set that is great for both beginners and for seasoned practitioners.

As with any exercise, you can overdo it with yoga. Be careful not to strain yourself, and have your instructor check to be sure you're doing it the best way for you.

The Green Exercise Standard

I agree with the American College of Obstetrics and Gynecology in recommending 30 minutes of moderate physical activity every day, or at least on most days.[40] We all know that this is a good idea, but having a baby is a fantastic time to make this resolution stick.

Talk with your pregnancy health care team before embarking on your activity plan. Some exercise is wonderful. Too much, or the wrong kind, is not. And some pregnant women should not exercise or should exercise in an even gentler way.

But for most women, exercise during pregnancy is a wonderful benefit, giving you stronger muscles, denser bones, healthier joints, and less chance of urinary incontinence. And exercise also wards off the baby blues or postpartum depression.

Personal Care Products

ONE OF THE DELIGHTS of being in love with a pregnant woman is watching the changes in her body, noticing the glow of motherhood suffusing her complexion, and taking in the scent of her femininity that now fills the room. I cherished this special time with my wife, Cheryl.

During pregnancy most women enjoy the wonderful array of hygiene and beauty products available today—soaps to cleanse and nourish the body, skin creams to soothe and moisturize, shampoos and conditioners to enhance and enrich their hair. Others are drawn to new perfumes and makeup that help them feel just a bit pampered.

If you have a sizable collection of personal hygiene and beauty products, this is the perfect time to take a closer look at their ingredients and trade in some of your products for healthier and greener versions.

According to the Environmental Working Group (EWG), the average American's daily use of shampoos, conditioners, deodorants, skin lotions, nail polishes, perfumes, hair gels, mousse, hair sprays, lip balms, and sunscreens deposits small amounts of 126 different chemicals on the skin every day. And unlike food ingredients, these chemicals are not always listed on the product label in a way that can be clearly and totally understood. So this is one more daily situation where you have the power to do something good for you and your baby by being informed and proactive.

Before you buy your next bottle of skin lotion, body bath, or even eyeliner, take a look at "Skin Deep," the searchable database offered by the EWG at *www.cosmeticsdatabase.com*. It rates products in terms of safety and toxicity, specifically for pregnant women. You might also want to jump ahead to Chapter Five, where I go into greater detail about beauty and personal care products.

If You Color Your Hair

Women often wonder whether they can continue with all their usual beauty routines during pregnancy. There's some question, for example, about whether hair dye is safe to use. Almost all hair dyes contain small amounts of chemicals called aromatic amines—well known to cause cancer in animals. (Dark-colored dyes tend to contain more.) Some studies have found a direct association between personal hair dye use in women and cancers of the bladder, breast, ovaries, and brain, and lymphomas and leukemias.[41] However, there are also good studies that have not found a problem.

The risk appears to depend on dye permanence, dye color, cumulative lifetime use, and the user's genetically determined ability to detoxify these damaging chemicals.[42] Regardless of whether hair dyes prove safe or not, I strongly recommend that expectant women avoid any type of hair coloring during pregnancy or while nursing. The EPA has concluded that carcinogens are on average ten times more potent for babies than for adults; some chemicals are up to sixty-five times more powerful.[43] We don't yet know much about hair dyes and babies, but I wouldn't want to experiment.

Safer Sunscreens

Many mothers slather on sunscreen to protect their skin and their bodies from damaging UV rays. Unfortunately, many sunscreens contain not only phthalates but also estrogen-like compounds as major ingredients. So stay away from this type of sunscreen lotion and instead use physical barrier lotions, such as zinc oxide or titanium dioxide products, which are not absorbed into the skin (unless they contain nanoparticles). We'll talk more about sunscreens in Chapter Five.

What's That Smell?

INHALE AND ENJOY THE warm aroma of fresh-baked bread, the spicy fragrance of a cinnamon stick, or the fresh scent of morning dew. These scents, like all aromas, are composed of the kinds of molecules that can and will go through the placenta and into the womb. These wonderful smells give your baby her first connection with your world.

Enriching Aromas

The sense of smell is the first of the five senses that babies in the womb develop.[44] Molecules that a woman can taste or smell tend to pass through the placenta, where they can also be detected by the amazingly sensitive olfactory cells of the baby.[45] During the months of gestation, your baby has become quite familiar with the aromas you are experiencing. As we will see in Chapter Two, the unborn baby's ability to smell the molecules in her own amniotic fluid will enable her to navigate to her mother's breasts in those first crucial moments after birth. This same experience will help her prefer and distinguish by smell alone her own mother's breast milk as opposed to that of other women. I suspect that this innate ability helps babies recognize, become familiar with, and prefer their own home, their own parents, and their cultural and ethnic foods. They seem to be drawn instinctively to those pleasant smells to which they have become accus-

Going Green

A Green Baby Shower

MANY MOTHERS-TO-BE are "showered" with lovely gifts that stock the nursery with all kinds of baby items, such as sleepers, quilts, toys, and so on. But rather than have to figure out what to do with some gifts that may be less than safe or healthy, spread the word before your shower that you're going green. Drop well-placed hints that you'd love to surround your newborn with pure, organic cotton clothing and with nontoxic toys, eating utensils, and bedding and bath supplies. You can sign up with gift registries at many online sites that sell wonderfully green baby products. Here are a few to get started:

- ❖ *www.ecobaby.com*
- ❖ *www.babynaturale.com*
- ❖ *www.purebeginnings.com*

tomed. In the best sense, these familiar aromas remind them of their experience in the womb. Surrounding your unborn baby with the scents of good nourishing foods may be an important way to begin to develop familiarity, acceptance, and longing for the kinds of foods that will sustain her in a healthy way for the rest of her life.

Harmful Fumes

Molecules of volatile chemicals from fumes and other harmful aromas, unfortunately, also pass through the umbilical cord into the placenta. Fortunately, many common sources of these odors are easily removed from your home.

The following are sources of harmful smells that you can reduce or eliminate:

- Glues
- Paints
- Furniture wax
- Household cleaners
- New carpets
- Dry-cleaned clothing
- Gasoline
- Gas from barbecues, fireplaces, and appliances
- Pesticides
- Incinerators
- Smog
- Cigarette smoke
- Flame retardants and stain protectors on some carpets, furniture, mattresses, and plastics

We can't possibly eliminate all of these fumes from our daily lives. But it is important to be aware of their potential danger and to avoid them when possible. The specific chemicals that make the fumes of many consumer products toxic are explored in later chapters, but for now, at this early point in your efforts to nurture your baby in utero, you might try one or two of the following suggestions today. Then, try another next week. Every time you make a choice to breathe in and supply your unborn baby with clean air, you move a step closer to creating a green world for your newborn:

- Take a break and stay out of the house during any painting or other home improvement projects that create fumes. (See Chapter Three for nontoxic products that are safer for you, your baby, and the environment.)

- Treat yourself to full service at the gas station. Don't pump your own gasoline. Most states require a warning on gasoline pumps that says something like:

  > Warning: Chemicals known to the state to cause cancer, birth defects, or other reproductive harm are found in gasoline, crude oil, and many other petroleum products and their vapors.

- Use nontoxic hobby paints and glues. To check on the safety of specific art materials, you can check with the Arts, Crafts, and Theater Safety group (ACTS) in New York at 212-777-0062, *www.artscraftstheater safety.org.*

- Switch to nontoxic organic household cleaners. (See Chapters Four and Five for nontoxic alternatives.)

- Find and use an environmentally friendly laundry service. But if your dry cleaner uses perc (tetrachloroethylene—also called PCE or perchloroethylene) or other dangerous solvents, ask someone else to help out so that you have no contact with this chemical.

Cigarette Smoke

As we've already seen, certain smells and fumes are not beneficial to the baby in your womb. One of the earliest fetal observations that hinted at the likelihood that babies in utero could "smell" their outer environment occurred when mothers were exposed to cigarette smoke. While watching babies on ultrasound, observers noticed that there was an immediate, obvious effect on fetal blood flow. Yes, even in the womb, babies don't like cigarette smoke.[46]

If you smoke, STOP. If other people in the home smoke, get them to stop. If you have a visitor who wants to light up, ask them to step outside. The nicotine and carbon monoxide found in cigarette smoke (whether inhaled directly or at second hand) are harmful to you and your baby and are known to cause complications in the pregnancy and serious health problems in a newborn. And you can see the effects in school-aged kids. Prenatal exposure to cigarette smoke appears, by itself, to account for more than a quarter million additional cases of attention deficit hyperactivity disorder (ADHD) in children.[47]

The list of proven problems is long, but none is more devastating than the sudden infant death syndrome (SIDS). On average, smoking during pregnancy doubles the risk of SIDS, and the odds increase with each cigarette. Or putting it the other way around, NOT smoking cuts the risk of SIDS in half.

There's no way to soft-pedal the negative effects of cigarette smoke on the unborn. The following are organizations and online sites that can help you purify the air your baby breathes:

- *Smokefree.gov.* An online resource sponsored by the federal government

- *Quit Now.* 800-QUITNOW

- *The Tobacco Research and Intervention Program (TRIP).* Offers an informational booklet to help pregnant women; call toll-free: 877-954-2548

- *The American Legacy Foundation.* A public health foundation that offers an online information program and a referral service to smoking cessation resources in each state; *www.americanlegacy.org*

And now onto the next room that you and your baby will visit: the labor and delivery room!

2

THE
Labor and Delivery Room

The labor and delivery room is the place your baby takes a first breath at the climax of pregnancy and childbirth. Pregnancy and childbirth are deeply natural processes—inherently green. This chapter will help focus the green elements of your labor and delivery that are most important to you and that you can comfortably incorporate into that important day. Even if you make only one green choice, you, your baby, and the planet will be better for it.

Who Will Deliver My Baby?

A LONG-STANDING RELATIONSHIP of trust and confidence in the people who will be helping deliver her baby is ideal for every pregnant woman. Many women will want to rely on the doctor, usually an obstetrician/gynecologist, who has been their physician in the past. Other women will decide to form new relationships with a doctor, midwife, or alternative delivery coaches early in the pregnancy, and also recruit friends and relatives to be on their "team" during childbirth.

Finding the person who will deliver your baby and building your delivery room team is a first step. The next is deciding how you want to make your childbirth and delivery greener. So my advice is that well in advance of your due date, you'll surely want to talk to your doctor or health care providers and write down your desires and decisions in a birth plan.

A *birth plan* (see page 81) gives you the opportunity to think about and express your desires for having a green delivery, addressing certain specific green elements and needs. It is important to remember that, regardless of the specifics of any birth plan, the outcome we most want is a healthy baby and a healthy mother. These considerations trump all others; always keeping them foremost, we want to find ways to be kind to the planet that our baby will inherit from us.

As a pediatrician working in home and hospital settings, I appreciate and am immensely grateful for the medical safety net of twenty-first-century bioscience. Many new, innovative procedures and cutting-edge technological resources can help babies during delivery, even those who are premature or born with dramatic problems that require quick intervention. Keeping tiny, low-weight, vulnerable babies alive and bringing them into normal maturity is one of the great accomplishments of modern medicine.

What I'm suggesting now, by adding the green baby perspective, is that we attempt to achieve this healthy delivery while minimizing any potential toxic exposures to the baby or the environment, reducing waste, and harmonizing a healthy baby with a healthy planet.

Choosing an Obstetrician

About eight women in ten will choose an obstetrician to manage their care during pregnancy.[1] I know how valuable it can be for an expectant mother to have a good relationship with an ob/gyn who becomes a friend and ally during the nine months prior to childbirth and of course at the time of the delivery itself.

If, however, you are looking for a new doctor, see "The Delivery Room" in the Green Information section at the back of the book for a list of sources of more information about providers and birth centers.

Recommendations are valuable in finding a health care provider, but the person who is best for one expectant couple may not necessarily be best for another. That's why I recommend that you have a sit-down talk with either your regular doctor or a new one whom you feel is most likely to be best for you now. It's important to get a feel for his or her personality and attitude.

During this interview process, show the provider your birth plan (detailed later in this chapter) and watch his or her reaction. You may also want to mention how having a baby has made you even more concerned about the environment and determined about doing things in an eco-friendly way. Is this a person who is excited about the ability of parents to make their own nonmedical decisions? Is this someone who respects your needs and desires as a person who is sensitive to the needs of your baby and our planet? Ask your provider if he or she has any suggestions for having a greener delivery. Whatever discussion follows will give you a lot of information. There are many practitioners out there who will create the kind of environment for your delivery that gives you comfort and happiness.

Let a Doula Help

A doula is a certified childbirth assistant whose purpose is to give comfort and aid to parents. (Interestingly, the word *doula* is derived from an ancient Greek word meaning "servant.") This person does not give any medical assistance; she helps the expectant couple get through the process of labor and delivery as smoothly as possible.

A doula can also be a great resource in your search for the best primary health care provider for you. An experienced doula is likely to have worked with many health care professionals in your area and will know who are the best and who are most likely to agree to your birth plan requests.

Unlike a physician and even some midwives, the doula stays with the expectant mom unceasingly throughout the labor and delivery. As an ever-present companion, she will shape, guide, protect, and encourage your efforts to make this most important day one that meets your needs and desires.

While the delivery staff is focusing on the baby's progress and health, the doula can be the one person who can best advocate for your green birth plan decisions. She will know ahead of time exactly what you desire. So if you deliver in a hospital or birthing center, for example, she might bring the organic cotton sheets and gown and exchange them for the facility-issued ones. She might remind the staff about your desire to avoid unnecessary medical intervention, even if the rules consider a procedure "routine." She is there to provide the pure soaps and cleansers you may have requested, and she will be the one to handle any disagreements regarding your green requests—allowing you to focus on the task of giving birth to your baby.

Research has shown that having a doula present during labor and delivery can indeed reduce invasive and often unnecessary medical interventions. A combined analysis of eleven clinical trials found that when a doula was present throughout labor, there was a 50 percent decrease in cesareans, a 36 percent decrease in the need for pain medication of any kind, a 70 percent decrease in the use of Pitocin, and a significant decrease in the length of labor.[2]

Doulas offer a wide range of services, including prenatal visits, labor and delivery coaching, and even family visits after the baby's birth. Their fees, therefore, also vary widely depending on their experience and how much time they actually spend with you; most are not covered by health insurance policies.

If you would like more information about doulas, contact:

- Doulas of North America (*www.dona.org*)

- National Association of Postpartum Care Services (800-45-DOULA)

Choosing a Midwife

Midwives are registered or legally licensed (or both) to assist in the delivery of a baby and can practice in any setting: home, birth center, or hospital. Midwives are growing in popularity, especially as they become more accepted in the hospital environment and as the popularity of birthing centers increases. In 2003, midwives attended 8 percent of births in the United States.[3]

Many women find that they can fulfill their desire to have a green birth more easily with the help of a midwife rather than with a physician, simply because the midwife often has more control over the environment in "her" birthing room. Unlike a busy physician, who usually is attending to other patients while a woman is in labor and under the care of hospital staff (and then pops in to deliver the baby), a midwife may stay with the expectant mom throughout the entire process and therefore be able to advocate with the staff and supervise the implementation of her green labor and delivery.

In my experience, midwives tend to be agreeable about meeting the expectant couple's birth plan requests. Whether in a birthing center or hospital, midwives may have no problem letting the dad-to-be bring organic cotton linens for the birthing bed; they are likely to agree to substitute facility food with the family's own high-nutrient organic foods; and they have a reputation for reducing the amount of invasive or unnecessary medical intervention that frequently accompanies a child's birth.

In your search for a midwife who will support your green pregnancy and delivery, look for one who understands and is willing to work with

Green Baby Story

Our Doula

I WANTED SOMEONE TO help me with breastfeeding when I came home from the hospital with our new baby girl, Eliana, so I called a postpartum doula recommended by my sister-in-law, who had used her when her son was born. This wonderful woman turned out to be a certified lactation counselor and a great coach during those first days of little Ellie's life, when everything was so new and sometimes overwhelming. A big bonus I hadn't anticipated, however, was her experience with green baby products. She recommended some terrific organic baby wash and lotions that had all natural ingredients and no weird chemicals or preservatives that could potentially irritate Ellie's skin or even worse, become toxic in her newborn body! I'd never been particularly aware of the choices I could make as a mother, but now I have a greener, more environmentally conscious point of view in selecting the best green baby products, household cleaners, and other green items for around the house that can impact our daughter's good health and also not damage the environment.

Jennifer Wenzel
San Francisco

your need for a green delivery room that has the least possible negative impact on you, your baby, and the environment. At the same time, make sure that your chosen midwife is expertly trained and licensed to meet your needs. See "The Delivery Room" in the Green Information section to read descriptions of the six types of midwife certification.

Where Will I Deliver My Baby?

IN MOST CASES, YOU'LL deliver your baby at the hospital where your health care provider has admitting privileges, so remember that when you choose a doctor or midwife, you're also choosing the place where you'll give birth. That could be an important consideration if the hospital has inflexible policies about issues important to you, so find out about this early in the process.

I recommend that you arrange for an on-site visit at the hospital you're considering. This is the only way to get a true picture of the culture, attitude, and feeling of the environment. You can tell a lot about a place just by sitting a while in the waiting room!

Your choice of a green location will add a few steps to the selection process that you won't find in standard birth plans. While searching for this perfect place, remember that a green location is one that uses the smallest amount of *unnecessary* medical intervention. It's also a place that has the least harmful impact on the environment in terms of its product selection, waste disposal, and recycling policies.

Giving Birth in a Hospital

The vast majority of women in the United States deliver their babies in a hospital delivery room.[4] A hospital birth is recommended for women with medical histories that put them at risk for delivery complications. Such complications might include being pregnant with multiples or having a preexisting medical condition, such as diabetes, high blood pressure, or a history of premature delivery. The hospital has the facilities and staff to give immediate medical assistance if needed.

Green Parent Report

Labor and Delivery Deluxe

SOME OF THE NEWEST trends in hospital labor and delivery services include amenities and conveniences once associated more with luxury hotel suites than with maternity wards. This list includes features offered by various hospitals throughout the country. I hope a higher level of green awareness will be next!

- ❖ Jacuzzi spa bathtubs
- ❖ Wireless Internet
- ❖ Entertainment center
- ❖ Salon services, such as haircut and style, manicure, and pedicure
- ❖ Room service menu of dining choices
- ❖ Complimentary candlelit dinner for new parents
- ❖ Complimentary thick terry bathrobe and mesh bag of spa toiletries
- ❖ Hardwood floors
- ❖ Sofabed for guests
- ❖ Kitchenette with granite countertops
- ❖ Refrigerator stocked with bottled water and juices
- ❖ Wireless fetal monitoring
- ❖ Lactation consultants and boutique
- ❖ Online nursery for out-of-towners to view the baby
- ❖ Breastfeeding pillow (to take home)
- ❖ Baby outfit (to take home)

Going Green

Packing for Delivery

By the end of your eighth month, you'll want to have your bags packed and ready for the big event! That way there won't be a last-minute rush and the possibility of forgetting something important. Some experienced moms recommend packing two bags for the ultimate in organization, one for the things you'll want during labor and another for afterward. A green delivery can require a bit more preparation, so give yourself enough time to gather the items you'd like to bring.

Paperwork

❖ A copy of your birth plan

❖ Your health insurance card and any necessary hospital forms

❖ Your marriage certificate in case of different last names

Comforts of home

❖ High-energy organic snacks and filtered water

❖ Ice pops (ask ahead if there's a freezer)

❖ Your own favorite pillow with an organic cotton pillowcase (use a patterned case so it doesn't get mixed up with the hospital's pillows)

❖ Warm socks and slippers

❖ A bathrobe and comfy nightgown. (Some women prefer to use the hospital's gowns so they don't soil their own and for ease of checking blood pressure and cervical dilation)

❖ Toiletries, such as your favorite natural body care products, a hairbrush, toothbrush, toothpaste, deodorant, shampoo and conditioner, and a hairdryer

❖ Massage oils and lotions

❖ Lip moisturizer

Gear

- ❖ A video camera and a backup battery
- ❖ A camera (bring the charger or extra batteries and extra film if your camera isn't digital)
- ❖ Cell phone and charger and a prepaid calling card in case cell phones are prohibited and the hospital phones are for local calls only
- ❖ Mp3 or CD player with your favorite music
- ❖ Laptop computer (one couple we know e-mailed regular updates and photos to friends and family directly from the labor and delivery room—check ahead to ask if there's wireless Internet available)

Extra Necessities

- ❖ Cash for parking and vending machines
- ❖ Your phone book

For Baby

- ❖ Organic cotton baby bedding in a print so it doesn't get mixed up with the hospital's linens (check ahead to see if this okay)
- ❖ Pure soaps, lotions, and creams for your baby, if the hospital requires using more than just water to cleanse your newborn
- ❖ Either organic cotton cloth diapers or disposable brands known to be environmentally low impact
- ❖ An organic fiber going-home outfit and a snowsuit if it's very cold
- ❖ A cap and a pair of socks or booties
- ❖ A natural fiber receiving blanket
- ❖ An infant car seat for the drive home (you won't be allowed to leave without one)

Postpartum

- ❖ A fresh nightgown
- ❖ Nursing bras, if breastfeeding, or if you plan to bottle feed, bring along premixed formula in the organic brand you prefer
- ❖ A roomy, comfortable going-home outfit

An expectant mother with a low-risk pregnancy also might want to deliver in a hospital because her trusted physician delivers only in the hospital setting, because she feels safer and more confident knowing there is immediate medical backup in the event of an unforeseen emergency, or because she simply feels more comfortable in what has become the "traditional" setting.

If you are considering giving birth in a hospital, take the time and effort to go on hospital tours, talk to the maternity nurses and personnel, and ask questions. If you haven't visited your local hospital maternity unit in the last few years, you might be surprised to see how it may have changed. Many hospitals offer comfortable labor and delivery rooms that are quiet, dimly lit, and attractively decorated. Some are now also recognizing the importance of a greener environment specifically for a baby's delivery room and are open to special requests.

Many entire hospitals are getting greener. Concerned individuals and organizations from around the world convened at the Environment Science Center in Augsburg, Germany, to create a guide for Greener Hospitals.[5] A number of hospitals from across the United States participated. They recognized that in the United States, hospitals rank second only to manufacturing facilities in electricity use per square foot. The group came up with specific plans to conserve energy and water; identify and reduce environmental pollution; use more nondisposable, multiuse materials; recycle paper products and packaging; serve nonpackaged food; control the handling of hazardous substances; and limit air emissions—all in ways that reduce operating costs and improve patient safety and health. Larger hospitals can save even more money by getting greener. And new building projects offer a great opportunity. The group also provided guidance for building new hospital buildings designed from the ground up to be more energy efficient.

Ask your local hospital about their environmental management plan. I know of one hospital for women and children in my area that is building a new green building from the ground up. As pressure from energy prices, regulations, consumer preferences, and conscience increase, I expect this green trend in hospitals to accelerate. And this is great for raising baby green!

Giving Birth at a Freestanding Birthing Center

Sitting halfway between the very medical environment of a hospital and the very nonmedical environment of a home birth is the freestanding birthing center. A birthing center is a facility designed for healthy, low-risk moms and babies that offers a more personalized and often greener atmosphere than a busy hospital can usually conjure up, but a more medically controlled environment than parents can create at home.

The National Center for Health Statistics estimates that, of the births that took place outside of a hospital setting in 2004, 27 percent took place in a freestanding birthing center.[6] Most U.S. birth centers are independently run facilities, but some centers can be found in hospitals (an interesting point to investigate if you are leaning toward a hospital birth).

The personnel at most birthing centers try to cater to the comfort of the expectant parents. They offer rooms designed to look like a comfy bedroom at home, with perhaps a queen-sized bed for both expectant mom and dad to rest. Many have comfortable chairs and cozy couches for family and close friends to hang out on before and after the birth, and showers for women to relax in during their labor. Many will have a kitchen where family can gather, cook, and eat. This can be a home away from home.

Although these amenities don't necessarily make the centers green, they do increase the potential for meeting your desires for a green labor and delivery. At a birthing center, your labor and delivery will be attended by a midwife and perhaps a doula, who are traditionally more open to meeting the individualized needs of the expectant couple. This choice gives you more control over the environment in your baby's delivery room.

However, freestanding birthing centers are not without their disadvantages:

- Birth centers may not be appropriate for women with high-risk or complicated pregnancies.

- They may not be equipped to handle medical emergencies.

- They often do not have a medical physician in the building.

- 12 percent of women who labor in a birthing center will be transferred to a hospital before their delivery.[7]

- Some health insurance companies do not extend maternity coverage to birth centers.

If you are considering a birthing center, you will want to ask about their emergency backup plan and how long it takes to implement in practice. I agree with recommendations that the time "from decision to incision" should be thirty minutes or less if an emergency C-section is needed.

Green Parent Report

Choosing a Nonhospital Birth Center

WHEN LOOKING FOR A birth center that is not within a hospital itself, ask these questions:

❖ Is this a state-licensed facility (if your state gives such licensing)?

❖ Is the birth center accredited by the Commission for the Accreditation of Birth Centers?

❖ Are the birth attendants licensed health care providers?

❖ Does the center have an established relationship with local obstetricians who agree to intervene in a medical emergency? If you have your own ob/gyn, will he or she be able to intervene if necessary?

❖ What are the arrangements for transportation to a local hospital if necessary?

❖ What is their average time "from decision to incision" if a C-section is needed?

❖ Does your health insurance cover the cost?

If you have a low-risk pregnancy and are unsure about whether or not a hospital in your area can give you the healthy, green labor and delivery experience you desire, use the questions in the Green Parent's Report box "Choosing a Nonhospital Birth Center" to help you determine if a particular freestanding birthing center is right for you.

Questions for Hospital or Birthing Center Staff

When you visit a hospital or birthing center, bring along from this list your birth plan questions that you feel are important to your goal of introducing your baby to a healthy world. Many details on creating a green environment for a newborn can be found in Chapter Three. Be sure to read through that chapter and Chapter Five before you make your birth plan:

- Is the delivery room cleaned with EPA-approved disinfectants?

- Is it possible to obtain fresh, healthy, organic food and filtered water while I am in this facility? If not, may I provide my own?

- Does the facility offer the option of organic cotton bed linens and gowns in the delivery room? If not, may I provide my own?

- Can I avoid medical intervention that is unnecessary to my health and the health of my baby? (Such interventions might include routine internal fetal monitoring—which may be at odds with my preference for "the least amount of unnecessary medical intervention.")

- What are the bassinets and baby bedding made of? If they are made of conventional materials, can I provide my own bassinet, pads, bed sheets, and blankets?

- Will my baby be cleansed with soaps, shampoos, lotions, and creams? Can I bring my own? (See Chapter Five for information about pure personal hygiene products.)

- Do I have an option as to the type of diapers used on my baby—organic cotton cloth diapers or perhaps disposable brands known to have a lower impact on the environment?

Giving Birth at Home

A home birth sounds so, well, *homey*—but it's not necessarily green. The fact is, many home births occur in environments that are filled with the same toxic cleaners, linens, paints, furniture, and baby products that are typically found in hospitals and some birthing centers.

But a home birth is a choice that gives you complete control over the environment—so you can make it as green as you desire. A home birth can most easily become a green delivery because

- It results in the lowest level of invasive medical procedures, such as episiotomy, vacuum extraction, or cesarean section (see the Green Parent Report box "Differences Between Hospital and Home Births").

- A mother in labor does not have to be tethered to IV lines or monitoring machines—something that may be an advantage or a disadvantage, depending on the circumstances.

- It allows the mother to enjoy the best possible nutrition after the delivery.

- The expectant couple can prepare the delivery room in ways that keep the baby away from any industrial cleaners and other products that a hospital might use.

- The mother and baby can use organic cotton bedding and clothing if they choose—without having to get special permission.

- The new parents can use diapers, lotions, cleansers, and creams that they feel are pure, nontoxic, and good for the planet.

- A home birth costs less than an uncomplicated vaginal birth in a hospital in the United States, while at the same time reducing the polluting medical waste that ends up as landfill.[8]

If the opportunity to create a green delivery room for your baby in your own home is appealing to you, you can be further encouraged by the fact that there is no additional mortality risk found in home births for low-risk pregnancies.

In 2005, the *British Medical Journal* reported the results of a study of the births of 5,418 babies born in the United States and Canada in 2000.

In the research group, some parents employed a professional midwife for a planned home birth; others had planned hospital deliveries. Among a variety of findings, the best news was that for low-risk pregnancies, the maternal and infant mortality rates were equally low whether the baby was born at home or in the hospital.[9]

In the United States, however, the American College of Obstetricians and Gynecologists (ACOG) has taken a strong stand against births outside a hospital setting. "We recognize that some women have concerns that the hospital setting for childbirth leads to more interventions. However, we cannot ignore the fact that childbirth . . . has become safer for mothers and babies over the last 6 decades due to improvements in medical technology and improved access to trained providers and emergency obstetrical and neonatal care."[10]

Green Parent Report

Differences Between Hospital and Home Births

THE DIFFERENCES BETWEEN HOSPITAL and home births identified in the study published in the *British Medical Journal* were most apparent in the level of medical interventions that some say are unnecessary and therefore nongreen.[11]

Episiotomies	*Vacuum deliveries*	*C-section deliveries*
• Home: 2 percent	• Home: 1 in 200	• Home: less than 1 in 25
• Hospital: 33 percent	• Hospital: 1 in 20	• Hospital: 1 in 5

Of course the cesarean deliveries weren't performed at home; after the labor began, about 12 percent of women who planned to deliver at home needed transport to a local hospital. For this reason, I believe that the key to choosing a home birth is the speed with which state-of-the-art emergency support can be obtained if needed.

Although there may be appealing advantages to delivering a baby at home, we know this choice is not for everyone, or even for most women. When exploring all possible locations for the best delivery for you, keep in mind that there are some disadvantages to a home birth. For example, a home birth is generally attended by a midwife rather than a physician, and therefore you may not be able to receive medical help as quickly if an emergency arises. If your labor is especially difficult and long, for example, you may not be able to receive medications that could reduce your pain if your birth attendant is not licensed to administer pain medications. Or, if the baby experiences fetal distress or if your health becomes endangered and therefore a cesarean delivery becomes necessary, you will need transportation to a nearby hospital. If you are considering a home birth, make arrangements to be able to have emergency backup so that you can go from decision to incision within thirty minutes if needed. Think carefully about the pros and cons before making your final decision.

The decision is up to you. Many healthy babies have been born in the comfort of their own homes, and some families may strongly desire to plan a home-based labor and delivery. If the mother has a low-risk pregnancy and if the family has a backup arrangement with a physician and nearby hospital in the event of an emergency, home birth can be a viable option, with the added advantage that the expectant couple can control the environment to include the green elements that are important to them.

What Kind of Delivery Will I Have?

IN THE SAME WAY that you can select where and with whom you'll deliver your baby, you can also choose the type of delivery you prefer (barring a special medical circumstance or emergency). While preparing your birth plan, consider the options of a natural vaginal birth, a medicated vaginal birth, or a vaginal birth after cesarean if appropriate.

Going Green

Celebrate Your Baby's Birth with a Gift to the Planet: A Carbon Neutral Delivery

DEPENDING ON WHERE YOU deliver your baby, many of the equipment and material choices may be out of your control. One thing you can do, however, is offset the carbon emissions generated by the energy used to run the delivery room and all its equipment. When you arrange for a carbon offset, you make up for the "dirty" emissions-producing energy you couldn't help using, by making a financial contribution to projects that promote "clean" renewable energy (wind and solar, for example) and other efforts to reduce global warming. There are now many organizations worldwide that make it easy to invest in carbon offsets.

Here are some ways to have a carbon neutral delivery:

❖ You can purchase a $15 Wind Power Card to ensure that the energy used by your baby's delivery is replaced on the national power grid with wind energy, while offsetting more than 1,000 pounds of CO_2 emissions. Go to *www.renewablechoice.com*.

❖ You can donate to CarbonFund.org and select from a menu of certified carbon offset projects that include planting trees in severely fire-damaged forests and an innovative project that converts cow manure into methane that then generates the electricity to run a water desalination plant. Because CarbonFund.org is a nonprofit, your contribution is tax deductible. Go to *www.carbonfund.org*.

❖ You can plant a tree yourself. Over its lifetime, a tree will absorb one ton of carbon dioxide.

Be sure to record this special gift in your baby book. Someday you'll be able to tell your little one that when born, the energy that was used in the labor and delivery was offset and at least a little bit of global warming never happened. (See Chapter Seven for more on carbon offsets.)

Natural Childbirth

A natural delivery is one that is nonmedicated. It is green in its reduction of medical intervention and medical waste and in the way it protects the unborn child from the effects of pain medications.

Women who choose natural childbirth prepare for their labor and delivery in advance so that they have a clear understanding of the birth process—regardless of where they plan to deliver. They take childbirth classes that explain the physical function of contractions and how the body reacts to those contractions. They learn coping strategies to deal with the pain, including such techniques as deep breathing, visualization, muscle relaxation, self-hypnosis, and massage. See the section for this chapter in Green Information for a description of three popular methods of natural childbirth.

Medicated Vaginal Childbirth

Some may assume that the only green delivery is a natural vaginal birth, but that is not necessarily so. A medicated delivery is not automatically a nongreen one. The goal of a green delivery is to minimize the level of medical intervention and the negative impact of a toxic environment on the mother, the child, and the planet, while making the childbirth experience a comfortable and pleasurable one for the mother. You choose how to achieve that goal.

If you have chosen a physician or a certified nurse-midwife to deliver your baby, you can also choose a medicated birth. (Note: not all midwives are licensed to administer pain medications, so if you have chosen a midwife to handle your baby's delivery, be sure to ask exactly what pain medications she can and cannot offer.)

Common pain medications for labor and delivery are analgesics, anesthetics, or a mix of the two types. Narcotic analgesics can transfer across the placenta and also drug the unborn child. In contrast, the effects of the anesthetics commonly used during childbirth (typically an epidural or spinal block) don't directly affect the baby. See pages 274–275 in Green Information for other details on various types of nerve blocks. The Green Parent Report box "The Effects of Medicated Versus Nonmedicated Birth" reports the results of studies comparing babies born to mothers who use no pain medication and those born to moms who had an epidural nerve block.

Vaginal Birth After C-Section

A cesarean birth (the birth of a child through an incision in the mother's abdomen and uterus) is major surgery that is sometimes necessary for the health and safety of the baby or mother: to save a baby that might be in fetal distress, to deliver an exceptionally large baby or one in a breech position, or to save a premature baby under stress from the trauma of vaginal birth.

Green Parent Report

The Effects of Medicated Versus Nonmedicated Birth

SOME MOTHERS CHOOSE A natural birth; others require an epidural to ease the pain. Either way, the baby's health is similar:[12]

❖ Apgar scores are the same.

❖ Blood pH levels are the same.

❖ There is no increased risk of meconium in the bowel.

❖ The rate of cesarean section is similar.

❖ Among women who want to breastfeed and who deliver vaginally, there is no difference in breastfeeding between those who choose an epidural and those who choose no medical pain relief. (In the event of a C-section, women who have an epidural are more likely to breastfeed than those who have any other kind of anesthesia.)

❖ Mothers who have an epidural report experiencing less pain during labor and feeling better immediately afterward.

In these circumstances, a C-section is not a choice; it is not a matter of being green or nongreen. It is a medical emergency and is not something that can be predicted or therefore approved beforehand in a birth plan.

But there is a circumstance in which an expectant mom who has had one previous cesarean birth has the option to choose a vaginal or cesarean birth for the second baby. In this case, a green delivery may call for VBAC:

Going Green

Gentle Birth Method

THE LEBOYER GENTLE BIRTH method is a wonderfully green approach to childbirth—natural or medicated. You might appreciate some or all of its ideas. It was first introduced in 1974 by the French obstetrician Frederick Leboyer, in his book *Birth Without Violence*, which called for a more sensitive and gentle approach to birth.

Even though many parents have never heard of it, this method has brought about some changes in nearly all deliveries. For instance, it called for an end to dangling babies upside down and smacking their bottoms to start them crying, the end of putting harsh silver nitrate in the eyes shortly after birth, and the end of separating healthy newborn babies from their mothers. Beyond this, whether for a natural or medicated birth, this method encourages limited or even no use of delivery tools (such as forceps or vacuum pumps) so that the stress of birth on the child is reduced. It advocates low lights and soothing music in the delivery room, where the newborn is immediately placed on her mother's abdomen, postponing umbilical cord cutting and suctioning. In some hospitals the baby can then be placed in a warm bath to enjoy a return to the weightlessness of the womb.

The Leboyer method has been found equally safe compared to conventional deliveries, with the added advantages of a more natural delivery setting, of using the mother's body as the baby's first external environment and heat source, and of increased participation by the father in the birth.[13]

The second revised edition (2002) of *Birth Without Violence* is available from Healing Arts Press.

vaginal birth after a cesarean. (More pregnancies or more babies, as you might expect, change the situation considerably.)

After a woman has delivery by cesarean, some physicians insist that all future births also be by cesarean. There is a concern that in very rare circumstances a vaginal birth after cesarean could cause the uterus to rupture. But there is no evidence from randomized controlled trials on which to base any such practice recommendations regarding planned cesarean section for nonmedical reasons at term.[14]

Despite this lack of evidence, fewer than one in ten women these days have a vaginal birth after a cesarean delivery. The statistics on cesarean deliveries are just as startling: the most recent data from the Centers for Disease Control and Prevention show that the cesarean delivery rate in the United States has climbed to 29.1 percent of all births, the highest in our history.[15]

There are good reasons to avoid cesarean delivery if possible. It is major surgery and therefore it requires a longer, more expensive hospital stay, a greater need for blood transfusions, and a prolonged recovery period.[16]

A C-section affects the baby as well. The sterile environment required for the surgery can change or delay the ability of beneficial bacteria to make their home in the baby's intestinal tract. Growing evidence suggests that these beneficial bacteria can improve health. For example, in one small study of 865 healthy, full-term, breastfed babies with a family history of allergies, the babies were about half as likely to develop food allergies if they were delivered vaginally.[17]

A cesarean birth scheduled before labor begins also increases the risk that the baby will be born suffering from respiratory distress syndrome. If the gestational age of the baby is miscalculated, the lungs may not be fully mature, and upon cesarean birth the baby will experience problems of prematurity that he would not have had had he been allowed to develop fully until labor contractions began. This can keep him on a respirator and out of his mother's arms, and prolong his stay in the hospital.

You want the baby's first interaction with the environment to be as natural as possible, and that comes by whenever possible entering the world through the birth canal where the mom's body and the baby's body are joined together in a way that prepares the baby for life outside the womb. That's why, unless there's a good reason for a cesarean, a vaginal birth is a solid first choice.

After Delivery

IF YOU WOULD LIKE your newborn to be wrapped in organic cloth diapers, organic fiber linens and blankets, and organic fiber clothing, why wait until day two or three? Babies' skin is softest and most absorbent in the first days of life, before the protective outer layer of skin (the stratum corneum) forms. Read in Chapter Three about the impact of linens, diapers, and clothing on your baby and on the environment and then decide if you want

to welcome your baby into this world in an organic environment. If you do, be sure that your birth plan includes these welcoming amenities upon the birth of your child. If they are not provided—and they probably won't be—you can bring your own!

Cleansing Baby's Delicate Skin

Your baby will enter the world covered with traces of a white, cream-cheesy substance called vernix, which protected her skin from the long exposure to the water of the amniotic fluid. Soon she will have her first bath. And during diaper changes, your newborn's bottom will be cleaned again and again.

Although you certainly do want your infant to be clean, you don't want her skin to be covered with cleansers and lotions in those first few hours and days. For the first week of life, I do not recommend using any soap, lotion, shampoo, or diaper ointments unless necessary. Simple water is usually quite effective in cleaning up your infant's sensitive skin.

If you are giving birth at home, your midwife and doula will follow your instructions to use only water to gently bathe and clean your baby. If you give birth at a hospital, you might want to ask about what cleansers, shampoos, lotions, and ointments are used on babies, and what options are available. If shampoos and cleansers are required, you might ask if you can supply your own products for your baby. In Chapter Five you'll learn about the many chemicals in baby cleansing products that are best left on the store shelf in favor of the many alternative pure and gentle products that are now available. You'll also read why it is important to use only safe cleansers on your baby's skin.

What Will Be My Baby's First Meal?

What your baby will eat during his first days is a decision you must make before you deliver your baby. If you choose to breastfeed, this choice should be recorded in your birth plan and clearly understood by your support team. If you prefer to feed your baby infant formula, this too must be determined in advance—especially if you want to use a particular kind of formula right from the start.

The details of breast- and bottle feeding are covered in Chapter Four, "The Kitchen." The next sections talk about information that may affect decisions you'll want to make early on.

Breastfeeding

Many new mothers state clearly in their birth plans that they want to breastfeed their newborn immediately after his delivery. This is a well-intentioned request because we have good data that show that if a baby breastfeeds before being taken from the mother to be bathed after his birth, the mother has a much higher chance of successfully breastfeeding that baby.

But an even more natural way to begin the breastfeeding process is to give the newborn time to seek out his first meal by himself. Ask someone to place your newborn on your stomach before he is bathed or evaluated.

Cuddle, make eye contact, and then watch what the baby will do instinctively. He will first begin to act hungry by smacking his lips. He will then start pushing his feet against your body to work his way up to the breast. (I believe this is why babies are born with the stepping reflex that causes them to move their feet and legs as if they are trying to walk when something is pushed against their feet.)

He will navigate his way to your breast by following the scent of the amniotic fluid. (The breasts secrete an oily substance containing some of the same ingredients.) He will suck on his fists, get the scent of the fluid that is still on his skin, and then head up toward the breast by pushing, stretching, and inching his way along.

When he makes this journey to the breast by himself, the latch-on is much more likely to be a healthy one in which he gets the whole nipple and areola. The breastfeeding is then far easier for both baby and mom and makes it more likely that the breastfeeding attempt will be successful.

Unfortunately, if the baby's hands have already been washed, or if your breasts have been overly cleansed, the baby won't be able to make the journey. That's why it's important to plan for this little bit of exercise in your birth plan.

This first supper is an Olympic achievement for both of you. And for most healthy babies, it's a good reason to delay washing, eye ointment, weighing, measuring, shots, or procedures for the first hour.

Consider a Lactation Consultant

Although very natural and green, breastfeeding isn't necessarily easy. It can feel uncomfortable at first, and it can take time for both the mom and the baby to get the hang of it. This too is natural.

If you plan to breastfeed your newborn, check on the availability of a lactation consultant. This is a certified health care professional who is trained to help new mothers breastfeed their babies. She will observe a feeding, troubleshoot, and give suggestions and advice. She will also share natural remedies for cracked or sore nipples and for the discomfort of engorgement. Lactation consultants are sometimes provided by birthing centers and hospitals as a routine service, but if they are not, you can hire a private one; the service may even be covered by your insurance.

The section for this chapter in Green Information has more information about breastfeeding resources.

Bottle Feeding

Although I encourage all new moms to breastfeed, I am well aware that there are circumstances in which this is not possible. Some new mothers are separated from their babies due to medical problems that need immediate attention or require isolation. Other mothers have their own medical difficulties that don't allow them the opportunity to breastfeed. Mothers of adopted babies also will bottle feed their infants, and mothers who return to a busy work schedule may not have the luxury of breastfeeding their children.

If you cannot breastfeed your newborn, you can still take steps to nourish her in a thoughtful, caring, and green way. There are now improved infant formulas and bottles and nipples that are made without chemical phthalates or bishpenol A (BPA) and are therefore safer for your baby. There are even human milk banks that can provide pasteurized donor milk. To learn more, go to the Web site of the Human Milk Banking Association of North America: *www.hmbana.org.*

Before it's time to head to the delivery room, read Chapter Four for important information about baby formulas, bottles, and nipples. That chapter will explain why you may want to talk to your health care providers about having your own DHA-enriched formula, non-BPA bottles, and silicone nipples on hand for your baby's first meals.

Going Home

SHORTLY AFTER YOUR LABOR and delivery, the mixed anxiety and joy of this life experience will be in your past, and it will be time to look forward to the future—to the time when your baby will live and grow in the protective environment that you will create in your home.

Choosing a Green Pediatrician

As you did when choosing an ob/gyn, you want to find a pediatrician who is top-notch medically. How much better if he or she is also on the journey to an environmentally sustainable perspective on pediatrics!

This may be the first time you have selected a pediatrician; if you already have children, you may have an established relationship with their pediatrician—or you may have inherited a treasured family doc from when you were a child. In any case, here are five representative questions you may want to ask politely to gauge physicians' thoughts on things green:

1. **What advice do you give to new parents about introducing solid foods?** If their first suggestion is to begin with processed white rice flour cereal or processed conventional jarred foods, they may still be working from a twentieth-century industrial mind-set. To learn more, continue the conversation by asking for their advice about introducing whole grains, fresh tastes, or organic foods. Green pediatricians are often conscious of nutrition and care about establishing the nutritional habits of today's babies in ways that are better than those of previous generations.

2. **How do you recommend treating ear infections?** If they say that all ear infections should be treated with antibiotics, they may be behind the times. The Academy of Pediatrics now teaches that, in many situations, ear infections will heal better on their own, without antibiotics (but pain relief should be given for the ear pain). (See Chapter Five for discussion of this newer approach.) The first steps toward sustainability that pediatricians often make in their practices are to reduce the unnecessary use of antibiotics.

3. **How do you recommend treating eczema in babies?** If their first response is to use steroids or prescription drugs, they may not yet be thinking green. Often, a better first approach is to reduce exposure to eczema triggers or to gently moisturize the skin. Green-oriented physicians are more likely to treat the cause rather than just the symptoms and will opt for the gentlest treatment possible.

4. **What kind of baby shampoo do you recommend?** If they mention a conventional brand, they may not yet be thinking about sustainable and pure products. If they mention any of a number of greener options, such as Baby Avalon Organics, Burt's Bees, or Tom's of Maine, that's a good sign that they are at least aware of a variety of greener options for common baby products.

5. **Do you buy organic foods for your own family?** Or **What kind of car do you drive?** The answers to these types of questions will help you get a sense of their own green lifestyle outside the practice of medicine. Often physicians will start thinking about green issues for their own lives before they start integrating them into their practices. If they have made even small steps in this regard, they may be more supportive of your efforts to raise your baby green.

In addition to conversations with prospective pediatricians, you can also get some insight into the green potential of a medical practice by making an office visit simply to observe. What kind of lighting is used? (Incandescent bulbs are very nongreen.) What kinds of cleaners are used? (A strong scent of bleach or ammonia is the tip-off that green cleansers are not yet in use.) Are there any babies in the waiting room who are wearing cloth or hybrid diapers? (This is a good sign that other parents with environmental concerns have chosen this doctor.)

And from the comfort of your home, you can learn a lot about some physicians and their practices by looking at their Web sites—many pediatricians have them now, but not all—and by talking to other parents. To make learning from other parents even easier, at DrGreene.com we've invited parents everywhere to rate their pediatricians and to share a little about what they like best about them. This feature, launched in 2007, is called CareSeek. I hope it will make finding the right pediatrician easier than ever.

Creating a Green Birth Plan Checklist

A GREEN BIRTH PLAN is a written checklist of your preferences during your labor, delivery, and hospital stay; the act of creating it will help you, your partner, and your health care providers talk about what you would like during this oh-so-important life event. It is also a tool that you can use to identify and inform the support people who will be there to help you. See the end of this chapter for a basic list of topics for such a birth plan.

A birth plan is not, however, a binding contract or a rigid set of rules. It is a list of your desires, a record that you would like all those involved in the delivery of your baby to know about and to work toward fulfilling, assuming that your preferences are medically feasible.

A birth plan encourages communication between you and all those who will care for you during labor and delivery. It allows everyone to put on the table their thoughts about your decision to have a green birth. Far better to find out now that one of your support team does not agree with your plan while there's still time to make adjustments, rather than when your little one is pushing to be born and you're in no position to discuss the problem. The following are the questions you will answer as part of creating your birth plan:

- Who will be my health care providers: medical doctor? midwife? doula?

- Where will I deliver my baby: hospital? birthing center? home?

- Is the birthing room designed and maintained in an eco-friendly way?

- If not, what can I bring so as to create as green an environment as practical?

- What kind of delivery will I have: natural? medicated? cesarean?

- What will baby's first meal be: breast or bottle?

- What kind of linens, diapers, creams, cleaners, and other baby products do I want for my green birthing room?

- How about something green or natural in the room, like a houseplant or seashells, or a piece of driftwood?

Depending on where you deliver, there may be some restrictions.

The next chapter, "The Nursery," will help you think about the many ways you can create a healthy and beautiful environment for your newborn.

MY BIRTH PLAN

1. **My baby will be delivered:**
   ____ at home
   ____ in a freestanding birthing center
   ____ in a hospital birthing center
   ____ in a hospital delivery room

2. **The health care providers on my team will be:**
   ____ my partner or other lay coach
   ____ a doula
   ____ a midwife
   ____ a medical doctor

3. **I would like the delivery of my baby to be:**
   ____ natural childbirth
   ____ medicated with narcotics
   ____ medicated with a nerve block
   ____ medicated only if requested during the course of my labor

4. **I would like my delivery room to:**
   ____ use natural-fiber sheets and diapers
   ____ cleanse my baby with pure water only, or if necessary pure cleansing products that I will supply
   ____ avoid using facility-issued cleansers, lotions, or creams on my baby

5. **I would like my baby's first meal to be:**
   ____ breast milk
   ____ supported by a lactation consultant
   ____ hospital-supplied formula
   ____ organic formula brought from home
   ____ my organic formula offered in non-BPA bottles with silicone nipples

3

THE
Nursery

The nursery is the perfect room to begin turning any house into a green home. The occasion of bringing a new baby into the world is an opportunity to apply green principles to a universe of new products, from cribs to diapers and toys to baby sleepers—and it's the ideal time to learn about new green versions of familiar home improvement materials, such as paints and flooring. The recommendations in this chapter for decorating, stocking, and maintaining a nursery are also practical and important to consider for other rooms of the house. In fact, if you plan to keep your newborn in the master bedroom with you—that room just became the nursery! Therefore, the information in this chapter about decorating green is applicable to any room in your home.

What Is a Green Room?

WHEN DECORATING OR REMODELING any room of your home, "green" means using products and materials that:

1. **Are locally manufactured.** Buying products manufactured nearby cuts down on the waste of fuel and the emissions that result from transporting goods long distances, and also supports your local economy.

2. **Conserve natural resources.** These include products that are made from rapidly renewable materials generally produced from agricultural crops, such as organic cotton, wool, sisal, cork, and bamboo, and products made from wood derived from certified well-managed forests. Examples include cork and bamboo flooring.

3. **Are salvaged.** Some construction and decorating components can be reused or rescued, thus reducing the consumption of new products

made from raw materials. Examples include period hardware and millwork.

4. **Contain recycled content.** These include products made of materials that have been diverted from the landfill and put into the production of new products. An example is flooring made of reclaimed wood.

5. **Are made to last.** Green products don't need frequent replacement. Well-made items constructed from quality materials stay out of landfills and incinerators and save the production costs of replacement products.

6. **Avoid toxic emissions.** Green products minimize toxic industrial chemicals and contribute to a healthy home environment. Examples include zero- or low-VOC paints, caulks, and adhesives.

Green Parent Alert

If You Decide to Remodel

FROM A GREEN PERSPECTIVE, the very first thing to consider if you decide to remodel, especially in an older home, is that you may be exposed to chemical residues in construction dust and debris. This is a common way to be exposed to lead and an array of other chemicals, pesticides, mold, and asbestos. Specific advice for reducing or eliminating harmful exposures depends on the age of your home and your particular project.

If you're pregnant, to be safe you should check with your doctor before pursuing remodeling or other home improvement projects. You may want to take special precautions because many chemicals can cross the placenta and harm your developing baby. If you've had your baby and you're now thinking about remodeling, check with your pediatrician first.

In either case, you may need to find an alternative place to stay during construction, and make sure that floors are well cleaned and rooms are thoroughly aired out for several days before you return.

With these criteria in mind, let's start the green nursery makeover with an empty room, then furnish, decorate, and stock it with products that are safe for both the baby and the environment.

Remember, every change you make in the green direction is a positive step. So whether you make one small change or redo the entire room "green," you're contributing to the green movement and giving your child a healthier home in which to have her sweet dreams. It's a good feeling knowing you are doing something that's right for your family and the planet—and at the same time creating a beautiful living space.

Paint

WHETHER USING AIRY PASTELS or bold primaries, a baby's room is a great place to show the joy of color. Years ago when my first child was born, paint was paint, and it was pretty toxic. There was no other option but to open the windows wide and bear the fumes as best we could. Today, we have knowledge and options that give us much more control over the healthiness of the air we breathe inside our home. When buying paint, we can choose to go green.

Checking First for Lead

Environmentally green paints are free of many elements that were previously standard in the industry. For example, rooms painted before 1978 may be coated with lead-based paints. The EPA says that in most cases, lead-based paint that is in good condition is not dangerous. But deteriorating lead-based paint that is peeling, cracking, chalking, or chipping is an immediate health hazard to you, your baby, and the planet.

Lead gets into the air and the human body primarily through dust particles. The chips, especially those around door jams and window sills, will turn into dust from the friction of movement and then get inhaled from the air. The dust also falls to the floor, and as the baby begins to creep around at six months or so, she gets microscopic dust particles on her hands, which then go into her mouth. This dust can also be found in the soil outside the windows and doors.

Step one in your decorating plan: if there is deteriorating lead-based paint in your home, you should attend to it before doing anything else. Fortunately, there are several ways to protect your child and the environment from the dangers of this kind of paint.

If you have an older home or apartment, don't start renovating or repainting until you get a paint inspection and risk assessment for lead paint hazards in your home. You can get started by calling the National Lead Information Center at 800-424-LEAD. The hotline will answer your questions about lead paint and will also send you detailed information about preventing lead poisoning.

At its Web site at *www.epa.gov/lead*, you can find a list of EPA-certified labs near you where you can send paint chips for testing, and you'll also

find a list of local specialists who can remove or seal the lead. You can also get a helpful free pamphlet from the EPA, *Protect Your Family from Lead in Your Home*.[1]

If the assessment tests positive or your home was built before 1978, it's time to call in the professionals. You might choose to paint over the lead-based paint to seal the lead, but this quick fix is just that—only a temporary solution. And it's simply not safe for you to peel away or scrape off lead-based paint on your own, and any attempt to make your baby's room fresh and lead free by yourself will likely make things worse! When scraping or sanding lead paint, the dust instantly creates a serious health hazard

Buying Green

Natural and Milk Paints

❖ The Real Milk Paint Company offers an assortment of twenty-seven colors of paints made from organic products. You just add water! Find them at *www.realmilkpaint.com* or 800-339-9748.

❖ Green Planet Paints allows you to shop online or find a store near you that carries the products, giving you the opportunity to see the colors firsthand. Their paints are made from natural minerals and are plant based. Go to *www.greenplanetpaints.com*.

❖ Bioshield Healthy Living Paints offers a range of the different types of natural paints. Choose from clay, solvent free, and color washes to name a few. They also offer Kinder Paint, which is specifically for nurseries and children's rooms. These colors are created to provide a calming environment. You will also find a pure white milk paint suitable for tinting and furniture. To order or to find a retailer near you, go to *www.bioshieldpaint.com*.

to you and your unborn child. What you need are lead abatement specialists who will enclose the room and then remove the paint and the dust safely. Or they will treat and cover it over in a safe and effective way.

Choosing Eco-Friendly Paints

Paints manufactured after 1978 no longer contain lead; however, many do contain other undesirable compounds that also pollute the air and disrupt our health. First on the list of paints to avoid are those that contain high levels of volatile organic compounds (VOCs). Because the danger of these compounds has been well established, the EPA has required the reduction of VOC levels in all commercial products. There are many paints on the market today that provide wonderfully green options for all your new decorating projects; they won't contribute to the growing problem of indoor air pollution—a real problem indeed.

Low-VOC paints use water as a carrier instead of petroleum-based solvents, thus reducing the level of harmful emissions. They also contain no,

---

Buying Green

Earth-Friendly Paints

Zero-VOC Paints

❖ Eco Organic Paints has won several environmental awards. They offer a color matching service and next-day delivery. You can find out more at *www.ecos organicpaints.com.*

❖ Safe Paint is Green Seal certified, and the company offers free custom color tinting and free shipping. You can find out more at *www.safepaint.net.*

❖ The American Pride brand of zero-VOC paints is Green Seal certified and low odor. You can find a wide assortment and clearance prices at *www.eco safetyproducts.com.*

Low-VOC Paints

❖ You can find low-VOC and zero-VOC paints and enamels that are geared toward the chemically sensitive and people with allergies at *www.alerg.com.*

❖ Sherwin-Williams adds a GreenSure designation to its environmental friendly products. Because this is a large dealer, you probably can find a store in your area, or go to *www.sherwin-williams.com.*

❖ AMF offers a wide range of low-VOC paints and other building and remodeling supplies. One advantage of this company is that it lets you order samples of the paint to see how you like it and if you have any allergic reactions. Go to *www.afmsafecoat.com.*

Green Parent Report

VOC Paint Facts

❖ According to the EPA, 9 percent of the airborne pollutants creating ground-level ozone come from the VOCs in paint.[2]

❖ In sunlight, some paint VOCs can react with nitrous oxide and create smog—we think of it as coming from auto exhausts, but it also comes from oil-based paints.

❖ The disposal of conventional paints causes landfill and groundwater contamination, whereas low- and zero-VOC paints are not considered hazardous waste materials.

❖ The use of chemical-laden paints year after year causes them to build up on walls and ceilings of homes, which when later demolished, release contaminants into the air, water, and soil.

or very low levels, of heavy metals and formaldehyde. Even better are zero-VOC paints (also called VOC-free or no-VOC paints) that contain five grams per liter or less of VOCs.

Although these paints make it easier for us to decorate our homes beautifully *and* safely, they're not the entire answer to the indoor pollution problem. They may still contain pigments, biocides, and fungicides that might not be good for anyone in your household.

If you're going to go green with the paint in your baby's room, why not take the extra step and look for either natural or milk paints?

Natural paints are derived from such substances as citrus, balsam, clay, chalk, and talcum. Water-based natural paints give off almost no smell and do not send out biocide gasses; they are petroleum free and very low in VOCs. They are now available in any color or shade, from soothing pastels to lively primaries.

Milk paints are made with milk protein or casein and lime and are colored with earth pigments, such as lime or clay. They are odorless and come in powdered form to be mixed with water. I have seen rooms painted with these pure-quality products. They are beautifully vibrant. And when you're done with the project, it's much easier to properly dispose of natural and milk paints than their toxic counterparts.

Wall Coverings

IF YOU PREFER THE texture and pattern of wallpaper for your nursery, you can find a wide choice of the green variety. I have seen super wall coverings made from natural renewable sources, such as bamboo, raffia, rice papers, flax, cork, arrowroot, jute, and recycled paper. There are also grasscloths made from honeysuckle vines; sisal coverings from recycled sisal carpets; and an organics line made from green tea, coffee, or mugwort. Other interesting products are made from hemp cloth in combination with cottons, cellulose, and plant skins. So many to choose from!

Conventional wallpaper is a nongreen product—waste, toxic glue, and chemical gasses abound! You should make a special effort to avoid vinyl. The manufacture of vinyl creates dioxins, among the most toxic industrial by-products. Dioxins enter the food chain and get into the fat of animals (including us), where they can cause cancer and harm the immune system. And the chemicals used to make vinyl soft and pliable include the phthalates—known endocrine disruptors. Healthy Child Healthy World (previously called The Children's Health Environmental Coalition or CHEC) has posted an article on its Web site that deems vinyl (PVC) "the worst plastic, from both an environmental and health standpoint."[3] You don't want vinyl in your baby's teether, bottle, cup, baby food jar, or bath toy—or on the wall where she will sleep every night.

Green wall coverings are better for your baby's health than conventional ones because the inks used in their production are usually water based, containing no heavy metals or VOCs. They are also better for the environment because they reduce both the amount of natural resources necessary for manufacture and the pollution produced.

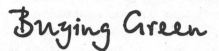

PVC-Free Wall Coverings

❖ You can find a large assortment of wall coverings that are PVC-free through Duron. The company carries Eco III, Texturglass, Tuffwall, and Verastone, which are all eco-friendly. You can find a local retailer by going to Duron's site: *www.duron.com.*

❖ ModGreenPod creates wallpaper made from 100 percent organic cotton and fabrics. Its coverings are vinyl free, for a healthier environment both in your home and in the outside world. By visiting the company's site you can pick colors and printed designs as well as find a location near you to check out samples and buy the product. Go to *www.modgreenpod.com.*

Flooring

GREEN FLOORS? YOU BET. Whether you choose to refinish an existing hardwood floor or to start fresh and install something new, you now have wonderful green options that allow you to decorate with style and at the same time protect your child's health and the environment.

Refinishing Your Old Hardwood Floors

Many homes have solid hardwood flooring that is either battered or hidden under carpets. If that's the case in your house, refinishing this old wood is a very green choice. The beauty of the original wood lies hidden beneath years of wear and grime, but it's there to be discovered anew.

Refinishing hardwood flooring, however, can be a dirty and toxic job. Every step of the way—stripping, sanding, sealing, varnishing, and polishing—can fill the air with pollutants that you want to avoid during your pregnancy, even if you use one of the new generation of sanders that do a better job of containing dust. So if you do decide to refinish the old wood, someone else should do it while you're out of the house entirely. In fact, it would be smart to make plans to live somewhere else during the entire refinishing process.

Eco-Friendly Floor Finishes

Beautiful natural floors made of such raw materials as wood, bamboo, and cork will need to be finished for lasting beauty and care. Unfortunately, the green quality of these materials can be diminished by the traditional finishing products that contain solvent-based polyurethane, known carcinogens that can be toxic to humans and pets.

Fortunately, today there is a comprehensive range of eco-friendly natural waxes made from sustainable raw materials that can be used for both interior and exterior applications.

The following are nontoxic alternatives to solvent-based polyurethanes:

- **Water-based polyurethane.** Water-based polyurethanes provide a clear finish and have low odor. If you start early enough in the day, you can apply the recommended four coats and sleep in the room that night. (Oil-based polyurethanes, in contrast, require fewer coats. But there is a five-hour wait between coats and then, due to the strong odor and fumes, you need to wait twelve hours after the last coat before you can live in the room.)

- **Drying oil.** This is an organic oil, such as tung oil, used as a binder in paints and varnishes. It dries into a tough elastic layer when applied in a thin film and exposed to air. Avoid the oil vapors before it dries completely.

- **Hardwax oil.** There is a whole range of hardwax oil timber floor finishes. Treatex and Osmo, for example, are highly accepted and widely used global brands. They are said to enhance the natural beauty of wood floors, are extremely durable and also safe to apply and easy to maintain and repair. Products like these are produced through an environmentally friendly manufacturing process and allow for safe disposal of used wax after sanding.

New Wood Flooring

Natural wood flooring can be green if it is manufactured and installed in environmentally sensitive ways. Otherwise, like other conventionally produced wood products, its use will increase the destruction of our forests and, by creating gasses from VOCs and formaldehyde, contribute to the air-quality problem.

If you'd like to use hardwood floors in your baby's room, this is a good time to look for FSC-certified wood. As explained in the section about wood furniture later in the chapter, these flooring materials are harvested according to the rules of the Forest Stewardship Council, which certifies environmentally managed forests the world over. Purchasing FSC-certified wood casts your vote for forest conservation—and as a side benefit reduces the indoor air pollution in your home that can affect the health of your baby.

Engineered Flooring

Engineered hardwood flooring is a product to consider if you want to add a new wood floor quickly without the dust and fumes that come with installing traditional solid wood floors. This kind of flooring material comes in prefinished planks that don't need to be sanded and finished in your home, and are easy and relatively inexpensive to install. In engineered flooring, a surface layer of hardwood is bonded to wood sublayers. Cross-ply construction makes the product even more stable than solid wood. And it's a good wood floor solution if you have a concrete subfloor.

It's now possible to purchase FSC-certified engineered wood flooring manufactured with low-VOC glues that eliminate off-gassing in your home, and some are completely formaldehyde free. You can choose from a wide array of FSC-licensed wood species, from traditional maple to exotic Brazilian cherry and Australian chestnut. Be sure to check for the above specifications of any engineered wood you're considering.

Reclaimed Wood

Wood floors offer classic beauty to any room, including your baby's nursery. But installing a new wood floor raises concerns about deforestation. To have both the beauty of wood and the peace of mind that comes with green building, you might give reclaimed wood flooring a try.

Sometimes called antique wood, reclaimed wood flooring is made of lumber rescued from deserted barns, old broken-down piers, deconstructed factories—even enormous old cider vats from breweries in England and Ireland! After every nail and bolt and any embedded debris is removed, the wood is resawn, kiln dried, and milled for reuse. Occasionally the cleaning process provides a peek into the wood's historic past and reveals tiny treasures like Civil War bullets, coins, and handmade nails. Vintage pine, oak, and chestnut planks are full of character and rustic appeal, and are considered especially desirable for their historic value. Reclaimed wood floors can be found in private homes and public buildings across the country, including the New York South Street Seaport Museum and the Portland Museum of Art.

Some folks prefer reclaimed wood because it came from old-growth forests of America, making it harder, denser, and more attractive in appearance than new-growth wood.[4] From a green perspective, reclaimed wood can be more resource efficient. It reduces the need for excessive foresting, diverts wood from landfills, and reduces the need for manufacturing new wood floor products.

Bamboo Flooring

Bamboo is a durable product that makes a great-looking floor covering, while addressing many of sustainability issues.

Bamboo propagates by spreading horizontally underground and is considered a rapidly renewable resource because it can be harvested in as little as three years. Twice as much fiber can be taken from a bamboo forest each year than from even fast-growing pine forest (a major supplier of wood flooring). Also, it needs little if any irrigation, pesticides, or fertilizers.

Although I have seen beautiful bamboo flooring and recommend it highly, low-quality bamboo has recently begun to flood the market in response to consumer demand. Unfortunately, many of these products contain high levels of formaldehyde in their binders. The finish can also be a

Buying Green

Wood Floors

❖ EcoTimber's wood flooring comes from FSC-certified forests. These are forests where trees are grown and harvested in a way that protects their longevity. Their wood is finished without harmful chemicals. EcoTimber sells many species of solid and engineered flooring, as well as some varieties of reclaimed and salvaged woods and bamboo flooring. Go to *www.ecotimber.com.*

❖ Floor Shop allows you to comparison shop for unfinished hardwood flooring from several manufacturers. Go to *www.floorshop.com.*

❖ Natural Home Products sells solid oak, ash, merbau, and beech hardwood floors without toxic adhesives. The wood comes from forests that are managed for sustainability. Go to *www.naturalhomeproducts.com.*

❖ Mountain Lumber specializes in reclaimed lumber, and for the past thirty years has rescued more than twenty million board feet of pine and other woods for reuse that otherwise would have gone to landfill or just quietly disintegrated. Go to *www.mountainlumber.com.*

Bamboo Floors

❖ Green Building Supply sells a range of nontoxic bamboo flooring. This company also offers a warranty. To find out more, go to *www.greenbuildingsupply.com.*

❖ Duro-Design uses a low-VOC finishing system on their bamboo flooring. They also offer free samples. For information, go to *www.duro-design.com.*

❖ EcoTimber sells both solid and engineered bamboo flooring derived from bamboo plantations rather than cultivated from wild habitats. The company works with suppliers in China to verify that the flooring is produced using low-VOC and formaldehyde-free adhesives. Go to *www.ecotimber.com.*

Natural Cork Flooring

❖ Livingreen offers product samples and design consultations, for a fee, on how to add cork flooring to your home. Go to *www.livingreen.com.*

❖ Green Building Supply offers a fifteen-year warranty on the wear layer of its cork flooring. You can check out its flooring options at *www.greenbuilding supply.com.*

❖ For cork wall tiles, parquet tiles, and underlayment as well as cork floating floors, check out *www.ecobydesign.com.*

source of these emissions. So if you're looking for a long-lasting floor that will reduce the cost and environmental impact of other types of nongreen flooring, choose bamboo, but only the higher-quality bamboo, and be sure to ask about the presence of formaldehyde in the binding.

If your bamboo flooring is installed unfinished, use a low-VOC, water-based polyurethane finish as your sealer. One site suggests applying a new coat of urethane every few years as maintenance. See more at *www.duro-design.com*.

Cork Flooring

Cork flooring is soft underfoot, quiet, stain and moisture resistant, and available in natural, tinted, and vivid colors. It is also exceptionally green. Cork is harvested from the outer bark of cork oaks, which continually produce this bark for 150 years. The flooring is made from scraps from the manufacture of wine bottle corks. Also, it does not off-gas or shed microfibers, and it is naturally resistant to moisture, mold, rot, and fire.[5]

Generally cork flooring comes in tiles, planks, or sheets of various sizes. Installation gives you more green options. It can be glued down (with nontoxic glues if you choose), or the tiles can be snapped together in tongue-and-groove fashion.

When purchasing cork flooring, ask if formaldehyde is used as a binder. If it is, keep looking. There are other brands that are manufactured without this toxin.

Cork is durable and long lasting. When it is removed at the end of its useful life, it can be applied to your yard, garden, or potted plants as a compost if it was finished with a natural sealer.

Stay Away from Vinyl and Linoleum Flooring

Vinyl flooring is common in American households, but as was discussed in the section on wallpaper, it is a poor choice environmentally. Linoleum is a better choice in general, but it's not for a nursery. Linoleum is made primarily from linseed oil, pine resin, sawdust, and cork dust; it is biodegradable, and it does not have the chlorine and plasticizers that vinyl does. However, linoleum raises the concern that in this form the natural linseed oil can continue the off-gassing of aldehydes—VOCs that can be harmful to young children.

Carpet with Caution

Wall-to-wall carpets—even those made from green materials—are not on the top of my list for decorating baby's room. All carpets are magnets for undesirable organisms that you would never knowingly allow to accumulate anywhere else in your home. Carpet fibers are ideal hiding places for mold, dust, bacteria, and other allergy-causing organisms. These fibers also can create the "sink effect" that holds on to noxious chemicals tracked into the home on your shoes. Dirt, lawn fertilizers, garden pesticides, road oil, snow salt, and the like become trapped in carpet fibers and remain there for years, creating real hazards for infants and children who play on the floor and put their hands in their mouths.

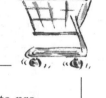

Buying Green

Two Ways to Find Green Carpeting

❖ Green Seal is an independent, nonprofit organization dedicated to protecting the environment by promoting the manufacture and sale of environmentally responsible consumer products. It sets environmental standards and awards a Green Seal to products that cause less harm to the environment than other similar products. The Green Seal Choose Green Report "Carpet" offers a list of recommended carpet brands, their manufacturers, and contacts. Find it at *www.greenseal.org/resources/reports/CGR _carpet.pdf.*

❖ Look for carpeting, cushioned underlayments, and floor covering adhesives that display the Carpet and Rug Institute's Green Label, which indicates that the product has met stringent indoor air quality requirements for very low emissions. To learn more, visit *www.carpet-rug.com* and type the words "green label" in the Web site's own search box.

Carpeting, moreover, is also relatively short lived, and according to the industry's own statistics, a staggering five billion pounds of it winds up in landfills each and every year.[6] Usually, the best choice is to go with a clean, hard-surface floor topped with an easy-to-clean natural fiber area rug.

Carpeting remains a popular choice, and many green options are now available. If you decide on carpet, consider these greener options.

You can choose carpeting made of natural fibers from abundant and renewable sources, such as wool, cotton, jute, sisal, reed, seagrass, and coir. Other types are made from recycled polyester. Yes, this is still a petroleum product, but at least it is recycled, so it doesn't deplete nonrenewable resources to the same degree as do new polyester carpets.

Green Parent Alert

Use Your Buying Power to Help Stop Child Labor

IF YOU'RE THINKING ABOUT buying a new rug imported from India, Pakistan, or Nepal, first check out Rugmark. This nonprofit organization was launched in 1995 to combat the terrible practice of using children as laborers in rug-weaving factories. The illegal practice is widespread in India, Pakistan, and Nepal, involving an estimated three hundred thousand children ages four to fourteen who suffer greatly from respiratory diseases, vision problems, malnutrition, and deformities from long hours spent crouching before looms in wretched conditions.

You can help end this practice by checking for the Rugmark label. It certifies that the rug was woven by adults in licensed factories that have passed random inspections. Your purchase also helps support Rugmark-sponsored rehabilitation programs, schools, and vocational training for children rescued from illegal rug manufacturers.

Go to *www.rugmark.net* for more information or to find an online seller or retailer in your area.

Wool is in many ways the best option. It's durable and naturally flame resistant, and it repels stains and liquids. It's more expensive at the outset, but is so long lasting that it's a bargain in the long run and in every way a green choice. Other natural fiber carpets may cost less but are more susceptible to mold, mildew, and fading from sunlight, and will probably need replacing long before a wool carpet begins to show wear.

Carpeting made of natural fibers does not contain the chemicals (as many as 120) found in a typical conventional carpet. Those chemicals (the ones that give off that "new carpet smell") are in the fiber bonding material, dyes, backing glues, fire retardants, latex binder, fungicides, and anti-static and stain-resistant treatments. In general, these chemicals will send off a chemical gas into your home for one to three months.[7]

Carpet underpadding can also be a green choice. Padding made from new, recycled, or natural renewable fibers such as cotton, felt, hemp, or jute are excellent alternatives.[8] Conventional carpet pads are made of foam and synthetic rubber manufactured from nonrenewable petroleum sources— very ungreen!

Wood Furniture

FOR SUCH A LITTLE person, it's amazing how much furniture a baby may use: cradle, bassinette, crib, changing table, rocking chair, bureau, and the like. And nothing brings nature indoors better than beautiful wood furniture.

But the depletion of the world's forests makes the purchase of wood furniture an important consideration for all consumers. The rapid destruction of our forests radically reduces one of our planet's most important ways to trap and use carbon dioxide, thus adding to the problem of greenhouse gases that cause global warming. Hmmm. We need to think carefully about our wood purchases. Of course, it's not just furniture that's using up all the forests. It's many things, including paper and paper products.

There are three ways to make buying wood furniture a green choice:

1. Buy recycled

2. Buy sustainable

3. Buy quality

Buy Recycled

New parents often cherish the thought of using heirloom baby furnishings that have been passed down through the family. Others delight in discovering beautiful vintage wooden baby items at estate sales and antique stores. And still others try to find great deals in used furniture in order to stretch the budget. All of these are green choices. The green movement is in part about salvaging, recycling, and reusing things, thus reducing the environmental impacts related to the extraction, processing, and transportation of virgin materials.

As green as recycling is, however, I do have to add a word of caution here. Before deciding to use an older piece of baby furniture, especially a crib, be certain it meets modern safety standards; otherwise, it's possible that this green choice will not be safe for the baby. Carefully inspect any used furniture with the following in mind:

- Some older furniture was manufactured before the U.S. Consumer Product Safety Commission set safety standards. For example, the spaces between slats or spindles on a crib can be no more than two and three-eighths inches (about the width of a soda can), and the corner posts must be less than one-sixteenth inch high to prevent entrapment or injury to the baby.

- Old cribs may have loose, missing, or broken hardware or slats, or may have unsafe cutout designs in the headboard or footboard.

- A crib must have a firm, tight-fitting mattress.

- Lumber and wood products made from salvaged wood may be coated with toxic paint, sealants, or preservatives.

- Much of the baby furniture found in attics and at garage sales is padded with soft vinyl. Best to steer clear.

You may be interested in supporting the efforts of the Rainforest Alliance Smartwood Rediscovered Wood Program, which encourages the use of existing wood and wood products that would otherwise go to landfills. Sources of reclaimed wood include demolition projects for antiquated buildings, dead or fallen trees, unproductive orchard trees, and trees carefully reclaimed from rivers and lakes. The Rediscovered Wood Program certifies that the wood is recovered using environmentally sound procedures. Most of the certified wood is now used for construction, flooring and cabinetry, rather than furniture. But keep checking for home furnishings that bear the Rediscovered Wood label as more products become available. For further information on this worthwhile program, see *www.rainforest-alliance.org/programs/forestry/smartwood/faq.html.*

In the meantime, consider the 100 percent recycled, wood-fiber-based heirloom-quality children's furnishings produced by a small company outside Sun Valley, Idaho, called Lilipad Studio. Their line of eco-friendly children's furniture includes step stools built of a wood product made of recycled wood fiber and formaldehyde-free binder. The classic stools are beautifully hand crafted and painted with intricate designs in rich, vivid colors using zero-VOC paints and then finished with three coats of a nontoxic sealer. See them at *www.lilipadstudio.com.*

Buy Sustainable

The Forest Stewardship Council (FSC) is an international, nonprofit group that encourages the use of sustainable forestry practices to harvest our forests but also keep them alive and abundant in an "ecologically sound, socially responsible and economically viable manner."[9] The FSC audits forestry operations and certifies those products that are produced in ways that meet fifty-seven different criteria, including protection of local wildlife and minimal use of chemical pesticides. If a forest or plantation passes the test, its wood products get branded with the FSC logo and a "chain of custody" number, which tracks the wood from its source, through milling and manufacture, right up to the point that you purchase the product from the store.

Wood and wood products may also be certified by the Sustainable Forestry Initiative established by the American Paper and Forest Association. This is an industry-based self-monitoring group, however, and its standards for certification are not as high as those of the FSC, nor does it require a chain of custody. When given the choice, I'd choose FSC certification. (Look for the FSC logo—a check mark with a tree.) You can find suppliers by visiting *www.certifiedwood.org* and clicking on "Certified Forest Products," then use the pull-down menus to choose your country and state to find the nearest suppliers.

Buy Quality

Being green doesn't mean avoiding wood furniture altogether. Co-op America (*www.coopamerica.org*) reminds us that if we invest in well-made furniture constructed from FSC-certified wood, the purchase can last a lifetime, be passed on to future generations—and keep a forest of cheaply made pressed wood products out of the landfill.[10]

Buying Green

Green Crib Mattresses

I RECOMMEND MATTRESSES MADE of **organic wool,** which is naturally resistant to dust mites and mold, and **organic cotton,** which is not treated with pesticides. Make sure any crib mattress you buy declares that it meets federal requirements for firmness and flame retardance.

Here are some sites that carry green mattresses:

❖ *www.ecobedroom.com*

❖ *www.nontoxic.com*

❖ *www.daxstores.com*

❖ *www.ecobaby.com*

Because the less expensive kids' furniture that's so popular with young parents is made to be used only temporarily while the child is small, it is often made of pressed wood that is manufactured using adhesives containing urea-formaldehyde (UF) resins. In even small amounts, this chemical can irritate a child's eyes, skin, and throat, and it can cause nausea and lethargy.[11]

The pressed wood furniture pieces sold by so many big box stores can include particle board used in shelving, cabinetry, and furniture; hardwood plywood paneling used for decorative cabinets and furniture; and medium-density fiberboard, used for drawer fronts, cabinets, and furniture tops. Medium-density fiberboard contains a higher resin-to-wood ratio than any other UF pressed wood products and is generally recognized as being the highest formaldehyde-emitting pressed wood product.[12]

In short, avoid pressed wood.

Bedding

YOUR NEWBORN WILL LIKELY spend more than sixteen hours sleeping every day during the first week at home. This will gradually decrease, but even at the first birthday most babies still sleep more than thirteen hours out of twenty-four.

So during this first year of spectacular growth one of the most important green purchases you make for your baby will be the mattress and sheets on which he sleeps.

Mattresses

From both a health and an environmental perspective, well-made green baby mattresses are far better than conventional ones. The batting, filling, and fabrics are made of clean, safe, certified organic cotton and organic wool. They are chemical free as well as waterproof and fireproof (see the Buying Green box "Green Crib Mattresses"). In fact, mattresses of organic material should meet or even exceed all federal and state flammability standards (including the stricter California TB603 and Consumer Product Safety Commission standards).

Your baby's body and face will lie close to her crib mattress every day and night for several years. This is one purchase that is worth going green for.

A Warning About Conventional Crib Mattresses

Putting children to sleep on their back has greatly reduced the rate of SIDS. I recommend this strongly, no matter what mattress is used. But I wonder if some part of the benefit comes from not having babies' faces pressed into the chemicals and gases of conventional mattresses.

Here is an overview of some specific chemical components of conventional crib mattresses that you can avoid by buying your baby a green mattress:[13]

- Polyvinyl chloride (PVC), the surface material used in nearly all baby mattresses, is widely considered to be one of the most toxic and environmentally unfriendly plastics in use today.

- Phthalates, associated with asthma, reproductive effects, and cancer, make up 30 percent by weight of the PVC surface of a typical baby mattress. The FDA and Consumer Product Safety Commission have issued general warnings regarding the use of phthalates, yet the PVC surfaces of baby mattresses still contain phthalates.

- The PVC surface of a typical baby mattress is also treated with toxic fire-retardant chemicals such as antimony, arsenic, and phosphorous. Various biocides are often added as well.

- Polyurethane foam, the predominant filling material used in baby mattresses, typically contains various problematic ingredients, including chemical catalysts, surfactants, emulsifiers, pigments, and other chemical additives. These frequently include formaldehyde, benzene, toluene, and other well-established toxic chemicals, such as organotin compounds.

- Polyurethane foam (essentially solid petroleum) is extremely flammable. To combat this hazard, toxic industrial fire retardants are added.

The most common chemical fire retardant used to treat polyurethane foam has been pentaBDE, a toxin associated with hyperactivity and neurobehavioral alterations. PentaBDE is not bound to the foam, so it leaches out into the surrounding air. PentaBDE has recently been banned in Europe. It has also been banned by the State of California as of 2006. However, there is currently no planned government action to recall the millions of baby mattresses presently in use that contain pentaBDE.

Organic Cotton Bedding

Crib sheets are made with the world's most popular fabric: cotton. I encourage you to choose organic cotton. It is so much kinder to your baby and to the planet.

Organic cotton is grown without the use of toxic pesticides or chemical fertilizers. Organic sheets are then produced without harsh chemical bleaches or dyes. They are natural and hypoallergenic. That's the kind of fiber you want caressing your baby's sensitive skin.

Unfortunately, the production of the world's conventional cotton supply has become an environmental mess, and now our everyday purchases— including crib sheets, diapers, and clothing—are a part of that mess.

Each year conventional cotton producers use nearly $2.6 billion' worth of pesticides, or more than 10 percent of total world pesticide use—including nearly 25 percent of the world's insecticides, making cotton the most insecticide-intensive crop in the world.[14]

This excessive use of pesticide in the cotton industry depletes the land of its nutrients by killing what's alive in the soil, requiring the use of more potent fertilizers to keep the land productive. The harmful chemicals are certainly bad for the land, but they may also be bad for your baby. The chemicals can end up in the cotton, and as the cloth lies against your baby's body, his skin may become irritated due to their toxicity, and the porous nature of human skin allows for the absorption of the toxins into the body.[15]

Thanks to the consumer demand of concerned parents like you, organic cotton baby supplies have gone mainstream. They are easy to find and competitively priced.

Go for Organic Wool

Organic wool comes from sheep that are raised organically and is processed without detergents, dyes, and other irritating substances. The resulting wool is luxuriously soft with just enough lanolin to retain the wool's natural characteristics.

If you buy something made of organic wool—let's say a warm and cozy comforter—you can be confident that the sheep it came from wasn't dunked into a pool of toxic organophosphate "dip" to kill parasites, as are conventionally raised sheep. Instead, beneficial insects and natural repellents handle parasites. And your sheep belonged to a herd that was carefully managed to protect the land from the damage caused by "overgrazing"— where too large a herd is allowed to strip away every shred of vegetation, leaving behind a barren, infertile landscape.

This sustainable approach to organic sheep ranching protects the environment for future generations, a concept we can support by making a special effort to purchase organic woolen products. Because wool is a renewable resource, is so durable, wicks moisture, and is fairly unflammable, organic wool is a green fiber of choice in my house.

For organic woolen and other natural fiber bedding and other products, check out *www.ecobaby.com*.

Diapers

AMONG THE FIRST ITEMS you'll stock in the nursery are diapers—lots of them. It has been estimated that you'll change about eight thousand diapers from birth to toilet training! With that many changes looming ahead, this is one baby product that may challenge your decision to go green— the convenience of landfill diapers can be hard to resist.

Most people call them disposable diapers, but this is misleading. It is a positive-spin marketing term invented by the diaper industry. These diapers are easy to get out of your home, but they are the least easy to truly dispose of. Because these diapers will spend far more time in a landfill than on your baby or in the trash, I call them landfill diapers.

Let's return to our definition of green nursery items at the beginning of this chapter: products that are locally manufactured, renewable, reused, recycled, durable, or healthier for us or the planet. Conventional landfill diapers don't get a clear nod on even one of these counts.

Some also believe that conventional diapers are bad for a baby's health. The literature on this subject is controversial and conflicting. Studies that have found links between conventional diapers and asthma, toxic shock, infertility in males, and simple diaper rash, for example, are strongly refuted in other scientific studies. Nothing is proven, but these studies bear watching.

Nevertheless, given that conventional diapers are convenient to use, it's no wonder that they have become the diaper of choice for 95 percent of North American parents.[16] Surely you would want cloth diapers or other alternatives to have some major benefits to make their use worthwhile. We'll consider today's cloth diapers as well as two newer options now available: "eco-diapers" and flushable diapers.

not your grandma's cloth diaper

New-Generation Cloth Diapers

Cloth diapers have changed over the years. Yes, the classic flat square is still sold, but even this basic choice now comes in a prefolded style that includes extra layering in the center, and in a contoured style that is form fitted to be less bulky under baby clothing.

Green Baby Story

The Never-Ending Diaper

MY INITIAL REASON FOR cloth diapering was to save money, but now the environmental benefits have also become a priority.

My brother is a chemical engineer and previously worked for one of the largest diaper makers in the United States. When I asked him just how bad disposable diapers are for the environment and how long it takes them to biodegrade he said, "Well, if it tells you anything, the diapers that we did recycle are used to make plastic fences." That pretty much said it all. Now I kind of cringe when I do have to use a disposable diaper because I realize that this piece of plastic is never going to degrade. If they were all made into fences that would be great, but the truth is, most of them will end up in a landfill for the rest of time.

Liz Bailey
Montrose, Michigan

Cloth diapers also now come in a fitted style that has an elastic waistband and leg openings. Most of these have closure systems, such as Velcro, or more innovative snaps, that eliminate the need for diaper pins.

Both the classic flat and the fitted diapers still need waterproof covers. The most common type is the old-fashioned plastic pull-ups that are lightweight and inexpensive, but do not breathe to allow ventilation and do not last long before drying out. New versions to the rescue. You can now buy polyester, wool, or fleece covers in a variety of vibrant colors and designs.

For the greatest ease, try the latest cloth diaper style called all-in-ones. These cloth diapers have a built-in waterproof cover. They have snap or Velcro closings and are size adjustable.

You can also get "pocket diapers" that have a soft, micro-fleece inner layer against the baby's skin, a waterproof outer layer to keep wetness contained, and a micro terry cloth insert that slips in between to absorb the moisture.

I also highly recommend what I call a hybrid arrangement, which is a flushable liner inside a cloth diaper. I discuss this in detail on the next page under "Two New Diaper Alternatives."

Make It Organic

If you do decide to go cotton, why not go all the way? Use organic cotton diapers. Organic cotton is grown without the use of toxic pesticides or chemical fertilizers. Organic diapers are then produced without harsh chemical bleaches or dyes and are hypo-allergenic. This is a far better choice for your baby's soft bottom.

The conventional cotton used in the production of crib sheets (as discussed earlier), by contrast, is produced with chemical fertilizers, toxic pesticides, and chlorine bleach, and these harmful elements are also present in cotton baby diapers.

See the Buying Green box "Cloth Diapers" for sources for these organic cotton diapers.

Cloth Diapers Could Save You Money

There are a number of studies that compare the cost of landfill versus cloth diapers, and the results vary. But all agree that buying and home-laundering cloth diapers is definitely less expensive.

One study found that savings of $800 to $1,600 over two and a half years could be realized through thousands of diaper changes. But is a dollar or two a day worth the time it takes to launder tons of diapers? It depends on your family. Using a commercial laundry service to wash cloth diapers is closer in cost to buying landfill diapers, but is still less expensive.[17]

Two New Diaper Alternatives

Take a good look at these new kinds of progressive diapers:

1. **Eco-diapers.** Somewhere between using landfill diapers or going with cloth ones is the choice to use disposables fondly called "eco-diapers." These diapers are made without dyes and fragrances, chlorine-bleached paper pulp, and sometimes even the polymer gels. Some are produced using wood pulp from sustainable forests. Sure, some consider organic cloth to be the best choice, but given that only 4 percent of U.S. families use cloth diapers,[18] eco-diapers are a satisfying step in the right direction.

2. **Flushable Diapers—True Disposables.** You can choose convenience while avoiding landfills by using disposable inserts inside cloth diapers. I call these diapers "hybrids"—with benefits of both convenience and cloth. The inserts are biodegradable and flushable, which allows for fecal matter to be properly disposed of: in the toilet. (The inserts that are wet as opposed to soiled can actually be used as compost.) This makes cleanup much easier and cuts down on the heavy-duty washing required for soiled diapers. For buying information, see the Buying Green box "Cloth Diapers."

Which Diapers Are Better for the Planet?

As a father and pediatrician, I've changed many diapers—enough to teach me that diapers are a daily reminder that as humans we deplete resources as we consume, and we make messes with our waste.

Those landfill diapers that are so easily tossed into the trash are clearly a major ecological issue. But what about the energy, water, and often chlorine involved in laundering cloth diapers? Comparing the environmental impact of different types of diapers has been the subject of a number of studies—with differing results often linked to the vested interests of those behind the study.

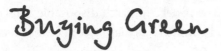

Cloth Diapers

❖ Fuzzi Bunz has a soft micro fleece layer against the baby's skin, a waterproof out layer, and a micro terry cloth absorbent insert. The snaps are easy to use, and the diapers are comfortably soft. For more information, go to *www.fuzzibunz.com*.

❖ You will find a wide variety of sizes and styles in cloth diapers, including special overnight diapers, at *www.greenmountaindiapers.com*.

❖ Ecobaby uses organic cotton and is part of the Organic Trade Association. For more information, go to *www.ecobaby.com*.

❖ You will find diapers and a wide range of accessories at *www.baby naturale .com*.

❖ To help save the environment and some money, you can check out *www .diaperware.com*. The company will buy back diapers that are still in great condition for a third of the purchase price. It then sells these diapers through its specials/clearance/used section.

Finding Eco-Diapers (a less problematic disposable)

❖ Tushies (*www.tushies.com*)

❖ Seventh Generation (*www.seventhgeneration.com*)

❖ TenderCare Diapers (*www.tendercarediapers.com*)

Finding Flushable Diapers—Hybrids or True Disposables

❖ gDiapers makes flushable snap-in liners that fit into a stylish outer diaper. Check out *www.gdiapers.com*. Starter kits include two outer pants and ten flushables for $25. Flushable refill inserts run about $15.

❖ Kushies sells flushable and biodegradable liners. You can order these liners at *www.kushiesonline.com*.

The largest and most objective study to date was carried out by the Environment Agency, the public body responsible for protecting the environment in England and Wales.[19] The panel compared disposable diapers to home-laundered cloth diapers and commercially laundered cotton diapers

Green Baby Story

Look Ma, No Pins!

By the time she was eighteen months old, my daughter Audrey was getting some serious diaper rashes. It was so horrible to see her in pain from the rashes that I tried to potty train her long before she was ready. Of course, that failed, but I noticed that her rash cleared up while she was wearing cotton panties against her skin, even when she soiled them.

That surprised me so I started learning about cloth diapers and how much they've changed since I was a kid. For example, I was relieved to find out that you don't have to use pins anymore. I can be a little clumsy sometimes and I didn't want to poke my little girl with a safety pin! Luckily there are cloth diapers now that use snaps or Velcro fasteners.

I'm completely sold on cloth diapers now. Not only did they take care of Audrey's rashes, I also just feel good about doing this for the environment. We wash ours at home and the amount of water we use per week for the extra laundry is about the same amount used by flushing the toilet a few extra times a day. We're definitely saving money over using disposables, but even if it were more expensive to use cloth diapers, I'd do it in a heartbeat. The main thing is that my children are learning to be good stewards of the earth and this is their first step in that direction.

Bev Morris
Covington, Georgia

in terms of global warming, ozone depletion, smog formation, depletion of nonrenewable resources, water pollution, acidification, human toxicity, and land pollution. The study did not include what I call hybrid diapers—the reusable diapers equipped with flushable, biodegradable liners.

This study found that overall environmental impact is about the same for all three options they did consider; the biggest impact is on global warming, resource depletion, and acidification. For disposable diapers, the most significant impact comes during manufacture; for home-laundered diapers, the primary impact comes from the electricity used in washing and drying; for commercially laundered diapers, the biggest impact comes from use of fuels and electricity.

Thus, according to the Environment Agency, if you choose cloth diapers, the first focus should be on reducing the energy used during washing and drying and reducing fuels and emissions during transportation (see Chapter Seven for more information about laundry). If you choose disposable diapers, focus first on greener manufacturing, such as used by the Eco-Diapers mentioned previously.

Although the Environment Agency report is more thorough than other analyses to date, it is still quite incomplete. For instance, it looked only at the major brands used—not the greener alternatives. It didn't look at making choices back at the very beginning of the manufacturing process: at the oil rigs where the plastic liners of landfill diapers begin, at the forests where the wood pulp starts as trees, and in the cotton fields long before cotton is a cloth. There is a big difference between cotton grown drenched in toxic chemicals and cotton organically grown, between sustainable forestry and irresponsible logging, between dioxin-producing chlorine gas in pulp mills and bleach-free diapers.

Whatever we choose for diapers, we have an unavoidable impact on the environment. But whatever we choose, we can make those diapers a little greener.

Putting Diapers in Perspective

When we say that two of the biggest environmental impacts of diapers are their contribution to global warming and depletion of nonrenewable resources, how big an impact are we talking about?

The Environment Agency report estimates that over the 2.5 years they assumed a child would be wearing diapers, the total impact, whichever diapers you chose, would be about the same as driving an average car thirteen hundred to twenty-two hundred miles over those thirty months. The highest estimates I've seen rate the impact as high as burning fifty-four gallons of gasoline a year for every year of diaper use.

A Natural Air Freshener

Changing dirty diapers can certainly foul the sweet baby smell in the nursery. But think twice before using commercial air fresheners. Many contain VOCs, and their use has been linked to minor infections, such as diarrhea and ear infections in children.[20] Instead squeeze a lemon into the diaper pail as a quick, gentle, natural alternative.

Diaper Cleaning Tips

There's no point in using cloth diapers if laundering puts harsh chemicals into the cloth and then back onto your baby's skin (not to mention into the sewer system and water table). So take a look at the recommended laundry soaps in Chapter Seven and keep the following cleaning tips in mind:

- Avoid commercial fabric softeners. They soften with various oils that can decrease the absorbency of your diapers. Instead, use vinegar in the wash load. This helps get the soap out of the cloth to minimize possible irritants, and it softens the material.
- Don't use bleach. This harsh product will be absorbed by the cloth, and you do not want this against your baby's skin.
- Weather permitting, dry diapers on the clothesline. They will last longer and smell sweeter. If they get stiff after drying, simply throw them in the dryer for just a few minutes to soften the material.

The Bottom Line

The negative environmental and social effects of conventional landfill diapers are quite clear. If I were to have a new baby now, I would use a combination of flushable "hybrid" diapers and new generation "pocket" cloth diapers to be equipped for a variety of settings. If the need arose for a "disposable," I would use one of the eco-diapers for its gentler manufacturing process.

Baby Clothing

BABY CLOTHES ARE SOOOOO cute. Those tiny sneakers and sleepers call to all new parents "Buy me!" But before you load up the nursery with extensive new baby wardrobe, remember to think green. Less is better when it comes to buying items you won't be using for very long.

Buying Green

The Well-Dressed Organic Baby

ORGANIC BABY CLOTHING STORES are sprouting online like happy dandelions. Here is a select list of Web sites that sell beautifully designed clothes made completely of certified organic fibers.

- ❖ *www.underthecanopy.com* is the company that coined the term *ecofashion*. They make comfortable high-quality clothes for babies and mothers.

- ❖ *www.sckoon.com* is based in New York and specializes in Japanese inspired kimonos, booties, caps, diaper covers, and bottoms called monkey pants.

- ❖ *www.betterforbabies.com* sells organic wool felt booties with an ankle cuff that holds the shoe on without being too tight. Because these are made of wool, they keep baby's feet at an even temperature. Natural cream color with a dark brown cuff.

- ❖ *www.speesees.com* offers fair trade organic cotton basics like jumpers and bodysuits in bright happy colors at reasonable prices.

- ❖ *www.sagecreeknaturals.com* has a big selection of infant gowns, playsuits, baby pants and tees, along with receiving blankets and sheets all made of soft organic cotton interlock knit. Lots of colors and designs.

Giant retailers Wal-Mart (the world's biggest buyer of organic cotton) and Target have also jumped into the organic baby clothing market.

- ❖ *www.walmart.com* sells infant clothing under its own label George.

- ❖ *www.target.com* carries the Organics by Tadpoles line of creepers.

Plan for Growth

Newborns have one primary job—to grow—and they do it very well and very quickly. Experienced parents can tell you stories about the bundles of baby clothes they bought and then packed away, unused, because their babies outgrew them before they had a chance to be worn.

For this reason, think before you buy. Yes, it's hard to resist that newborn dress shirt with the bow tie or that adorable party dress, but it's unlikely that your newborn will be attending any formal affairs in the first few weeks of life, and after that, the outfit won't fit anymore anyway. The same goes for those oh-so-useful one-piece sleepers and undershirts that babies often live in. They are wonderful, but don't buy too many at once. Your baby will jump from one size to the next faster than you can unpack your latest purchase.

Consider shopping for baby clothes in consignment shops and resale stores. And donate or resell those your own baby outgrows. This is a very green concept. So rather than buying that handsome baby bow tie and tuxedo set, invest instead in saving the resources used up by manufacturing, packaging, and distributing clothing that may be worn only once.

Buy Organic

Buying baby clothes made of organic fabrics is one green parenting decision that is getting easier to follow through on every day. Brands such as Under the Canopy are providing eco-friendly clothes with a great sense of style. Thanks to increasing consumer demand, organic baby clothes are now standard stock in many children's clothing stores. In fact, sales of organic fibers for infant clothes and cloth diapers rose 40 percent between 2004 and 2005, to $40 million. This surge in popularity has encouraged retail giants like Target and Wal-Mart to take these products mainstream.[21]

In addition to the health and environmental benefits of avoiding the toxic pesticides and chemical fertilizers used in conventional fibers (outlined in the diaper section earlier), organic clothing also allows you to protect your baby's delicate skin from other chemicals used in the manufacture of children's clothing. These include flame retardants, wrinkle resisters, stain repellants, colorfastness treatments, and chemical dyes. In fact, formaldehyde and PVC are often used as fabric finishers.

Although cotton is the most popular organic fiber, you can also wrap your baby in fabrics of organically grown wool, bamboo, hemp, and linen (flax). As demand increases, so will the availability of these green fabrics.

Toys

I AM A BIG fan of high-quality wooden and cloth toys for children. Both can be delightfully green—but not always. So when toy shopping, take time to examine the materials used to make the product and then choose wisely. And be sure toys are easy to clean if they will be shared.

Wood Toys

Well-made unfinished solid wood toys are safe for baby and the planet. There are no toxins to leech out, no toxic paint or sealant residues, and none of the urea-formaldehyde (UF) resin adhesives found in pressed wood. (You can tell if a toy is made from pressed wood by looking at any unfinished edges; they appear bumpy, and you can see the layers.)

Environmentally, solid wood toys are a sound choice. As explained earlier when we were discussing wood furniture, a solid wood toy has staying power, lasting through a family of children without adding clutter to our landfills. If you take time to search, you can even find wood toys made from FSC-certified wood or recycled wood that preserves forests from clear-cutting.

If adding a finish on a wooden toy, use a natural oil finish such as a walnut oil or beeswax. Mineral oil, linseed oil, and any plant-based oil with a strong smell are not recommended on the toys of children under age three.[22]

Cloth Toys and Stuffed Animals

Soft toys and cloth-covered stuffed animals that babies love to hug and chew (but should not sleep with) are now available in organic fiber fabrics—often of cotton, hemp, or wool. The outer-cloth fibers and the stuffing are made of materials that are grown without the use of pesticides or chemical fertilizers (which could be bad for baby to be chewing on and also known to be heavy polluters of groundwater and oceans). As a bonus, these soft toys are colored with nontoxic, colorfast dye (and not azo dyes made up of carcinogenic chemical compounds), and they are not chemically stain- and mothproofed as are most conventional fabric toys.

Toys to Love

You can find wonderful toys for your baby made of earth-friendly materials such as organic fibers and sustainably grown woods. Some toy sellers, furthermore, make sure that the toys they offer are manufactured according to fair trade policies, follow environmentally sound practices, and do not use sweatshop labor. Here are a few recommended sources to get you started:

- *www.mamasearth.com* offers delightful stuffed bunnies and baby dolls made of organic untreated cotton inside and out.

- *www.waldorfresources.net/nstoys* is one place to find classic baby rattles and toys made of walnut and oak to push and pull.

- *www.underthenile.com* sells a line of stuffed toys made completely of Egyptian organically grown cotton. Take a look at the cute crate of teething veggies, including a carrot, a string bean, and a mushroom safe for babies to chew on.

- *www.naturescrib.com* carries toys made of responsibly harvested hardwoods and handcrafted in Vermont. The baby items have a whey-based finish, come with a lifetime guarantee, and are meant to pass on to the next generation.

Avoid the Wrong Plastic Toys

Research on the health effects of many plastics is still in its early stages, but it is known that some of our children's plastics toys contain toxic chemicals, including lead, cadmium, and toxic softeners, that may cause permanent damage to the brain, liver, and reproductive system.[23]

Soft plastic toys are particularly troublesome. Many conventional products still use phthalates to make the plastic soft and pliable. (Yes, the same phthalates that are in vinyl flooring and mattress covers, widely considered to be one of the most toxic and environmentally unfriendly plastics in use today.) This toxic chemical is used in teethers and soft squeeze toys, beach balls, bath toys, dolls, and many other soft plastic products.

Soft plastics are especially dangerous for babies, who put everything in their mouths. The Consumer Product Safety Commission has asked U.S. manufacturers to remove phthalates from baby pacifiers and toys for children under age three (which the European Union has already done), and many companies are doing so. However, reports on phthalate and other hazardous chemical levels in children's products show that many manufacturers are far from compliant.[24] The environment is also damaged by plastics. The manufacture and incineration of PVC result in highly toxic dioxins and furans. Also, plastic manufacturers are the single largest users of chlorine that reacts with organic matter in drinking water to produce toxic by-products. And to top off the list of assaults, the heavy metals lead and cadmium are added as stabilizers in children's soft vinyl products and packaging. They can be released into the environment during both manufacture and decomposition, contaminating water, soil, and air.

As the problem of toxic plastics begins to hit the mainstream media, manufacturers may soon be pushed to remove them from children's toys. In December 2006, *Time* magazine ran a feature article titled "What's Toxic in Toyland." The story covered San Francisco's ban on the sale of certain plastic toys for children under age three.

Green Baby Story

The Urge to Remodel

A Cautionary Tale

WHEN I WAS PREGNANT with my son, it seemed like a good time to embark on a little remodeling project. "If not now, when?" we reasoned. Nothing big, just enlarging a bedroom window and building a window seat, adding a closet, installing some lights, replastering the walls, and getting the baby room painted and wallpapered. So we talked to a contractor who was cheap and available. I was more than five months away from my due date and we figured this project would take around six weeks.

"No problem!" the contractor said. You can probably guess what happened next.... Our project dragged on with one delay after the other. My due date came and went and we were still sleeping in a temporary room filled with boxes. There was construction debris everywhere and I worried about breathing in all the dust and paint fumes. More than anything I just wanted our house back so I could settle in and prepare for our new baby. In the end, as soon as the builder finished and left, I went into labor—three weeks overdue! Maybe it was just a coincidence, but I've wondered if the stress of living in a construction zone, not to mention a thwarted nesting instinct, somehow contributed to my delayed labor.

My advice is to plan as far in advance as possible and consider whether remodeling during pregnancy is really necessary. If so, I would choose a contractor very carefully, and try hard to find one familiar with green building concepts to minimize the exposure to noxious fumes. I would get a finish date carved in stone and try to find another place to stay during the course of construction.

Caryl D. Reed
Kalamazoo, Michigan

Green Parent Alert

Boycott PVC

Greenpeace USA has been active for several years in efforts to pressure manufacturers to stop using plastics containing PVC because their manufacturing processes consume approximately 30 percent of the chlorine used in industrial processes and release many other toxic chemicals, some of which accumulate in the body. In a strongly worded statement on their Web site, Greenpeace explains: "Few consumers realize that PVC is the single most environmentally damaging of all plastics. Since safer alternatives are available for virtually all uses of PVC, it is possible to protect human health and the environment by replacing and eventually phasing out this poison plastic."[25]

If you do buy any plastic toys for your baby, look for products that are PVC free. These companies have removed PVC from their products:[26]

- ❖ Brio
- ❖ Primetime Playthings
- ❖ Sassy
- ❖ Little Tikes
- ❖ Lego
- ❖ Early Start
- ❖ Tiny Love

If you aren't sure if a product contains PVC, call the manufacturer's 800 number, usually located on the bottom of the package label.

Although the targeted toys comply with U.S. law, the results of a study funded by the *San Francisco Chronicle* are quite troublesome. The study found, for example, that "one rubber ducky contained the phthalate DEHP at thirteen times San Francisco's allowed level. A teether contained another phthalate at five times the limit. And a rattle, two waterproof books and a doll contained BPA, which is prohibited by the city at any level."[27] Protect your child and our world by avoiding toys made of the wrong plastics.

Now that we've considered the many choices available for making your baby's nursery green and beautiful, it's time to move on to the kitchen, where it's easy to find more ways to keep things green.

4

THE
Kitchen

For many families, the kitchen is the center of domestic life and the favorite room in the house. We come home, we head for the kitchen to have a quick snack, a glass of water or cup of tea. You'll be spending more time than ever in the kitchen with your baby, who will also come to associate this room with good smells and tasty meals. The kitchen is also a room where your efforts to go green can have an immediate and powerful impact not just on the health of your child but also the planet. Every bite of food you and your baby take is an investment in your bodies' future. And, as we'll see later in the chapter, what you eat can have a bigger impact on the environment than the kind of car you drive!

First Feedings

FOR NEWBORNS, ALL NUTRITION comes either through milk from the breast or through a formula from a factory. This will be the core of the diet for the entire first year, so if breastfeeding can be an option for you, it's important to make this choice very carefully. Both can have a significant impact on the health of the child and on the world.

Breast Milk

Human milk is precisely optimum for human infants. You can see this even in their stool. By two months of age, breastfed babies are using this food so efficiently that they produce little waste. It can be normal for a breastfed baby to go a week or more without a stool.

This ideal design is reflected in improved health. Many studies have found that breastfed babies have fewer illnesses and less severe illnesses than do formula-fed babies. Research reported by the American Academy of Pediatrics,[1] for instance, shows that there is "strong evidence" supporting the findings that breast milk reduces the incidence or severity of such diseases as

- Diarrhea
- Lower respiratory infections
- Ear infections
- Bacterial meningitis
- Urinary tract infections

In addition to supporting a baby's growth and development, breastfeeding can also expand the baby's taste palate for nutritious foods. When Mom eats a variety of flavorful and nutritious foods, her baby will taste them in the breast milk and will be more open to eating those same foods during his lifetime.

The health benefits of breastfeeding are not just for the baby. Mother Nature bestows health advantages to breastfeeding moms, too. The following are some of these gifts:[2]

- Right after birth, breastfeeding helps contract the uterus.
- Breastfeeding helps shed the extra pounds of the pregnancy.
- It releases hormones such as oxytocin and prolactin that can be associated with a general feeling of well-being and contentment (and increased maternal behavior).[3] The hormones can also help you feel relaxed after milk let-down.[4]
- Women who have breastfed for many months have significantly lower rates of urinary tract infections; osteoporosis; and breast, ovarian, and uterine cancers.

It's fitting that such a natural food is also exceptionally good for the environment. Its delivery system is the most efficient on the planet: no pollution is caused in its transport (talk about eating local!), and it neither uses packaging nor produces industrial waste.

Baby formula production, packaging, and delivery, in contrast, cause a tremendous amount of industrial waste:[5]

- The mechanical production of baby formula causes air pollution and uses natural resources for its fuel.

- Formula is then shipped great distances to the consumer market—resulting in gasoline consumption, vehicle exhaust, and other unnecessary pollution.

- Tin, paper, and plastic used in packaging baby formula create even more pollution.

- Bottles and nipples that require plastic, glass, rubber, and silicon add to the production and disposal pollution problems. The popularity of disposable bottles and liners makes this a major problem.

- Because these materials involved in formula-feeding a baby are rarely recycled, their disposal in landfill or through incineration causes even more pollution.

Infant Formula

You may be surprised to hear that commercial infant formulas can be a green choice in some circumstances. These formulas have been developed to substitute for breast milk when nursing is impractical, undesirable, or even impossible due to physical illness, separation, or adoption. I am deeply grateful for such formulas because my wife's critical illness once prevented my son from breastfeeding (they are both vibrant and healthy

Going Green

Money in the Bank

ACCORDING TO *Consumer Reports*, the cost of using baby formula is between $1,500 and $4,000 a year—much more expensive than breast milk.[6] Also, according to the U.S. Department of Health and Human Services, breastfeeding reduces health care costs. It reports, "Total medical care costs for the nation are lower for fully breastfed infants than never-breastfed infants since breastfed infants typically need fewer sick care visits, prescriptions, and hospitalizations."[7]

today). I'm glad to report that some of today's infant formulas are very good substitutes for mother's milk.

If you use formula at any point, you can make choices about the type that will be healthiest for your baby and kinder to the planet and your pocketbook. The ready-to-use variety is most convenient: open the can and pour. However, the decision to choose powdered formula substantially reduces the amount of waste from liquid single-serving cans that are then either trashed or recycled. (Keep in mind that even recycling requires an expenditure of natural resources in collection, transportation, and processing.) Using filtered tap water and a container of powdered formula is a greener choice you can make for the good of both your baby and our world.

Please note that it may be best to use water without added fluoride for mixing baby formula or baby food. The American Dental Association in November 2006 issued an alert urging parents to avoid fluoridated water

Buying Green

Organic Baby Formula

ALL THE ORGANIC BABY formulas listed here are fortified with at least some of the lipid DHA, a nutrient found in breast milk that is a key factor in infant health and development.

❖ Ultra Bright Beginnings (*www.brightbeginnings.com/products/organic-baby-formula.asp*) makes an organic formula with excellent levels of DHA.

❖ Parent's Choice (*www.parentschoiceformula.com*) offers an organic formula that is properly fortified with DHA.

❖ Similac (*www.similacorganic.com*) offers an organic version of its formula, the first organic infant formula from a major formula brand.

❖ For other organic formulas, check out *www.babyorganic.com*. You can get free shipping with every case purchased.

for babies because they believe it can damage teeth, not protect them. There are several fluoridated water products for babies; the leading one is marketed as "Nursery Water" and is sold nationwide at Wal-Mart and other major retailers. So take care to read the labels.

The Kitchen Pantry

As you're creating a green home and lifestyle in which to raise your child, you cannot overlook your own diet—for the health of your baby if you are breastfeeding, for the eating habits you will pass on to your child, and for the example you set.

In Chapter One, I outlined the benefits of going local, organic, and seasonal for the pregnant mom—those benefits certainly remain the same after the baby is born. Seasonal, local, and organic foods may have more vitamins, minerals, and health-promoting antioxidants than conventional foods, while minimizing the unwanted chemicals, drugs, and hormones. For a general guide to stocking your pantry and simple, great cooking you may want to pick up *The Organic Cook's Bible* by Jeff Cox (Wiley, 2006) and *Your Organic Kitchen: The Essential Guide to Selecting and Cooking Organic Foods* by the chef Jesse Cool (Rodale, 2000).

If You Are Breastfeeding

Your diet is of immediate importance to your baby if you're breastfeeding. Just as the nutritious foods taken into a woman's body during pregnancy pass through the placenta to the baby to give him an early boost of good health, so they do now through the mother's breast milk.

The medical literature makes it unquestionably clear that this natural milk is the food of choice for giving babies a strong start at a healthy life, whatever the mother's diet may be. Even so, if a mother's diet is filled with nongreen elements from unhealthy or contaminated foods, the quality of breast milk, though still far higher than formula, will not be as high as it could be: the very milk that boosts immunity may now also contain some immunosuppressive chemicals; the very nutrition that protects a child

Buying Green

Baby-Safe Bottles

WHEN SHOPPING FOR BABY bottles, look for products made of glass, polyethylene, or polypropylene. Polycarbonate bottles (about 95 percent of the bottles on the market) can leach BPA, a hormone disruptor that acts like human estrogen. Even tiny amounts of this have been associated with health problems such as early puberty, hyperactivity, and decreased sperm count. *I do not recommend using any polycarbonate products for babies.*

❖ The Institute for Agriculture and Trade Policy (IATP, *www.iatp.org*) says bottles made of milky, soft, translucent plastic usually contain no polycarbonates.

❖ Highly rated bottles by the Ethical Consumer include Born Free (*www .newbornfree.com*), which are guaranteed to be free of BPA (I like the air vent in these bottles as well) and the Medela Breastmilk Storage and Feeding set, which is made from polypropylene. Find it at *www.target.com* and other stores.

❖ Glass bottles do not contain the same potentially harmful chemicals as plastic bottles. Evenflo glass bottles are recommended by the IATP and are available online at *www.babysupermall.com.*

❖ Replace the conventional rubber or latex bottle nipples that come with some plastic and glass baby bottles with a nontoxic, clear silicone variety. (Conventional nipples may contain cancer-causing nitrosamines.) Evenflo and Circo both make silicone nipples, sold separately from their bottles.

❖ Quick tip: Remember when shopping for plastic items for babies, including bottles and pacifiers, check the recycling symbol. Products numbered 3, 6, and 7 may contain harmful chemicals, whereas 1, 2, 4, and 5 may be safer.

Baby Safe Cans?

A 2007 analysis by the Environmental Working Group found BPA in 33 percent of the cans of concentrated soy- and milk-based infant formulas tested. BPA is in the plastics and epoxy resins that line some food cans, and can leach into the liquid formula. *I strongly prefer powdered formulas until BPA is no longer allowed in the cans.*[8]

against cancer may now also contain some carcinogens. Some chemicals in a mother's diet even appear capable of interfering with her ability to produce milk in the first place.

The chemical contaminants that most concern me are those that become more concentrated as they move up the food chain. Human breast milk, which is distilled from the food that mothers eat, exists high on that chain; therefore, it can contain more persistent pollutants if the mother's diet is nongreen. If you've made the decision to breastfeed, you make a great choice even better if you ensure that your own diet contains the kind of healthy foods you want to feed your baby.

The information on whole, local, organic, and seasonal foods in Chapter One and in this chapter will guide your choices and help you give your breastfed baby the nutrients he needs without the added toxic chemicals.

Baby Food

Throughout the history of our species, humans were breastfed as newborns and then they quickly graduated to mashed adult foods that were grown locally. Until the twentieth century, that is. This modern period ushered in an age of baby food in jars, infant formula in cans, and kids' meals in boxes.

Many of these foods are not the best choice for your child or for our environment. Far from being green, what we feed most babies in the United States is like a conveyor belt leading them to a childhood (and adulthood) diet of unhealthy, artificial, chemical-laden, and overprocessed foods. Sadly, children's excessive intake of these foods is responsible in large part for the obesity rate among elementary school children, which has more than quadrupled in the last thirty years and is projected to keep increasing. The American Dietetic Association in 2006 concluded that toddlers and infants over four to six months of age who are eating solid foods should eat a wide variety of fruits, vegetables, and whole grains, as well as foods naturally rich in iron.[9]

In addition to these health considerations, the production, packaging, transport, and disposal of processed foods all contribute in untold ways to water, air, and food-chain pollution. Whereas organic fresh foods, and even organic packaged foods, support the growth of organic farming, which in turn protects the health of the environment.

In this twenty-first century, we have an opportunity to give back to our children pure and nutritious foods that will better nourish their bodies and the world they will inherit.

Starting Solid Foods

Between the time that babies start moving across the floor and when they begin to walk with confidence, they will put almost anything in their mouths to sample and explore. This is an excellent time to introduce a variety of healthy foods because this window of opportunity will soon close. Toddlers often restrict their food choices to those they have come to trust during pregnancy, nursing, and early taste experiences. This makes historical sense: you wouldn't want a new walker to toddle away from parents and sample a new berry or an unfamiliar leaf.

I don't personally agree with the twentieth-century idea of introducing only one food at a time, spread five to seven days apart, processed-flavored and devoid of spices. I understand this used to be considered state-of-the-art advice. I understand the fear of allergies and of strong flavors behind this blip in nutrition history. However, it did nothing to decrease food allergies; it only made it a bit easier to identify the culprits—not worth the huge cost, in my opinion. The 2006 American Academy of Pediatrics guidelines for feeding children forgo any suggestion of waiting three or five or seven days between foods. And real flavors have been an important part of baby food in almost every culture in history except the second half of the twentieth century.

So as you introduce solid foods, whether it be with intervals between each new food or with several foods at once, choose as many healthy, real flavors as possible—again with an eye to the foods that you will want your child to enjoy at age two and then throughout life. Grab this opportunity to introduce a culture of delight and spice, not of fear and blandness.

Typically kids need to be exposed to a flavor at least six to nine times (often as many as fifteen times) before they acquire a taste for it. (Some of these exposures may happen even before the baby is born.) This need for repeated exposures is normal and beneficial (so kids don't learn to love debris from the floor the first time they put it in their mouths!). The key is to offer a bite of the new flavors each day, but not to push or coax kids beyond that first bite. Let them taste and explore before you expect a food to become a real meal.

Go for Color

Nature has very wisely given bright colors to many of its best foods. The purpose, I believe, is to attract our attention to the foods that are filled with the vitamins, minerals, and phytonutrients essential for healthy growth and development. Sometimes the color is in the food itself (beets); sometimes the color is in the peel (bananas). You may think of bananas as white, but they are rich in vitamin B_6, vitamin C, potassium, and fiber—a great food for babies. Babies love them, and they don't require cooking. Just smushing or slicing, depending on your baby's stage.

As you begin to introduce solid foods (whether homemade organic pureed foods or organic commercial-brand baby foods), lean toward vibrant, natural color. Later, when teaching your preschooler colors, I love using foods, flowers, and abundant colors of nature. For now, here are a few ideas to link vibrant color with health foods:

Orange. Carrots, sweet potatoes, and squash are packed with nutrients, especially vitamin A, so necessary for vision.

Green. There is a reason the movement to save the planet uses the green moniker—green is rich in so many elements necessary for a healthy life. Steamed and blended broccoli, for example, is a powerhouse of nutrients. Ounce for ounce, it contains more calcium than a glass of milk and more vitamin C than an orange. And be sure to give your baby a taste of avocado; it offers more than twenty-five essential nutrients, such as fiber, potassium, vitamin E, B vitamins, and folic acid, and also has healthy monounsaturated fat. The creamy texture makes it easy to add to your baby's first meals.

Blue. Yes, blue is supernutritious when it comes in the form of a blueberry. This little berry brims with fiber, phytochemicals, vitamin C, and antioxidants. Smush some up and mix with a bit of baby cereal to encourage the joy of eating.

The Joy of Eating

As babies progress to finger foods, they're at a great age to turn the high chair into a treasure map. For many kids the best way to do this is with a muffin or ice cube tray. Each slot can hold a few tasty, bite-sized treasures.

I like using one or two of the slots for a dipping sauce. Applesauce, yogurt, or pureed baby fruits or vegetables can all be good choices. Other slots might contain cubes of sweet potato (easy to steam); small half slices of banana; half medallions of soft-cooked carrots; shredded apple or carrot; small pieces of cheese; quartered grapes; diced bits of pear, kiwi, avocado, or soft-cooked green beans; bite-sized pieces of toast or oat cereal O's. Imagine all the possible combinations!

Herbs and Spice and Everything Nice

Learning to love the smell and taste of herbs and spices can help kids accept the tastes of unfamiliar vegetables and whole grains as they get older. Spices can serve as what I call taste threads to guide the development of a healthy set of food preferences. And as a bonus, herbs and spices are among the healthiest of foods.

Turmeric heads my list of healthy spices for babies. Curcumin, found in turmeric, is powerful at destroying cancer-causing molecules. Many studies are finding it effective in helping prevent or treat several forms of cancer (including breast cancer). Perhaps turmeric is one reason that leukemia is so much less common in cultures where curry is commonly used. In India, it affects less than one child in a million.[10] A growing body of evidence also points to turmeric's powerful antioxidant and anti-inflammatory effects as providing natural environmental protection.[11]

Similar health benefits can be described for a number of spices, including cinnamon, ginger, rosemary, and oregano. Pick your favorite spices, start with tiny amounts, and let spices become a regular part of your baby's diet.

Dr. Greene's Organic Prescription Just for Babies

Picture your treasured, pristine newborn, just beginning the voyage of life—a baby who hasn't yet picked up some of the habits or tastes you might wish you never acquired. Next consider that what you feed your baby now will help establish her habits of eating, her taste preferences and food favorites.

If I were going to pick only one time of life to eat organic, it would be from conception through age three. Our bodies and our brains grow faster during this period than at any later time. Babies eat more than adults, pound for pound, and, as we discussed in Chapter One, they are more vulnerable to environmental toxins.

Here are seven very important choices to keep in mind for the health of your baby and of the planet:

1. **Organic milk.** The best choice by far, when practical, is for breast milk to be the exclusive milk for at least the first year. But if you are using milk-based formula for your baby, either partially or entirely (or if milk is an ingredient in other foods), consider organic.

Babies shouldn't be given cow's milk directly during the first year of life. Nevertheless, most American babies consume a lot of milk during their first year, in the form of infant formula. At some points, formula-fed babies take thirty-two ounces a day—more milk than older kids or adults. And later in the first year they might get milk in foods that contain yogurt or cheese.

There's more to a bottle of conventional formula than meets the eye. You see the formula, but hidden from view is the cow where the milk came from, the dairy where the cow was raised, and all the land devoted to growing food for that cow. When you choose a bottle of conventional milk-based formula, you are buying into a whole chemical system of agriculture.

Each bottle of organic formula, however, represents a whole organic ecosystem. Rich, living soil, responsibly nurtured, produces healthy organic pasture and nutritious organic feed, which leads to healthy organic cows. (Organic cows must, by regulation, be allowed to graze on pasture during the growing season.) If you give milk-based formula, choose organic every time.

An astonishing *two hundred million acres* of farmland in the United States are devoted to growing feed for our livestock.[12] By choosing organic formula, your small choice affects a big segment of our agricultural system.

2. Organic soy. Almost all babies in the United States are fed soy in the first year, usually without their parents knowing it. Infant formula is based on three core parts: protein, carbohydrates, and fats. Most parents are surprised to learn that the fat in formulas in general, whatever the type, almost always features soybean oil. For a variety of reasons, I prefer avoiding soy formula for most babies, especially in the first six months. But even if you don't use soy formula, there may still be soy in your baby's diet.

Soy turns up as an ingredient in a surprising array of products. Almost the entire soy crop in the United States is crushed to make soybean oil and meal. Only a tiny proportion is consumed as whole soybean products. Soybean oil, in contrast, is huge, accounting for about two-thirds of all vegetable oils consumed in the United States.[13] You'll find it in all kinds of infant and toddler foods—teething biscuits, baby pasta, arrowroot cookies, vegetable puff finger foods, and those ubiquitous little crackers moms carry with their strollers. And when you think trans fats, think partially hydrogenated soybean oil.

More than seventy-two million U.S. acres are planted in soy. Soybean pesticide use in the United States ranks second only to the rate of use for corn.[14] In recent years, soy has been the domestic crop found most contaminated with organophosphate pesticides.[15] Beyond this, soy leads the way in genetic modification: 87 percent of the soy planted in the United States, about sixty-two million acres, is genetically modified (GM).[16] The U.S. Department of Agriculture (USDA), in its report on the first decade of GM foods, observes that most U.S. consumers have concerns about GM foods but routinely eat them "largely unaware" that they are doing so. This contrasts starkly with the European Union and Japan, where consumer preference has largely eliminated GM ingredients from store shelves.[17]

Because labeling regulations do not require companies to specify whether or not their products contain GM ingredients, it can be difficult to know for sure what you are getting—particularly considering that soy is an ingredient in so many processed foods. Choosing organic is one way to be sure you are not choosing foods grown from GM seeds.

Less than 0.17 percent of our massive soy crop is organic. We need to make a dent. Let's start by choosing exclusively organic soy for our babies. If soy or an unidentified vegetable oil or protein is on the ingredient level, either choose a different food or go with the organic version.

3. **Organic baby cereal.** Suppose a baby has begun to show interest and excitement while watching her parents eat. Her parents decide that today is the day. For some it is a bittersweet day—she is growing so fast! Before today, all of her nutrition may have come directly from her mother. Doting parents mix the cereal and grab the camera. They prop up their little girl and move the spoon toward her mouth. In goes that historic first bite . . . and it may come right back out again. The first few days, many babies will tend to push the cereal back out with their tongues. This is because young babies have a thrust reflex in response to anything unfamiliar in their mouths.

Within several days, however, your baby will get the idea of closing her lips around the spoon and swallowing. Once she does, she begins to figure out how to eat just the right amount of solids (which is not a predetermined amount, but varies from child to child). Attentive parents are also learning. Keep moving the spoon toward the baby's mouth and look for signs that she is losing interest. If she turns her head away, clamps her lips shut, or appears bored, it is time to stop. Otherwise, keep moving the spoon to her mouth as long as she keeps opening it and looking happy.

And what is the fateful first bite of food, the focus of so much learning and attention? For most U.S. babies, it is heavily processed conventional white rice flour (usually containing soybean oil!). I'm not surprised that U.S. toddlers tend to reject foods made from hearty whole grains. Their earliest comfort food is white flour.

For a healthier alternative, I recommend organic whole grain cereals for babies. They are also a great choice for the planet. Organic rice is grown without the use of toxic pesticides and chemical fertilizers that can harm our environment. In one small study of family farms, directly comparing organic to conventional rice farming methods, organic techniques improved the quality and biodiversity of the soil. Organic methods used only 18 percent of the fossil-fuel-based energy used by the conventional farms, a dramatic reduction in oil waste and greenhouse gases. For every calorie of fossil fuel used on the conventional rice farms, four food calories were produced. On the organic farms, the same amount produced an impressive nineteen calories—nearly five times as much food![18]

4. Organic fruits and vegetables. After babies have mastered cereals, they usually cycle through a variety of fruit and vegetable experiences. Most parents haven't yet learned that food quality from chemically intensive agriculture is going down. According to USDA data,[19] your baby is likely getting less protein, iron, calcium, phosphorus, riboflavin, and vitamin C—to say nothing of the thousands of important food phytonutrients that hadn't been discovered yet when the measurements began. When compared head to head, organic fruits and vegetables average about 30 percent higher antioxidant levels than their conventional counterparts.[20]

So don't skimp on food for your baby. You don't want foods with declining nutrients, grown from depleted soil. You don't want overprocessed baby foods that may prepare her to prefer processed foods as a toddler.

And you don't want all the toxic pesticides that get into our food, our water, and our soil from the cultivation of conventional produce. In my organic prescription for adults, I suggest starting with apples and potatoes as the most important fruit and vegetable. With babies, I prefer to make organic first choice for all fruits and vegetables.

5. **Organic baby food meat.** If you feed your baby meat or poultry, I urge you to switch to organic. Consider beef, for example. Conventional non-organic American beef is corn-fed or grain-fed beef. And it is not natural. Cattle are biologically designed to graze. When fed corn, their stomachs can become ten to one hundred times more acidic,[21] welcoming bacteria such as *E. coli* O157:H7.[22] And the amount of antibiotics used to promote growth in livestock dwarfs the total amount used to treat diseases in people. Grass-fed organic beef tends to be leaner, and yet have five times the omega-3 fatty acids of conventional beef.[23] I suggest replacing conventional baby beef either with grass-fed organic beef or organic poultry, or with a variety of other plant sources of protein, such as garbanzo beans—a source of plant protein around the world—and quinoa, a complete protein.

6. **Corn.** Corn fattens up America's beef cattle, accounting for 90 percent of U.S. feed grains.[24] High fructose corn syrup fattens up America's human population. Corn syrup is the carbohydrate in a number of infant formulas and in many products for babies and toddlers. (A parent recently told me about a "healthy fruit treat" she had discovered for her nine-month-old. The first ingredient was corn syrup, followed by sugar.) Corn starch, modified corn starch, and corn flour are some of the other ways that corn enters our diets. I've heard a number of parents say they haven't fed their babies corn. Most have, though, without knowing it.

More American land is planted in corn than any other crop. More pesticides and more chemical fertilizer are used to grow corn in the United States than any other crop.[25] Most of the corn, almost fifty million acres of it, is GM corn.[26] *If we change corn production, we change agriculture.*

Commercial corn production is the biggest culprit in an environmental disaster looming in the Gulf of Mexico. There is a marine dead zone the area of New Jersey, which doubled in size between 1985 and 1999. Aquatic life cannot survive in the oxygen-depleted water. According to the Institute for Agriculture and Trade Policy, a primary cause of the dead zone is fertilizer runoff from the midwestern corn belt that filters first into the Mississippi River and then dumps into the Gulf. It's a powerful picture of the cost of industrial corn production.[27] The industrial production of conventional corn has had a devastating impact on the American landscape—on our soil, air, livestock, and waters. Switching from conventional to organic corn could do wonders for the health of your family. And no other change would improve the health of so many acres of cropland.

Green Baby Story

Feeding Organic

I GREW UP IN a family that enjoyed our small vegetable garden and fruit trees. I remember loving our fresh apples, peaches, and cherries, especially how they tasted so delicious. Now that I'm grown, I don't have the luxury of growing my own foods where I live and have to struggle with my kids to eat their fruits and vegetables. I was finding half eaten apples with the skin spit out in the trash. This was really frustrating as a mother, as produce is expensive, so I decided to see what the problem was.

When I asked my five-year-old daughter, "What's the matter with the food?" she simply said, "It tastes bad on my tongue."

So I decided that organic food was the only way to provide the most beneficial nutrition for my children. I began to get only organic baby cereals, formula, and jar foods; organic fruits and vegetables for snacks; organic pastas for dinner. It was easy to find substitutes for things that my family once rejected or maybe weren't as good for us.

I've easily incorporated organics into my family's life with rave reviews! I've noticed a difference in the way the foods taste, how much more my kids enjoy their fruits and vegetables (THEY DISAPPEAR!!), and I can feel good as a mother making this small contribution to their future and their health. I thought paying extra for organics was crazy, but it turned out to be a money saver as I am not throwing out ANY produce anymore!

Amy Bowker-Prather
Hesperia, California

7. Cotton. Babies wear and use a lot of cotton in the first year. If we choose organic cotton for our babies, we can make a big environmental difference and improve the food supply for older kids and adults.

The World Health Organization estimates there are twenty-five million global poisonings and twenty thousand deaths from all pesticides each year, not to mention the enormous damage to wildlife.[28] Cotton is a major contributor. Cotton is also one of the top three GM crops in the United States, along with soy and corn.

Without our being conscious of it, much of the cotton crop ends up in our food. According to the National Cotton Council, about two-thirds of the cotton crop is harvested as cottonseeds.[29] The oil from the seeds is used in our food supply, appearing in vegetable oil (cottonseed oil) and in such snack foods as crackers, cookies, and chips. The meal from the seeds has primarily been fed to dairy cows.[30]

If a product lists cottonseed oil or an unidentified vegetable oil on the label—choose an organic brand instead. And choose organic cotton for your baby to wear, play with, and sleep on. Organic cotton is a safe choice for your baby and far healthier for the planet.

For updates about my organic prescription for babies and families, please visit DrGreene.com.

A Word About Food Allergies

The great majority of kids never get a food allergy and can enjoy the full spectrum of nutritious foods. Nevertheless, food allergies can be serious problems for many kids (and adults). It's likely that allergies in babies are related, as we've seen, to the tendencies to have allergies in the family history. Allergies related to cow's milk protein are the most common in babies, followed by soy protein. Babies might be exposed to some form of these in an infant formula. Even exclusively breastfed babies can sometimes develop food allergies. Cow's milk protein in the mother's diet is the most likely culprit for an allergic reaction through the breast milk, followed by peanuts, soy, or egg.

Although a child can develop an allergy to almost any food, well over 90 percent of food allergies in children are caused by one of only six foods: milk, eggs, peanuts, wheat, soy, and tree nuts. The symptoms of food allergies in kids may be minor, such as increased fussiness, a little blood in the stool, a minor rash, runny nose, or itchy eyes. Some allergic reactions to food are severe, including swelling and difficulty with breathing. Thankfully, most babies can outgrow their food allergies. About 85 percent of milk allergies are outgrown by age three. Outgrowing soy and egg allergies is very common. Even 20 percent of children with peanut allergies, once thought to be lifelong afflictions, may outgrow them, but they should be retested regularly under a doctor's care.

Green Parent Report

The Surprising Impact of Eating Meat

What you eat can have a much bigger impact on the environment than what kind of car you drive. Livestock and manure methane alone directly release greenhouse gases equivalent to what's produced by thirty-three million cars. But it's not just the livestock; it's the resources that go into its production.[31]

- It takes seven pounds of corn to add one pound of weight to one feedlot head of cattle (and of course, only some of this weight is edible meat). In fact, 66 percent of the grain in production in the United States ends up as livestock feed.
- Grain production creates the heavy use of fertilizers—about one pound of fertilizer use for every three pounds of cooked beef.
- It takes forty-five hundred gallons of water to produce just four ounces of raw beef (precooked weight).
- Sixteen hundred calories of fossil fuel energy are required for every hundred calories of grain-fed beef we eat (compared to fifty calories of fossil fuel for every hundred calories of plant food).

The production of corn-fed or grain-fed beef uses an exceptional amount of fossil fuel. For this reason, one way to have a greener diet is to eat less meat, or at least to switch to organic or pasture- and grass-fed animals—dramatically altering the use of chemical fertilizers, toxic pesticides, and energy.

Nevertheless, food allergies appear to be getting more common. If you think you're hearing more about peanut allergies now than when you were a child, you're right! Researchers at Mt. Sinai Medical Center estimate that peanut allergies in the United States doubled in just five years, between 1997 and 2002. Now, a little over 1 percent of Americans are allergic to peanuts. What caused this rapid rise? Perhaps it is partly due to the increased use of antibiotics and our more antiseptic environments—living more removed from nature. Maybe it is the increase in chemicals and artificial ingredients in our foods. Or the decrease in fresh fruits and vegetables. Or perhaps the introduction of genetically modified soy and other foods in the late 1990s contributed to this rise (soy and peanuts are closely related). Whatever the cause, I suspect that organic agriculture and organic foods could be part of the solution.

Preventing Food Allergies

Breastfeeding might keep some babies from getting food allergies. I also recommend you avoid directly feeding babies common allergenic foods while their stomachs are immature (especially in the first year) or inflamed (as from antibiotics, illnesses, or chemical irritants). For families with a strong history of food allergies (two or more parents or siblings with any food allergies, or one with severe food allergies), I suggest no milk, soy, or wheat for the first year; no eggs for two years; and no peanuts, tree nuts, or fish for three years.

For all kids, I prefer organic foods for the first three years, without chemical additives. There is also some evidence that probiotics (beneficial bacteria), either given directly to babies or to their pregnant and nursing moms, may help prevent allergic reactions.

Fruit Juice for Babies

Fruit juice seems like a good idea for babies because it is a natural source of fluids and vitamins, and kids like the taste. But I'm not a big fan, and neither is the American Academy of Pediatrics (AAP).

In a policy statement released in 2001, the AAP urged pediatricians to steer parents of children under six months of age away from fruit juice. They reported that there is no nutritional value to be gained from drinking juice at that age, and in fact drinking juice may reduce the child's intake of the protein, fat, vitamins, and minerals found in breast or bottle milk. They also warned that excessive juice consumption in childhood has been linked to both obesity and short stature in children.[32]

For children older than six months, I encourage parents to introduce organic fruits that are mashed or pureed. Parents can then introduce juice if they want to, but only in a cup—not from a baby bottle, due to the risk of dental cavities. In general, I recommend no more than four to six ounces per day of fruit juice through age six (and then no more than eight to twelve ounces a day).

If you buy packaged juice for your baby, it should be pasteurized to prevent serious illness. After that, it doesn't matter if the juice is a brand marketed specifically to babies or one enjoyed by the entire family. I do suggest, however, that you cut the juice with water to reduce the sugar content while still introducing the taste—in fact you might use a cup of water spiked with just a few spoonfuls of juice for a hint of flavor.

And to stay on the green side of juice consumption, minimize juice boxes and juice sold in plastic bottles. The production and waste of these juice containers are often unnecessary: you can buy a large glass jar of your favorite juice and then recycle the glass responsibly.

Even better would be to forego store-bought juice altogether and go natural. This is a good time to introduce vegetable juice made from thoroughly-washed fresh vegetables and perhaps some fruit while your little one is developing a discerning taste for naturally good foods. I learned when I began juicing at home that the taste of fresh juice is unlike anything in a bottle. (I also found out that while it is fresh, apple juice is not brown—it is white, with a hint of the color of the apple peel!) My whole family has come to prefer fresh juices for maximum nutrition and taste. And I've come to like the many ways this choice is kind to the environment. It eliminates the energy consumption, pollution, packaging, transportation, and bottle disposal of store-brand juice.

Green Parent Report

The Benefits of Soft Water

THE SIMPLEST FILTER CAN soften hard water, and that's good for you and your baby, but it's also good for your wallet and the environment. According to the Water Quality Research Council, hard water can clog pipes and appliances, reduce clothing longevity by 15 percent, leave a soapy film on bathtubs and shower tiles, and increase water heating costs by nearly 30 percent, while shortening the life of the heater. A water softener reduces the hardness of water, eliminating these problems and resulting in substantial savings.[33]

At the Kitchen Sink

IF YOU HAVE A baby, you need pure water! Baby formula is made with water; eating utensils, bottles, nipples, and so on are all washed with water; you bathe your baby in water; you'll clean up her spills and hands and mouth with water. Her toys, crib, and all the other paraphernalia that go with babies will all be washed down with water. Yes, you need to be sure about your water supply.

Tap Water

First the good news about tap water: more than 90 percent of the water systems in the United States meet the EPA's standards for tap water quality.[34] And by law, water suppliers must send you an annual drinking water quality report before July 1 each year, telling you what contaminants have

Try This Today

Improving the Taste of Water

MOST COMMUNITY WATER IS treated with chlorine to disinfect against viruses and bacteria. If your water has a chlorine taste, place the water in an uncovered pitcher in the refrigerator overnight—doing so may help reduce the chemical content and improve the taste.

been detected in your drinking water and how these levels compare to drinking water standards. Many consumers can access their water report online at *www.epa.gov/safewater/ccr/whereyoulive.html*.

Now the not-so-good-news: in an analysis of tap water conducted by the Environmental Working Group, more than half of the contaminants found in water across the country are unregulated and therefore not considered when the EPA gives high marks to water systems. In fact, the study reports that the EPA has set safety standards for fewer than 20 percent of the many hundreds of chemicals that it has identified in tap water. And it gets worse: forty-one of those unregulated contaminants are linked to reproductive toxicity.[35]

With good cause, many Americans are concerned. A 2005 Harris Interactive poll found that Americans ranked water pollution as the number one environmental concern facing the country, topping global warming, ozone depletion, and air pollution.[36]

But you are not totally at the mercy of your local water supplier. You can make sure that the water you drink and give to your baby is pure. You can also have a positive impact on the water supply in your area.

Double-Checking Your Local Water Supply

Even though your annual water quality report (also called a consumer confidence report) may say that your local water supply is safe relative to established drinking water standards, you may still want to have your water tested by a private testing lab, for two primary reasons:

1. The levels of some contaminants vary according to season of the year, so your annual report may not be entirely accurate.

2. The lead pipes, joints, and faucets in your own home may be leaching lead into your water.

If your water comes from a household well, you should definitely have your water tested, as you won't receive a yearly report and are responsible for your own testing. This is especially important in areas where homes and nearby businesses are on septic systems. Because many contaminants are colorless and odorless, testing is the only way to determine whether your well water is safe to drink. Wells should be tested annually for nitrate and coliform bacteria to detect contamination problems early. If you suspect a problem, test more frequently and for other potential contaminants, such as radon, pesticides, or industrial chemicals.[37]

Green Parent Alert

Testing for Nitrates in Your Drinking Water

WHETHER YOU HAVE LOCAL or well water, during your pregnancy and again during the first six months of your child's life it is a good idea to test for the presence of nitrates. Nitrates are rarely a problem for humans after the age of six months (a good thing given that approximately 4.5 million people in the United States are served by water systems that exceed the EPA's maximum contaminant level for nitrates), but this toxin can be dangerous for unborns and newborns.

Nitrate contamination comes from fertilizers, animal waste, and septic tank waste; therefore, the water supplies most vulnerable are in agricultural areas and in areas with large numbers of septic tanks. Fortunately, when the nitrate-contaminating source is removed, the effects of nitrate are reversible in babies. But it's important to test your tap water for nitrates and to use an ion-exchange water softener, distillation, or reverse osmosis filtration system to reduce their presence in your water.[38] (See the Green Information section on pages 277–278 for more information on these filtration systems.)

If you need information on how to test your local water, see "The Kitchen" in the Green Information section for information about certified drinking water laboratories. Green Information also discusses water filtration systems, which you may want to install in your home if you have concerns about the purity of your tap water.

Home Water Filtration Systems

Even when the annual drinking water quality report gives a thumbs-up to the safety level of your water, it's often a good idea to buy a bit of "insurance" to further improve the quality. If you haven't already, this is a good time to purchase a home water treatment unit to increase the purity of your tap water.

Choosing the right water filter will depend on the contaminants you're trying to filter out. That's why before laying down your money, you should at the very least examine your annual drinking water quality report; even better, get the water tested yourself. This will give you a clear picture of what it is you'd like to filter out—not all home treatment systems filter out all contaminants. In fact, they vary widely in complexity, price, and efficiency.

For an overview of common types of filters and information about water filter certification, recommended filter models, and locating certified drinking water laboratories, please refer to the section for this chapter in Green Information.

Moving to Greener Wraps and Containers

The chemical components in many plastics can create both health and environmental problems. Switching from plastic to nonplastic or to a safer plastic product can be easy. It won't be long before your kitchen is free of toxic plastic if you follow these suggestions.

- Switch from plastic to glass storage containers.

- Switch from plastic cling wrap to non-PVC cling wrap or waxed paper.

- Switch from plastic picnic cutlery to Spudware (see page 155).

- Switch from plastic to wood cutting boards. I use Epicurean Cutting Surfaces (*www.epicureancs.com*). I find them elegant, easy to clean, and

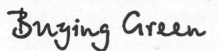

Buying Green

Non-PVC Cling Wrap and Nonplastic Storage Containers

BUTCHER PAPER AND WAX paper provide safer alternatives to cling wrap. However, if you choose to use cling wrap, look into products using low-density polyethylene (LDPE), which is safer than polyvinyl chloride (PVC). Although it is less clingy than PVC, LDPE is not known to contain traces of potentially toxic additives. The following are some popular brands that are LDPE based:

❖ Glad Cling Wrap.

❖ Saran with Cling Plus (new version of Handi-Wrap).

❖ Saran Premium Wrap (new version of Saran Wrap).

❖ Diamant Food Wrap contains no plasticizer or chlorine, is noncarcinogenic, and is completely recyclable. *www.diamantfilm.com*

And here are some earth-friendly products I recommend for safer food storage:

❖ BioBag made of GMO-free cornstarch and is compostable. *www.biobag.com*

❖ Glass, porcelain, and stainless steel containers provide safer alternatives to plastic for food storage.

❖ Greenfeet carries eco-friendly kitchen storage supplies, including glass containers, PVC-free plastics, and even recycled aluminum foil. *www.green feet.com*

❖ Anchor Hocking Glassware makes glass containers and lids. Find them at *www.instawares.com* and in department and discount stores.

❖ Corningware, available at large home stores and at *www.corningware.com*, has a large assortment of glass containers and lids.

❖ You can also reuse glass food jars that you would otherwise throw out or recycle. Just wash them and remove the label.

easy on knives. And they are easy on the environment (made from natural wood fiber from certified sustainably managed forests).

- Switch from beverages sold in plastic bottles to beverages sold in glass bottles.

- Switch from water bottled in individual plastic bottles to water delivered in large glass coolers.

 In general, reduce your use of food, water, and beverages sold in cans, plastic containers, and bottles destined for the trash whenever possible. Always try to buy minimally packaged goods. Less packaging saves you money and spares the environment.

Green Baby Story

Learning His 1, 2, 3s

When my two-year-old was learning to recognize numbers in all fonts, colors, and shapes, I'd give him a bunch of clean plastic containers. We looked at the "numbers in the arrows" and he learned that in his neighborhood 1, 2, 3, 4, and 5 can be recycled, but 6 and 7 can't be. Now it's a game, and he helps me. He puts the recyclables in the recycling bag and the nonrecyclables in the trash. He knows which trash can outside is for recyclables and which is for trash, and proudly tells visitors about them. For a field trip, we are planning to go to Metro Nashville's recycling headquarters (*www.nashville.gov/beauti?cation/recycle_room.htm*), so he can see what happens to our recyclables.

 Pretty cool, and the child knows his numbers!

Liz McLaurin
Nashville, Tennessee

When it comes to that eternal supermarket question, "Paper or plastic?" you may be surprised to learn that the energy required to produce one paper bag may make plastic a better choice (unless you're a very determined saver of paper bags)! Plastic requires 600 BTUs; paper, 2500 BTUs.[39] But the materials for the plastic bags usually come from a nonrenewable source. Resuable bags are an eco-friendly alternative.

Know Your Plastics

To avoid plastics that can be harmful to your baby and the environment, get to know the easy-to-identify plastic recycling codes you'll usually find on the underside of the bottle or packaging. Look for these numbers and symbols before you buy; they will help you find products that are kinder to the environment and safe for your baby.

The safer plastic choices are coded 1, 2, and 4. Try to avoid 3, 6, and most 7s. Although technology exists to recycle most plastics, some centers offer only recycling of select plastics (such as numbers 1 and 2).

Code 1: PET or PETE (polyethylene terephthalate). Found in soda, water, and cooking oil bottles. Can be recycled once, then it's made into new secondary products, such as textiles, parking lot bumpers, or plastic lumber—all unrecyclable products.

Code 2: HDPE (high-density polyethylene). Found in toys and bottles containing milk, juice, detergent, water, shampoo, and motor oil. Recyclable once into products similar to those for code 1 plastics.

Code 3: PVC (polyvinyl chloride). Found in pipe and tubing, shrink wrap, and a few food and detergent containers. May be discarded at the recycling plant. AVOID

Code 4: LDPE (low-density polyethylene). Found in soft, flexible plastics such as those used in bags for dry cleaning, produce, and garbage.

Code 5: PP (polypropylene). Found in hard but flexible plastics, such as those used for ice cream and yogurt containers, drinking straws, syrup bottles, and diapers.

Code 6: PS (polystyrene). Found in rigid plastics, such as those found in coffee cups, meat trays, plastic cutlery, and take-out food containers. AVOID

Code 7: Other (including polycarbonate, nylon, and acrylic). This is a grab bag symbol. It includes polycarbonate, an important source of BPA, and found in baby bottles. But it also includes some of the newer, compostable green plastics, such as those made from corn, potatoes, rice, or tapioca. AVOID number 7, unless it is labeled as one of these new bio-based plastics.

Kitchen Appliances

THE KITCHEN THAT PROVIDES your family's nutrition is a warehouse of energy consumers: refrigerator, dishwasher, compactor, toaster, microwave, toaster oven, blender, and so on. Generating that energy uses up natural resources and contributes to greenhouse gas emissions.

Your kitchen is a solid place to go green as your old appliances eventually break or wear down. Choose a replacement that has earned the Energy Star label. These appliances meet strict energy efficiency guidelines set by the EPA and the U.S. Department of Energy that will save you money and help the environment.

Products in more than fifty categories are eligible for the Energy Star. These include appliances, electronics, lighting, heating and cooling devices, and office equipment. If a product uses a form of natural resource energy, it is likely to be readily available in any standard brand as an Energy Star product at a retailer in your area.

This seems like a small step for an individual consumer, but the results of your Energy Star purchase will add up to make a significant difference. With the use of Energy Star products, Americans saved enough energy in 2005 alone to avoid greenhouse gas emissions equivalent to those from twenty-three million cars—all while saving $12 billion on their utility bills.[40] If just one in ten households bought Energy Star–qualified heating and cooling products, the change would keep eighteen billion pounds of greenhouse gas emissions out of our air.[41] This would be like planting 1.7 million acres of new trees. You can personally save about a third on your energy bill, with similar savings of greenhouse gas emissions, without sacrificing features, style, or comfort. The average family spends $1,900 a year on energy bills, much of which goes to heating and cooling. By following the EPA's recommendations for home energy efficiency, consumers can save about $600.[42]

There is a wealth of information about energy efficient appliances online at *www.energystar.gov*. Visit the Web site to learn about the latest certified models and to find a store in your area. There is even a "rebate finder" to help you track down any special offers your local utility companies might be offering.

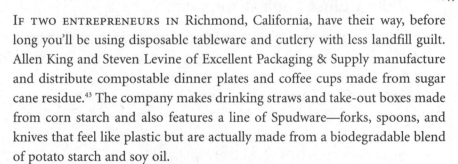

Buying Green

Spudware and Other Eco-Disposables

IF TWO ENTREPRENEURS IN Richmond, California, have their way, before long you'll be using disposable tableware and cutlery with less landfill guilt. Allen King and Steven Levine of Excellent Packaging & Supply manufacture and distribute compostable dinner plates and coffee cups made from sugar cane residue.[43] The company makes drinking straws and take-out boxes made from corn starch and also features a line of Spudware—forks, spoons, and knives that feel like plastic but are actually made from a biodegradable blend of potato starch and soy oil.

Watch for new products to emerge from the rapidly growing field of bioplastics and compostable disposables. Companies are experimenting with renewable materials such as corn and tapioca starch, cellulose, and soy protein, which aren't hazardous in production and decompose in the environment when discarded.

❖ Treecycle *(www.treecycle.com)*

❖ World Centric Eco Store *(www.worldcentric.org)*

Washing Dishes: By Hand or Dishwasher?

The EPA tells us that an efficient dishwasher (without an initial rinse cycle) is by far the most energy-conserving way to wash those dishes, in terms of the annual gallons of water consumption (g) and annual energy consumption in kilowatt-hours (kh).[44] Whichever dishwasher you have, be sure to run it with a full load.

• Efficient dishwasher:	868 g	276 kh
• By hand, two-basin sink:	1,419 g	295 kh
• Standard dishwasher:	1,563 g	334 kh
• Efficient dishwasher, rinsing first:	2,778 g	677 kh
• Standard dishwasher, rinsing first:	3,473 g	735 kh
• By hand, water running:	5,974 g	1,243 kh

Take a Close Look at Your Fridge

The refrigerator is the single biggest power consumer in most households. This is not surprising, as it runs twenty-four hours a day. Buying an Energy Star fridge would save on the utility bill, and if all U.S. households used Energy Star refrigerators, they would keep more than forty-eight million metric tons of carbon dioxide out of the atmosphere.[45]

But whether your refrigerator is conventional or Energy Star, you can make it more green if you do the following:[46]

• Vacuum the coils on the back of the refrigerator twice a year. This will maximize efficiency, cut down on the electric bill, and reduce consumption of energy.

• Make sure there is space between your refrigerator and the wall behind it, as well as space on either side. This will allow air to circulate around the condenser coils, eliminating the possibility of trapped heat, which increase energy consumption.

• Check the door gasket to be sure there is a tight seal. If cold air is escaping, more energy is required to keep a constantly cold temperature.

- Trade in an old one for a newer model—new, more efficient refrigerators can typically save you $70 to $80 a year by reducing energy consumption. A newer refrigerator can reduce your carbon dioxide emissions by more than a thousand pounds a year.

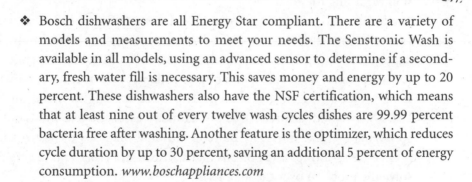

Buying Green

Dishwashers

❖ Bosch dishwashers are all Energy Star compliant. There are a variety of models and measurements to meet your needs. The Senstronic Wash is available in all models, using an advanced sensor to determine if a secondary, fresh water fill is necessary. This saves money and energy by up to 20 percent. These dishwashers also have the NSF certification, which means that at least nine out of every twelve wash cycles dishes are 99.99 percent bacteria free after washing. Another feature is the optimizer, which reduces cycle duration by up to 30 percent, saving an additional 5 percent of energy consumption. *www.boschappliances.com*

❖ Miele Slimline Series model number G818 is rated one of the most energy-efficient dishwashers by the American Council for an Energy-Efficient Economy. This dishwasher offers six wash programs and a built-in water softener. *www.miele.com*

❖ The stainless steel Kenmore twenty-four-inch built-in dishwasher has the Energy Star seal as well as giant tub capacity, delay wash cycle, and Quiet-Guard. *www.sears.com*

Under the Kitchen Sink

MANY OF US HAVE a catchall space under the kitchen sink, with a lot of bottles, toxic cleansers, and rusty old spray cans jumbled together with the funky garbage bags and crushed up against shiny silver water piping from the sink or garbage disposal.

We may ordinarily not pay much attention to what's under our kitchen sink until there's some kind of sudden demand for these old cans and cleansers, but there are very good reasons why we should reconsider what's stored down there and how we use it.

Household Pest Control

When we discover ants, cockroaches, rats, or other invaders living in our house, most of us want to start spraying, poisoning, and exterminating these creatures as quickly as possible, without too much concern or caution regarding the method.

Insects and rodents carry diseases, rodent-damaged electrical wiring causes house fires, and insect food infestation destroys our family food supply. Coexisting is not an option, and the wait-and-see approach is ineffective, because once you spot a bug or rodent, you know it's got a whole family it'll be inviting for dinner. (Two mice starting to breed on New Year's Day could theoretically have as many as thirty-one thousand descendents by December 31!) But conventional methods of pest management consist of traps and poisons that are toxic and cruel, and they seldom solve the problem over the long term.

Fortunately, there are pest management options now available that keep our families on the green side of insecticides and pesticides. And remember, you can't just toss old toxic cans and sprays in the garbage; they need to be disposed of in a way that does not damage or pollute the environment. Disposal of dangerous poisons and toxins is a process that is becoming increasingly mandated by your local town or state. (See Chapter Six for more details on the safe and legal way to dispose of toxic waste.)

Buying Green

Earth-Friendly Household Cleansers

Keep your home clean and fresh, your baby safe, and the planet a little greener by using cleaners free of chemicals, solvents, dyes, and fragrances. Look for products that are labeled nontoxic, chlorine and phosphate free, and that are biodegradable, such as those made by these companies:

❖ Seventh Generation is one of the nation's leading makers of environmentally safe household cleaning products. The ingredients used in its cleansers, dishwashing, and laundry products are renewable, nontoxic, phosphate free, and biodegradable and are never tested on animals. *www .seventhgeneration.com*

❖ Ecover is a Belgium-based company that sells its ecological household cleaners in more than twenty countries. In operation since 1980, Ecover products include a wide array of dishwashing, household, and laundry cleaners for every purpose, and its packaging is fully recyclable. *www .ecover.com*

❖ Begley's Best is one of my personal favorite brands of household cleaners. I use this eco-friendly spray cleaner all over the house. Made of extracts of pine, de-acified citrus, maize, fermented sugar cane roots, and olive seeds, this all-purpose cleaner cuts through dirt and grease on any surface compatible with water. Find it at *www.begleysbest.com.*

❖ Restore is a Minneapolis company that makes earth-friendly household products for every purpose, from oven-cleaners to laundry detergent to furniture polish. If you live in the Midwest, you can visit one of twenty-five Restore "refilling stations," where you can fill up your empty bottle instead of buying a new one. *www.restoreproducts.com*

Prevention

Prevention of infestation is the greenest move you can make to keep your home insect and rodent free. Look around your kitchen and make sure to

- Securely wrap and store all food. A box of cereal with the inner bag and box top wide open says "Come on in" to hungry pests.

- Keep the kitchen table and counters food free. Do not let crumbs from breakfast lie on the counter for cleanup later in the day.

- Clean thoroughly before going to bed. Do not leave any food or drink on the kitchen table or counter overnight. Many insects and rodents are nocturnal and will wait until you're fast asleep to seek their midnight snack. A single drop of juice left behind on a countertop can attract hundreds of ants by morning.

- Empty your kitchen garbage can regularly. The smell of old food is an open invitation to hungry critters.

- Keep your outdoor garbage cans securely covered and far from the house. The smell of garbage draws bugs and rodents.

- Keep the outside area around your home free of wood piles and weeds. Locate and seal any holes in the walls or floors that rodents can use to enter your home. Check air vents and crawl spaces.

Safer Ant and Insect Solutions

If it's too late for prevention, you need to move fast to get rid of pests in the kitchen. The morning you walk into the room and see the line of ants scurrying from the back door to your pantry, you'll have to resist the desire to grab the nearest toxic product at hand and obliterate them. So plan ahead: properly dispose of that can of bug spray (the one containing the very poisons you're trying to avoid by buying organic products) and choose a green indoor pest solution that is not toxic to your own children.

Soapy water or citrus oil and water can kill ants on contact. Sugar and boric acid ant baits can help eliminate ants back in their colonies. You can make your own traps with equal parts borax, sugar, and water in jars with a few holes in the lid. Afterwards, sealing holes and cracks in the kitchen with a no-VOC sealant can stop more outside ants from getting in.

The sugar and boric acid baits may also help with a cockroach problem. Sticky traps baited with pheromones can also be effective. Pheromones are the signals released by roaches to attract other roaches. You can sprinkle boric acid directly into cracks or under appliances, but be sure it does not get in the mouths of kids or pets. Borax does not pollute the air and is safer than most commercial pesticides but still toxic if ingested.

Household Cleansers

MANY HOUSEHOLD CLEANSERS THAT you may also store under your kitchen sink (with child-guard locks!) bear a warning label alerting you to one of the three federal safety ratings: (1) "Caution," (2) "Warning," or (3) "Danger." These labels are necessary because the products contain toxic ingredients, often including such volatile organic compounds (VOCs) as formaldehyde and harsh acids that we all know are not ingredients we want in our green homes.

In general, I recommend choosing cleaning products that don't require any such labeling. If a cleanser is not good for you and at its most acceptable level requires "caution," it is probably not good for others or for the environment either. Instead, as your household cleansers need replacement, switch to simple, green cleansers that are safer for you and your family and also reduce the environmental harm caused by the manufacture, use, and disposal of nongreen products.

You have choices here. You can make your own cleansers with readily available ingredients (most of which are probably already in your kitchen cabinet), or you can buy products that are healthier and environmentally responsible alternatives. Many of these are 100 percent biodegradable and do not contain the unnecessary ingredients found in conventional cleansers, such as artificial fragrances, antimicrobials, chlorine, coal dyes, or phosphates. (See the Buying Green box "Earth-Friendly Household Cleansers" for a list of these products and also see "The Bathroom" in the Green Information section for Web sites offering information on alternative cleansers.)

Green Baby Story

Things I've Learned as a Green Baby Mom

❖ My son's skin rash was from our detergent and dryer sheets.

❖ The cause of some respiratory irritation was the bleach that I was cleaning everything with.

❖ Distilled white vinegar can be diluted and used to clean many different things.

❖ Peroxide can be used instead of bleach in the laundry. (It can also be used to clean humidifiers, and disinfect toothbrushes.)

❖ It's important to change kitchen sponges often.

Cheryl Hill
Fort Benning, Georgia

Home-Grown Cleansers

Here is a list of basic ingredients that are great cleansers themselves and from which you can make cleansing formulas for almost any household need:

- **Baking soda** eliminates odors and softens water; can also be used as a scouring powder in the bathroom. To clean your oven with baking soda, sprinkle it on the oven floor and spray with water until damp; let set overnight; scrub clean in the morning.

- **Castile soap** cuts grease, disinfects, and makes a great all-purpose cleaner; "castile" means that it is a vegetable-based rather than animal-based soap.

- **Club soda** removes stains; polishes. Put it in a spray bottle and clean—great on windows!

- **Cornstarch** cleans windows and picks up spills on carpets (especially good on acidic spills from juice, coffee, and wine).

- **Lemon juice** bleaches, deodorizes, cuts grease, and removes stains.

- **Olive oil** polishes furniture.

- **White vinegar** kills bacteria; cuts grease, odors, and wax buildup; removes mildew; also dissolves hard water lime buildup on the inside of teapots—add four ounces of vinegar to a pot of water and boil, then rinse well.

Green Kitchen Design

IF YOU REMODEL OR choose to make changes to your kitchen, keep in mind the green decorating suggestions in Chapter Three. Kitchen paint, wallpaper, flooring, and cabinets are all available as green products that are kind to your home and the environment. Check back in that chapter for a list of product brands and recommendations.

In addition, the following green ideas for kitchen design are suggested by Berkeley, California, architect Andrea Traber:[47]

- Locate work surfaces near operable windows or install operable skylights or suntubes for improved lighting and ventilation.

- For additional lighting, use high-efficiency compact fluorescent light fixtures, with a color-rendering index of 84 or greater and a color temperature of 3,500 Kelvin or greater, and with a quick-start electronic ballast.

- Avoid standard particle board cabinets and use formaldehyde-free medium-density fiberboard, plywood, or wheatboard for cabinet boxes.

- Consider bamboo, reclaimed or sustainably harvested wood, and wheatboard for cabinet doors and drawers; seal with a no- or low-VOC clear finish. (There's further discussion of these building materials in Chapter Three.)

- For countertops, consider salvaged stone slabs or tile, and other unique salvaged materials. One green home used recycled wood from a bowling lane—solid one-and-a-half-inch maple—for countertops.

- Many environmentally responsible options exist for flooring, including stained and sealed concrete floors, sustainably harvested or reclaimed wood, bamboo, tile made from recycled materials, and even cork if well sealed.

The kitchen offers us so many opportunities to create a green world for our children. Make the switch to green foods, beverages, water, plastics, appliances, cleansers, and decor, one step at a time, in this hub of the home.

Now, on to the bathroom!

5

THE
Bathroom

The ideal bathroom for some people is a retreat, a quiet spa designed for long relaxing soaks surrounded by favorite scented candles. But when you have a baby, that concept goes right out the window. The bathroom becomes a place of joyous laughter and splashing, and perhaps, home to a fleet of rubber duckies. This is one room where small green changes can make a big difference. You can save more water here, for example, than in any other room in your home. And you'll be making lots of decisions about products related to your baby's health, from the top of her head to the tips of her toes.

Body Care

WITH A NEW BABY in the house, it's likely that the number of cleansing and soothing products in your bathroom will soon expand dramatically. Now, without even thinking, parents add baby wipes, diaper creams and ointments, baby powder, baby shampoo, body wash, soaps, baby oil and lotion, and sunscreen.

It's just amazing how such a tiny body seems to require so much cleaning!

Let's take a moment to look at the many adult products you've purchased to cleanse, moisturize, refresh, deodorize, sanitize, and beautify your own body. If your family is anything like mine, you have an impressive collection of personal care products that includes various brands of shampoo, toothpaste, soap, deodorant, hair conditioner, moisturizers, lip balm, shaving products, and cosmetics.

We can make our bathrooms more green simply by reducing the number of products we buy, try, and then discard or store in the back of the cabinet. By not purchasing that extra unnecessary bottle you can cut down on the pollution caused by its production, packaging, transportation, and disposal. Thinking green can be that simple.

Going Natural

The first and best way to protect the environment and your own child is to ignore the worry and hype about needing so many baby cleansing products, at least throughout your child's first year.

With skin that is highly permeable and sensitive, most babies

- Do not need a daily bath. A gentle sponge bath to clean the genitals and buttocks is all that's needed.

- Do not need to be washed often with soaps of any kind. Warm water is usually just fine for such delicate skin.

- Do not require constant slathering with diaper creams and lotions. Frequent diaper changes and a daily dose of fresh air is often the best preventive.

- Do not need antibacterial soap and wipes. The excessive use of antibacterial chemicals inhibits the development of our natural resistance and can contribute to creating resistant bacteria!

- Do not need to be doused in baby powder. Talc, in fact, is a known problem for baby lungs.

When you feel you must use cleansing products on your baby, be sure to think before you buy. Try to find products without artificial colors, synthetic fragrances, toxic preservatives, or cancer-causing chemicals and irritants.

The Scoop on Sunscreen

I've slathered sunscreen on my body for most of my life, without ever thinking twice about what was in it. I wasn't aware that what I put on my skin would be absorbed into my body and would be carried in the blood that bathed my cells. If I had known that the chemicals used in many sunscreens are estrogen-like, it wouldn't have concerned me, because I thought the skin was a more-or-less impenetrable barrier. Not so.

Buying Green

Body Care for Babies

THERE ARE MANY PURE cleansing products for babies on the market. I recommend the following products, which are all free of parabens, petroleum products, fragrances, and other harsh chemicals.

❖ Avalon Organics flushable biodegradable baby wipes are gentler on babies and reduce landfills. Also try Gentle Tear-Free Shampoo & Body Wash, which is free from petroleum, synthetic fragrances, and other chemicals. Sold at many stores and online retailers, or visit *www.avalonorganics.com.*

❖ Terressentials organic baby massage oil is made from organic sunflower and jojoba oils combined with organic calendula and chamomile. Check it out at *www.terressentials.com.*

❖ Nature's Gate body lotion is sulfate and paraben free. Other products include baby wash, oil, and diaper rash cream. Sold through many stores and online retailers. *www.naturesgate.com*

❖ California Baby is a nontalc powder that contains all-natural cornstarch and moisture-absorbing bentotite and kaolin clays. California Baby No Fragrance SPF 18 Moisturizer is formulated without PABA or invasive chemicals. Sold at many online retailers. *www.californiababy.com*

❖ You can also find healthier baby products at these online stores:

• Earth Mama Angel Baby products are free from artificial preservatives, fragrances, or dyes. The company uses eco-friendly recyclable or reusable packaging. Products include Angel Baby shampoo, body wash, and baby lotion. *www.earthmamaangelbaby.com*

• The Erbaviva baby line is made with pure botanical ingredients, free from harsh detergents, chemical fragrances, and other unhealthy additives. The company's products include baby shampoo, baby soap, baby cream, diaper cream, baby lotion, and more. *www.erbaviva.com*

• Simple. Pure. Baby. is a line of baby products that doesn't contain harsh chemicals or synthetic fragrances or preservatives. Its line includes baby wash, baby bottom wash, baby lotion, and diaper rash cream. *www.simple purebaby.com*

When researchers looked at adult volunteers using sunscreen, they found the estrogenic active ingredients from the sunscreen in their blood. And in their urine. Thankfully, it didn't appear to affect their overall estrogen or testosterone levels.[1] But what effect could it have on a prepubescent child, awaiting a single drop of sex hormones to start puberty? We just don't know. And what effect could it have in a young baby? Again, we don't know.

We do know that babies have about three times the relative surface area of an adult. If a baby were covered in sunscreen, and the skin were equally absorbent, you would expect three times the concentration of chemicals in the blood. But babies' skin is far more absorptive than adults throughout the first year. The actual levels of these chemicals in babies are probably far higher.

So sun protection is important for babies, all the more so because of what we have done to our ozone layer. But I recommend avoiding ordinary sunscreens. It's better to guard against too much direct sun exposure in the first six months and to dress your baby in sun-protective clothing when outdoors. When it comes to sunscreens currently available in the United

Green Parent Alert

Say No to Nanoparticles

BEWARE OF NANOPARTICLES, WHICH are being introduced as a rapidly emerging technology. These particles are smaller than a microparticle (one micron equals one thousand nanometers) and are now found in many products, such as commonly used sunscreens. Because of their small size and unique, unpredictable properties, nanoparticles quickly permeate the skin and body tissues and are also difficult to control and remove from the environment. Unless there is a compelling environmental or health benefit to be gained from using a nanoparticle option, it makes green sense to use nano-free personal care products. Our family uses Baby Avalon Natural Sunscreen, a mineral sunscreen without any nanoparticles. You might also try Ecolani, Alba Botanica, or Jason's Chemical-Free Sunblock.

States, I recommend using a natural mineral sunscreen that physically blocks the harmful UV rays with active ingredients such as zinc oxide or titanium dioxide—in microparticle, not nanoparticle, size. But the bigger immediate issue is that when it comes to what goes on babies' skin (or on pregnant or nursing mothers' skin), the product ingredients do matter.

Understanding the Label

The major green issue with personal hygiene products, whether for adults or babies, is the ingredient list. The global eco-movement has encouraged the manufacture of natural products made of healthy ingredients that are nontoxic when absorbed into body tissues and organs and whose manufacture does not contribute to air, water, or food pollution. (See the Buying Green box "Personal Care Products" product ideas.)

So, you might wonder, if these wonderful products are so readily available, why aren't the majority of parents using them? Good question.

Many consumers have no idea that conventional toiletries contain questionable chemicals. The FDA does not regulate personal hygiene products or their ingredients for safety before their release, and it has no legal authority to require safety assessments of cosmetics. This leaves the consumer unaware of potential dangers.

Of course, the FDA wants the ingredients to be safe, but its authority is limited. Consider these statements from the cosmetics handbook on the FDA Web site (emphasis mine): "Although the FD&C Act *does not require that cosmetic manufacturers or marketers test their products for safety,* the FDA strongly urges cosmetic manufacturers to [do so]" and "With the exception of color additives and a few prohibited ingredients, a cosmetic manufacturer may . . . *use essentially any raw material as a cosmetic ingredient and market the product without approval.*"[2] The FDA also warns consumers that "the law does not require cosmetic manufacturers to substantiate performance claims."

Manufacturers are not always required to list the toxic ingredients on the product label, even though these chemicals may permeate the skin and are found in body fluids and body fat, and that they may pollute the water supply and accumulate in our seas and rivers every time we wash them down the drain.

This is astonishing! I was surprised when I learned of the loopholes in protecting children from ingredients in cosmetics and personal care products. If you find something labeled "fragrance" or "flavor," you don't have any idea what chemicals are lumped under that term. The same goes for proprietary names and "other ingredients": the law allows a manufacturer to ask the FDA to grant "trade secret" status for a particular ingredient. If trade-secret status is granted, the ingredient does not have to be listed on the label.[3]

But as consumers go green, awareness is becoming more widespread. More parents are tracking down the real ingredient list and are learning how to identify the toxic chemicals they want to avoid. The following is a list of the cosmetic and personal care ingredients that I think are most important to avoid, especially during pregnancy and for a young baby:

- **Parabens.** This family of preservatives has generated controversy lately with the publication of some studies indicating that parabens may be associated with carcinogenic and weak estrogenic activity that could lead to tumors and even cancer. The results are not conclusive, so stay tuned to this controversy, which has generated a lot of emotion on both sides. You may see parabens listed on ingredient labels with many variations, such as methylparaben, propylparaben, or butylparaben. They are found in many popular baby products, including baby lotions, baby soaps, baby sunscreens, baby wipes, baby bubble baths, baby powders, baby oils, and baby shampoos—as well as in many products a mother may use, such as deodorants, moisturizers, shaving gels, and toothpaste.

Buying Green

Personal Care Products for Grown-Ups

THE VERY BEST PERSONAL care products are made with wholesome ingredients, are mild and gentle, yet effective enough to get the job done. The products listed here have each earned top safety rankings at *www.cosmeticsdatabase .com*, a resource I highly recommend. Visit the products' Web sites for more detailed information, to find store locations, or to order online.

CLEANSERS
- ❖ Kiss My Face Pure Olive Oil bar soap. *www.kissmyface.com*
- ❖ Dr. Bronner's Castile Soaps. *www.drbronner.com*
- ❖ Terressentials Fragrance-Free Gentle Bath Gel. *www.terressentials.com*
- ❖ Aubrey Organics Meal & Herbs Exfoliation Skin Care Bar. *www.aubrey organics.com*

DEODORANTS
- ❖ Crystal Body Deodorant Spray Mist. *www.thecrystal.com*
- ❖ Avalon Organics Roll-On Deodorant. *www.avalonorganics.com*

MOISTURIZERS
- ❖ Terressentials Silken Velvet Body Lotion. *www.terressentials.com*
- ❖ Ecco Bella Botanicals Organic Facial Treatment Revitalize. *www.eccobella .com*

TOOTHPASTES
- ❖ Tom's of Maine. *www.tomsofmaine.com*
- ❖ Nature's Gate Crème de Mint Natural Toothpaste. *www.natures-gate.com*
- ❖ Desert Essence Tea Tree Oil Toothpaste, from Australia. *www.desert essence.com*

HAIR PRODUCTS
- ❖ Avalon Organics Therapeutic Shampoo. *www.avalonorganics.com*
- ❖ Terressentials Fragrance-Free Pure Earth Hair Wash. *www.terressentials .com*
- ❖ Kiss My Face Natural Styling Gel (Upper Management). *www.kissmyface.com*
- ❖ Perfect Organics Mandarin Rose Coconut Body Glow, a moisturizing treatment for hair and body. *www.perfectorganics.com*

- **Phthalates.** Found as ingredients in fragrances, sunscreens, moisturizers, shampoos, conditioners, and nail products, this family of endocrine disruptors may also appear with many variations on the name, such as dibutyl phthalate, diethyl phthalate, or cetyl triethylammonium dimethicone copolyol phthalate. They are controversial because some studies have shown that rodents receiving high doses of phthalates have shown hormonal activity and damage to the liver, the kidneys, the lungs, and the developing testes. In humans, preliminary research suggests a link between these chemicals and smaller penis size. Again, more study is needed, but some parents have found this worrisome.[4]

- **Coal tar.** This is included in many FD&C or D&C colors and may be found, for instance, in some baby soaps, baby shampoos, and baby bath products. You might also find coal tar listed directly on the label as an active ingredient in dandruff and scalp treatments or shampoos. I still hear of pediatricians recommending coal tar shampoos for cradle cap in young babies, even though coal tar is a known carcinogen.

- **Phenylenediamines (especially P-phenylenediamine, or PPD).** These are used in hair color and bleaching and have been known to cause throat irritation (pharynx and larynx), bronchial asthma, and sensitization dermatitis.

- **Lead acetate.** Used in some hair-coloring products and in many facial cleansers. We all know that lead isn't so good for us, right?

- **Mercury.** (This may appear as thimerosal on the label.) Found in some mascara. Mercury, like lead, is to be avoided.

- **Formaldehyde.** May appear as formalin on the label. Used largely as a preservative.

- **Diethanolamine (DEA).** Risk of cancer. Particularly dangerous to fetuses, harming brain development by blocking choline. Also seen on labels as lauryl diethanolamide, coco diethanolamide, or several similar names.

- **Toluene.** Found in some nail treatments. Exposure of pregnant women to toluene during critical stages of fetal development could cause serious disruption to neuronal development.

- **Petroleum derivatives.** (These may appear as petroleum distillates.) Found in some fragrances, mascaras, lipsticks, and lip balms.

- **Methylisothiazolinone (MIT).** My concern is about the possible risk of using during pregnancy. Found as a preservative in a wide variety of products, including some shampoos, conditioners, body washes, facial cleansers, hair colors, styling gels, moisturizers, fragrances, and baby wipes.

- **Benzophenone.** This is an estrogenic sunscreen.

- **Homosalate.** This is another estrogenic sunscreen.

- **Octyl-methoxycinnamate.** Also called octinoxate, this is yet another estrogenic sunscreen.

Some consumers continue to buy these products because they have heard that the chemical ingredients fall within the "acceptable" range of body toxins. It's true that many of the synthetic chemicals used in these products have been tested and found to be acceptable for human use. But no one has yet tested the long-term effect of the cumulative dose we get each day from the little bit of toxin in the shampoo that adds to the little bit in the hair conditioner, which adds to the bit in the skin lotion, and the mascara, and the perfume, and so on and on throughout the day and over many years.

In the near future, it's possible that manufacturers will voluntarily remove known and strongly suspected toxins from their products—as they must when the products are sold in Europe. In fact, the Campaign for Safe Cosmetics (a coalition of U.S.-based health and environmental groups working to protect cosmetics consumers from toxic chemicals) has led more than four hundred cosmetic and body care product companies in the United States to sign the "Compact for the Global Production of Safe Health and Beauty Products," pledging to phase out toxic ingredients within three years.[5] The names of these companies can be found at *www.safecosmetics.org.*

If we continue to pressure manufacturers to produce products without these known toxins, it's likely that eventually the formulation of most of your hygiene products will be much safer than it is today. But until then, I'm sure you're wondering what you can do if you want to wash your hair and face and keep your baby bathed and moisturized. Well, fortunately there are plenty of products available online and in your local stores that do not use the most toxic chemicals.

You can find these, and also double-check on the products you are currently using, at the Safe Cosmetics Web site. This site offers an interactive personal care product safety guide with a searchable database of the ingredients and safety ratings of over fourteen thousand shampoos, lotions, deodorants, sunscreens, and other products. Check it out at *www .cosmeticsdatabase.com.* Please also refer to "The Bathroom" in the Green Information section at the back of the book.

Don't Be Fooled

Because of the growing popularity of pure hygiene products, many manufacturers are putting words on their labels to attract green customers. But don't be fooled. The Women's Environmental Network alerts us that

- "Hypoallergenic" is a word manufacturers can use without having to verify or prove their claim.

- "Organic" can be used on a hygiene product even if only 1 percent of the content is of organic origin.

Buying Green

Earth Friendly TP

THAT LOVELY BRIGHT-WHITE toilet paper is an ecological pollutant. The bleaching of toilet paper produces dioxins, which damage earth, air, and water. Next time you shop for toilet tissue, buy a brand that's made from recycled, non-chlorine-bleached paper. The recycling issue is also important when you consider the impact on forests. You can find toilet tissue made from recycled paper (and similar feminine hygiene products as well) at your local grocery or health food store.

- "Natural" is a meaningless word that can be applied to any toiletry.

- "Unscented" implies "with no added fragrance," but it does not mean that at all. In fact, fragrance is often added to these products to mask the odor of the other ingredients so that they appear odorless.

Making Your Own Personal Products

You'll find some of the ingredients for pure personal hygiene products right in your own kitchen pantry. Others you can find at the corner drug store or supermarket. The rest you can easily purchase from online natural cosmetic supply stores, such as From Nature with Love (*www.from naturewithlove.com*) or Essential Wholesale (*www.essentialwholesale.com*), who sell botanical ingredients such as vegetable oils, butters, essential oils, hydrosols, cosmetic clays, detoxifying muds, naturally harvested bath salts, herbs, and many other nutritive or functional ingredients.

Here are a few ideas to get you started:

- **Toothpaste.** Use plain baking soda instead of commercial paste perhaps flavored with a drop of peppermint oil.

- **Tooth whitener.** Add a bit of plain baking soda into your regular toothpaste; you'll see results after several weeks.

- **Mouthwash.** For a natural breath freshener, chew on a few sprigs of fresh parsley or fresh mint.

- **Deodorant.** Sprinkle on plain baking soda, or purchase white clay as a rub-on substitute.

- **Bath water softener.** Add a sprinkle of baking soda.

- **Soap.** Use castile soap or other plant-based soaps. (Stretch your soap use: save that last sliver of the soap bar, shave it into a bottle of water, shake, and use as liquid soap!)

- **Moisturizers and conditioners.** Soften your skin or condition your hair with common household products. Whip up a batch of egg yolks, or use milk or yogurt right out of the container. You can also use safflower oil (for light moisturizing), olive oil (for dry skin or hair), or jojoba oil (for regular skin or hair).

- **Perfumes.** You can use pure essential oils to scent shampoo, bathwater, or even the bathroom itself.

The Medicine Cabinet

WHAT'S IN YOUR MEDICINE cabinet right now? If you're like most of us, it's a good bet that you can make a major move in the green direction by cleaning it all out and starting over again.

Unfortunately, the contents of conventional medicine cabinets contribute significantly to world pollution—specifically dubbed PPCP pollution, for "pharmaceuticals and personal care products." Our frequent use of nanoparticles and chemical pharmaceuticals, including antibiotics and steroid hormones (cortisones), has serious side effects on our health and also on wildlife and the environment.

Fortunately, we now have the option of choosing remedies for common ailments that are both effective and kind to our bodies and our planet.

Reduce Your Use

Green living in general asks us to be mindful of our intake of chemical substances and to reduce their use unless the advantages clearly outweigh

Green Baby Story

Why I Love Castile Soap

In four words: It doesn't leave scum! What this means is that my shower stays clean without purchasing chemical "soap scum removers." This is clean soap! It has a very short list of ingredients and I can pronounce each one. There's nothing untoward in it, just a combination of organic vegetable oils (coconut, palm, olive, jojoba and hemp, some fragrance [I especially like almond]) and that's about it.

"Simplify" is one of my favorite green concepts. Castile soap is a great simplifier. You get to spend more time with your kids and less time cleaning. Check it out at *www.drbronner.com*.

Janie
Austin, Texas

the disadvantages. It is often best for our health to stay organic and natural, and it is best for the environment to reduce the amount of pollutants created in the manufacture, packaging, transport, use, and disposal of these items.

The contents of a chemical-laden medicine cabinet can be especially harmful. As these products wash off our bodies or leave through our digestive waste process, they go down the drain and into rivers, streams, and open water. They don't just disappear—PPCPs are key environmental contaminants.

Although the sheer number of different ingredients has made isolating the effects difficult, synthetic fragrances from personal care products, for instance, have been found in marine and freshwater habitats, where they accumulate in fish and invertebrates.[6]

Try Natural Home Remedies

As a pediatrician, I know there are times when a prescription or over-the-counter medication can save a life. So I would never advocate the elimination of synthetic chemical pharmaceuticals. In fact, I consider many of them among the greatest inventions of the last century.

However, I also know that many medications are overused, unnecessary, and often ineffective. Therefore, when it's appropriate, I often advise the parents of my little patients to try natural remedies first for the minor ailments of childhood before moving on to anything more potent.

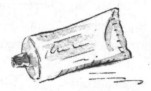

Here are a few simple green solutions to common infant problems:

Diaper rash. Ouch! This most common infant ailment calls out for treatment and fast relief. Soon the medicine cabinet fills with ointments, creams, and powders. However, many of these products offer a solution that's worse than the problem. Talc powder, for example, used to be a standard item in many bathrooms. But we now know that talc-based powders contain tiny particles that irritate the skin and the delicate tissues of the lungs. (As an aside, several studies have linked talc to ovarian cancer.)

Conventional diaper creams and ointments too often contain parabens and other questionable preservatives and harsh chemicals. The parabens are known to have estrogen-like effects, and the long-term impact is yet unknown. I see no reason to use them on babies (or for that matter on pregnant or nursing moms: parabens also get into breast milk). Better alternatives are available.

Remedy. Fresh air! A baby's bottom needs air to stay smooth and avoid irritation. As often as practical, each day, allow your baby to go diaper free. And change diapers frequently to keep the skin dry. If a rash should develop, I recommend soothing zinc diaper balm or an A, D, and E ointment made without harsh chemicals.

Colds. You can clean out the medicine cabinet of decongestants and antihistamines for your baby. There is no evidence that they reduce con-

Buying Green

Baby Supplies for the Medicine Cabinet

WHEN YOU BUY CREAMS and salves to apply to your baby's painful diaper rash or dry flaky skin, you want to be certain they're the very best available products. You can find detailed information and safety ratings for these products, thanks to the searchable database at *www.cosmeticsdatabase.com*, which has a special section devoted just to baby care products, including diaper creams, lotions, and wipes. The products listed below have received top marks for safety. Visit the Web sites for more information or to order online.

DIAPER RASH TREATMENTS
- ❖ Badger Diaper Crème, widely available in stores and online. *www.badger-balm.com*
- ❖ Terressentials 100% Organic Terrific Tush Treatment, which you can buy in a push-up version for easy one-handed application. *www.terressentials.com*
- ❖ California Baby Non-Burning & Calming Diaper Area Wash, comes in a spray bottle to use in place of diaper wipes for irritated skin. *www.californiababy.com*

TEETHING SOOTHERS
- ❖ Ecobaby sells small teething rattles that are made from organic cotton. You can wet or freeze these rattles to help soothe your baby's gums. *www.ecobaby.com*
- ❖ You can find organic cotton, machine-washable teething rings at *www.kidbean.com.*
- ❖ Global Exchange's Fairtrade Online Store sells naturally dyed and pesticide-free teething toys. *www.gxonlinestore.org*

gestion, runny nose, or sneezing in young children.[7] But they can cause side effects that affect both the health of the baby and the environment. The U.S. Centers for Disease Control and Prevention has reported that such cough and cold medications are no more effective than a placebo for reducing acute cough and other symptoms in children younger than two years, and the American College of Chest Physicians has advised health care professionals against using cough suppressants and other over-the-counter cough medications for young children because of actual deaths documented with their use. These deaths were related to dosages high above the recommended amount, but nevertheless, these products present a risk with little if any benefit.[8]

Remedy. Saline nose drops (a simple saltwater solution) will loosen mucus so it is easily removed with a bulb syringe. They also have a gentle decongestant and antiviral effect.

Gravity too plays a sound role in treating congestion. You've probably felt the way sinus congestion eases when you sit up after lying down for a while. Your baby will gain the same benefit if you keep her head a bit higher than her heart.

Thick mucus can be treated with a vaporizer or humidifier. The mucus will become thinner as it pulls in the moisture from the air, allowing it to discharge more easily. (Keep in mind, though, that if the air stays too moist too long, it can encourage mold growth.)

Eczema. The conventional medicine cabinet remedy for one of the most common skin problems in children—eczema—is a steroid cream such as hydrocortisone. In cases of acute inflammation, this treatment can be very helpful, but for medical and environmental reasons, it may not be the best long-term therapy for this condition, which can recur for years.

Remedy. Prevention is key in managing eczema and reducing (or even eliminating) the need for treatment with cortisone or even stronger prescription products. Many different things can be the irritating agent or trigger, which if avoided or eliminated will help avoid an outbreak. When first using these prevention strategies, you may not see an immediate improvement, but if you are going to successfully manage eczema without cortisone, it is important to be vigilant and persistent. Here are some helpful prevention tips:

• Eczema in babies is quite often a reaction to one of these six foods: cow's milk, soy, peanuts, eggs, fish, or wheat. Getting the offending food out of your baby's diet (or your diet, if you are nursing) may make a huge difference without medicines, usually visible within a week or so. If your baby is on a milk or soy formula, this would mean switching to a hypoallergenic formula. If a food is the culprit, the sensitivity may well be outgrown.

- Avoid putting products containing fragrances, masking agents, or harsh chemicals directly on your baby's body.

- Wash your baby's clothes in a laundry detergent good for her sensitive skin and the planet, such as the vegetable-based Seventh Generation Baby Laundry Detergent (nontoxic; biodegradable; and no dyes, fragrances or masking agents, phosphates, chlorine, petroleum-based cleaners, or optical brighteners).

- Avoid situations that will make your baby perspire—don't pile on blankets or put her in a blanket sleeper.

- For some children, wool is the eczema trigger. If so, avoid dressing your baby (or yourself for that matter) in wool or any harsh material (smooth-textured organic cotton is excellent). Also, she may need to avoid crawling on wool carpeting.

- Give brief baths in lukewarm water without a soap or body wash. If needed, use a small amount of very mild cleanser. You can add bath oil to the tub after she is mostly done, to seal in the moisture, not keep it out. Or you may want to slather her with a good moisturizing cream or lotion when her skin is still damp from the bath.

- If the air in your home is very dry, consider a humidifier to keep the air moist and prevent the skin from getting dry.

To treat an outbreak, first apply a pure, moisturizing lotion to the affected areas at least twice a day. These steps are often as effective as just reaching for an over-the-counter or prescription cortisone cream. (See the Buying Green box "Personal Care Products" for recommended moisturizers.)

Teething pain. Benzocaine teething gels are in many parents' medicine cabinets, but I find they are a mixed blessing. Although they can reduce pain, they do it by numbing the mouth and causing that "just left the dentist's" feeling. Some babies find this swollen, numb sensation as annoying as the teething pain itself. Also, the effect of teething gels is quite short lived, and the gels carry a small risk of allergic reactions and decreased gag reflex.

Remedy. Babies' painful gums are often soothed by a massage, so as the first line of treatment, simply rub the gums firmly but gently with a clean finger. You may find that your baby resists at first, but don't give up right away. Many babies settle down and become relaxed as the massage continues.

You can also offer your baby cold teethers to chew on. However, keep in mind that the toxic plastics found in many baby toys (which contribute directly to both body and world pollution) are also found in some teething rings. So if you choose plastic, it is important to purchase teething rings made of nontoxic plastics.

I prefer organic cotton teethers. Or your baby might find relief just by chewing on a washcloth that has been moistened and cooled in the freezer. This is a good idea if the washcloth is made from organic fibers.

See the Buying Green box "Baby Supplies for the Medicine Cabinet" for safe teething products for your baby.

Ear infection. This common childhood problem is the number one reason that children are given antibiotics (more than 10 million antibiotic prescriptions for the 5 million ear infections diagnosed in children each year). Of those 10 million, somewhere between 8.5 million and 9.5 million of them didn't actually help the children, according to the best medical research (and the American Academy of Pediatrics), and in fact may have caused harm because each time a child takes a course of antibiotics, future infections can become harder to treat.[9]

Remedy. Antibiotics may or may not be the appropriate remedy for acute ear infections that start abruptly, with the eardrum becoming suddenly tender, red, hot, swollen, and painful. For babies over six months, antibiotics and at least twenty-four hours of pain relief are usually best if the diagnosis of an acute ear infection is certain. (It must be of abrupt onset, with physical certainty of fluid in the ears and clear evidence of an inflamed eardrum.) If any of these symptoms are not clearly present, the babies are often better treated with pain relief and observed for 48 to 72 hours without antibiotics, unless they've had a fever of 102.2 or higher in the last twenty-four hours, or severe symptoms. For babies under six months, however, antibiotics are usually best if an acute (red-hot) ear infection is strongly suspected, even if the supporting evidence isn't clear-cut.

But for a garden-variety ear infection (what doctors call otitis media with effusion, or OME) in which germ-filled fluid is present in the middle ear, I recommend a period of simple observation. In most cases, the infection will clear up just as quickly without antibiotics, and the baby will have avoided common side effects, which include nausea, vomiting, diarrhea, and skin rashes—and also will have avoided the development of resistant bacteria in his body as well as in the environment.

Whatever other actions you choose to take, I recommend offering the baby something to treat pain or discomfort. If the eardrums are intact, I favor ear drops (some of which are available over the counter). The home remedy of a few drops of warm baby oil or olive oil can also be effective. If more relief is needed, perhaps give some baby acetaminophen or ibuprofen for the pain.

Whenever it's appropriate to treat with pain relief rather than antibiotics, the choice is clear, and it's a green one.

Baby Vitamins

There are some people in the green movement who believe in the value of giving babies a health boost with vitamin and mineral liquid supplements. I have found that such supplementation is generally not needed in the first year because babies receive almost everything they need through breast milk and fortified infant formulas.

I say "almost everything" because I do believe that vitamin D supplementation is often necessary—not because breast milk is lacking in this vitamin, but because the sun-exposure habits of both moms and babies have changed, cutting down on our natural supply. Vitamin D has important preventive capabilities that make it a necessary component of good health.

Try This Today

Turn off the Faucet

IF YOU LET THE water run while you brush your teeth, remember that standard faucets use 2.5 gallons of water per minute. So turning off the faucet for one minute while brushing twice a day can save 1,825 gallons per year.

Disposing of Old Thermometers

Old rectal and oral thermometers contain mercury that should never be let loose in the local environment. Immediately replace these in your medicine cabinet with a new digital one. Call your waste management center for direction on proper disposal of the old mercury one. It should not be placed in the household garbage where it will end up contaminating a landfill.

Going Green

The Latest in Bathroom Energy Efficiency

IF YOU PLAN TO remodel a bathroom in the near future, be sure to investigate the latest green options:

❖ Tankless water heaters are 34 percent more efficient than traditional storage tank heaters. They use intense flame to heat water *only* when you turn on the hot water tap.

❖ Composting toilets so popular in parts of Europe are gaining attention in America. Some of these toilets do not use water at all and produce safe and usable compost, free of bacteria or other pathogens.

❖ Gray water systems recycle water used in the shower and at the sink back to the toilet, so the toilet is not using fresh water with each flush.

❖ Drain-water heat recovery systems transfer heat from the hot water going down the drain to water flowing into the water heater. This allows the heater to use less energy to raise the water temperature again.

❖ Hot water recirculation pumps can be placed on the water fixture farthest from the water heater. This saves energy by cycling the water in your pipes back to the heater, thus cutting the amount of energy needed to heat colder water drawn from its source.

Conserving Water

MOST OF THE WATER you use in your home each day—about 75 percent—flows in and out of the bathroom. That's a huge slice of the pie! So implementing some water-saving strategies in this room is a terrific way to make a quick but significant green impact. You'll find more general water saving strategies in Chapter Seven, "The Whole House."

The Toilet

Think twice before you crumple up that stray tissue and dispose of it by flushing it down the toilet. Toilets eat up more water than any other user in the home—up to 28 percent (GreenHomeGuide Staff).

If your toilet was purchased before 1994, it uses about five gallons of water per flush. Newer toilets cut that amount to about 1.6 gallons per flush. And an ultra-low-flow dual-flush toilet drops the water use to a mere .5 gallon. Some quick math says that a family of four, who each flush the toilet an average eight times per day, can save 13,000 gallons of water per year by using a dual-flush toilet instead of a standard modern toilet, and 52,000 gallons of water compared to the older toilets.

Here are two quick ways to be sure your toilet isn't wasting water:

- Check for leaks in your toilet. Squeeze a few drops of food coloring in the toilet tank. If the toilet leaks, the color will seep into the toilet bowl within fifteen minutes.

- Reduce the amount of water used by older toilets by placing a half-gallon plastic jug filled with water and a bit of gravel in the tank. This will displace some of the water, reducing the amount used with each flush.

The Shower

Showering uses up about 20 percent of your home's water consumption (GreenHomeGuide Staff). Showers installed before 1992 put out 5 gallons of water per minute. After that date, the Energy Policy Act required showerheads to limit water output to 2.5 gallons of water (and you can now buy showerheads that reduce this flow to 1 gallon per minute).

By switching to a low-flow showerhead, a family of four people who each shower for ten minutes per day, can save about 58,000 gallons of water per year!

You might also install a showerhead shutoff valve above the showerhead. This allows you to reduce water flow while lathering up, without losing the hot water in the pipes.

A Clean and Fresh Bathroom

We're fortunate that safer cleansers are now readily available (see page 159), so we're not stuck with conventional bathroom cleaners, which contain ammonia, chlorine, and phosphates, emit fumes, and leave residues.

Natural Bathroom Cleaners

There are many effective alternatives that you can make right at home using simple household products. Give these a try:

- **Disinfectant.** Use isopropyl alcohol.
- **Porcelain and glass cleaner.** Use lemon juice.
- **Air freshener.** Add a half cup of borax to the bottom of the garbage can or diaper pail to reduce the growth of mold and bacteria that causes odors.
- **Drain cleaner.** Prevent clogs before they begin: use plastic hair catchers to keep the biggest clogger from going down the drain. When necessary, use a plunger or mechanical snake to dislodge clogs, and as a last resort, shun the caustic products that contain lye and sulfuric acid and instead try a half cup of baking soda poured down the drain, followed by a half cup of white vinegar.
- **Toilet bowl cleaner.** Use borax and lemon juice.
- **Tub and tile cleaner.** Use baking soda.
- **Scouring powder.** Use baking soda or dry table salt.

Air Freshener or Pollutant?

We'd all like the air in the bathroom to smell like a mountain breeze, but the air fresheners that promise us this kind of scent often contain common toxins like formaldehyde, petroleum distillates, p-dichlorobenzene, and aerosol propellants, and quite commonly they do their olfactory magic by adding a nerve-deadening agent to interfere with your ability to smell or by coating your nasal passages with an undetectable oil film.

And air fresheners and aerosol sprays can lead to sicker babies, sicker moms, and moms who are depressed, according to the University of Bristol.[10] This news came from the "Children of the 90s" study (the Avon Longitudinal Study of Parents and Children—ALSPAC, in which fourteen thousand children have been followed from pregnancies in the early 1990s to the present day). About 40 percent of the families in the study regularly used aerosol sprays (hair sprays, deodorants, furniture polish, and so on) or air fresheners. The more these products were used, the higher the levels of volatile organic compounds (VOCs) in the home. Those who used one or more of these products daily—especially during pregnancy and early childhood—were far more likely to have babies with minor infections, such as diarrhea or ear infections, compared with those families who used them once a week or less.

Mothers in the aerosol/freshener homes also reported more physical symptoms (especially headaches) than did their peers. Maternal depression was 26 percent more common in those families. The scientists suggest squeezing a lemon as a quick, gentle, natural alternative to chemical air fresheners. This seems like a wise idea to me, especially during pregnancy and infancy. The chemicals in air fresheners are among those that cross the placenta easily. It's better to give babies a fresh start without them. Open a window, open a box of baking soda, or add a few drops of an essential oil like lavender to the sink or a sprinkling of borax to the garbage pail.

Your bathroom has many opportunities for going green. The body cleansing products you buy, the natural health remedies you choose, and the products you clean with all affect the health of your baby, your family, and our planet.

In the next chapter, we'll consider the importance, beauty, and pleasure of eco-friendly gardens.

THE
Garden

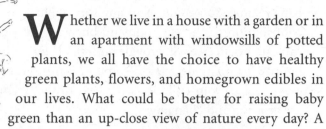

Whether we live in a house with a garden or in an apartment with windowsills of potted plants, we all have the choice to have healthy green plants, flowers, and homegrown edibles in our lives. What could be better for raising baby green than an up-close view of nature every day? A garden, whether indoors or out, is the perfect setting for teaching our children about the care and appreciation of our precious planet earth.

The Outdoor Garden

A GARDEN IS AN especially wonderful extension of your home when you have a baby. It's an outdoor room where together, you can enjoy fresh air, observe nature, breathe in the perfume of favorite flowers, dig in the dirt, and pick a sun-ripened fruit for lunch from your own organically grown tree.

A Garden for Baby

Think about creating a special corner of the garden where you can introduce your baby to the delights of the great outdoors. Choose plants that invite butterflies and hummingbirds, flowers that are especially fragrant and colorful, and tasty edibles for your baby's developing palate. Hang a bird feeder (fill it with organic seeds) to encourage feathered visitors. And be sure to include a comfy chair where you and your baby can cuddle and watch nature unfold.

Check out the organic gardening methods described later in this chapter for tips on getting started and shop around for certified organic seeds and plants. Use native plants whenever possible because these will be perfectly adapted to your climate and natural soil conditions, and you'll find them easiest of all to grow. Here are some suggested plants for this special garden, but check first with your local supplier for varieties or alternatives suitable for your area. Pick and choose from among these ideas, and remember that the main thing is to enjoy your garden, the fresh air, nature, fun, and nourishment—and to pass these joys on to your child.

- **A tree for baby.** A great way to begin is to plant a legacy tree in your baby's name. You could plant any sort of shade tree and make a fine contribution to the environment, but why not plant something you can eat? A fruit tree will provide both shade *and* delicious home-grown bounty for many decades to come. A fun project is to take a picture every year of your child standing next to the tree to record how both are growing and changing.

- **Fragrant annuals and tender perennials.** Try planting common stock (*Matthiola*) with spikes of blossoms that smell like cinnamon, or old-fashioned violets (*Viola odorata*). If you can find a violet that's native to your area, you'll be rewarded with the sweetest perfume of any wildflower.

- **Herbs.** Grow lavender (*Lavandula*) in a sunny spot and peppermint in the shade (this potentially invasive plant is best confined to a pot) for flowers and leaves to crush in your fingers and sniff. For a soft and dewy green carpet underfoot, plant aromatic chamomile (*Chamaemelum nobile*).

- **Fruits and vegetables.** For a special summer treat, try growing plump, delicious, and so-good-for-you blueberries (*Vaccinium corymbosum*). You'll have the best yield if you plant several varieties for cross-pollination. And watch for the brilliant scarlet or yellow foliage produced in the fall by this outstanding edible landscape plant. Other yummy edibles for baby's special garden include sweet "Nantes" carrots and tender sugar snap peas (*Pisum sativum*). But be careful! Don't confuse edible sugar snap peas with the decorative flowering sweet pea (*Lathyrus*), which is a poisonous plant.

- **To attract butterflies.** Sunny gardens attract the most butterflies, so pick an open, unshaded area to plant the nectar-producing plants that butterflies love. One aptly named shrub is called butterfly bush (*Buddleia davidii*), which creates a fountain of lavender or pink flowers. Butterflies are said to be nearsighted and attracted to swaths of bright flowers, so think about planting patches of scarlet zinnias, sunny marigolds, and colorful cosmos. Include as many native plants as possible.

- **To attract hummingbirds.** "Hummers" are drawn to tubular flowers, and their favorite color is red, so consider coral bells (*Herchera*), columbine (*Aquilegia*), and trumpet vine (*Distictis*). Once these fascinating birds discover your garden, they will enjoy other flowers, especially those you've planted to attract butterflies.

Edible Landscaping

If you've given edible plants a try in the baby garden, you might be interested in what else you can do if there's room left in the rest of the yard. Some of the most exciting gardens I've seen incorporate the idea of "edible landscaping" into the yard's overall design. In these gardens you might see fruit and nut trees, vegetables of all varieties, berries, grapes, and every kind of culinary herb, all blended with ornamental shrubs and flowers. With careful design, this kind of garden combines all the pleasures of a traditional landscape with the deep satisfaction of producing your own organic food for the table.

The idea of integrating edible plants into a traditional garden setting has been around for thousands of years. In the wonderful resource *The Complete Book of Edible Landscaping*, author Rosalind Creasy describes ancient Egyptian gardens dating back to 1400 B.C., with grapevine-covered trellises, and fig, pomegranate, and date trees laid out in a formal design with decorative flower beds and fish ponds.

Borrowing from that distant past, it makes perfect sense these days to create a garden that both looks great and is productive at the same time. A single mature apple tree can provide your family with enough fruit so that

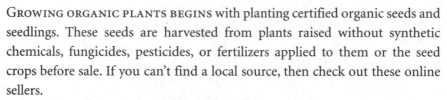

Buying Green

Start with Organic Seeds

GROWING ORGANIC PLANTS BEGINS with planting certified organic seeds and seedlings. These seeds are harvested from plants raised without synthetic chemicals, fungicides, pesticides, or fertilizers applied to them or the seed crops before sale. If you can't find a local source, then check out these online sellers.

Seeds of Change offers more than 600 distinct varieties of 100 percent certified organically grown seeds for the home gardener. Pick from varieties of gourmet leafy greens, culinary and medicinal herbs, flowers, and vegetables. You can also get a jump start on planting if you purchase seedlings, which make it easy to grow some of the perennials and herbs that are trickier to propagate from seeds. Check out their handy combination six-packs, such as the salsa pack that includes seedlings of all the right tomatoes and chile peppers for making your own dipping sauces. Go to *www.seedsofchange.com*.

Wild Garden Seed is a seed farm in Oregon certified organic since 1987. All their seed is open pollinated, untreated, and germ tested, an ecological approach that Wild Garden says produces "fat seeds with exceptional seedling vigor, a key trait for organic crop success." Go to *www.wildgardenseed.com*.

you can pick what you need at the point of sun-ripened perfection instead of driving to the store to buy apples that were grown in another state and trucked to your town. Or think about cutting fresh herbs from the garden exactly when you want them instead of resorting to the dusty dried variety or expensive little bunches sold in the gourmet produce aisles.

Edible plants grow best in certain conditions. Fruits and vegetables generally thrive where they get at least six hours of sunlight each day. Most also like well-drained soil. The areas of your yard that satisfy these requirements are good places to plan an edible landscape. You can start out just by substituting a traditional garden plant with an edible in its place. Where you might have planted a shade tree, plant a fruit tree instead. Where you want a shrub, try planting a blueberry bush. Where you usually grow sun-loving annuals, plant some colorful nasturtiums—you can toss their peppery leaves and flowers right into your salad.

Like the other suggestions I've made in this book, you can do as much or as little as you like. You might decide to turn your entire yard over to edible landscaping, or you might be satisfied with the juicy yield of a few tomato plants each summer. Every bit helps.

The Great American Lawn

IF YOU HAVE A lawn, you're in good company. At least 80 percent of households in the United States have lawns, and I confess that mine is among them. A patch of lawn can be a wonderful place for a baby to lie and sleep on, crawl around, and eventually play outdoors. It's green (we hope), and it provides oxygen to the environment. It feels good to walk on, and personally, I love my little lawn and care for it avidly.

Nevertheless, as a doctor and environmentalist I realize that there's no such thing as a natural lawn. Lawns don't occur in nature without intense human intervention, except historically in places like Great Britain where it rains all the time and grazing sheep trim the grass. The kind of lush green lawns we love to have in our backyards, on our golf courses, and surrounding our corporate headquarters actually cause huge capital expense and, more important, exceptional damage to the environment. According to the U.S. National Wildlife Federation,[1]

- 30 percent of water consumed on the East Coast goes to watering lawns; that figure rises to 60 percent on the West Coast.

- 18 percent of municipal solid waste is composed of yard waste.

- The average suburban lawn receives ten times as much chemical pesticide per acre as farmland.

- More than seventy million tons of fertilizers and pesticides are applied to residential lawns and gardens annually.

- "Small SI engines (as in lawnmowers, leaf blowers) produce approximately one tenth of U.S. mobile source hydrocarbon (HC) emissions and are the largest single contributor to nonroad HC inventories. A typical SI engine produces as much pollution in 7 hours as a modern car driven for over 100,000 miles."[2] Put another way, per hour of operation, a gas lawn mower emits ten to twelve times as much hydrocarbon as a typical auto. A weed eater emits twenty-one times more, a leaf blower thirty-four times more.

- Where pesticides are used, 60 to 90 percent of earthworms are poisoned. Earthworms are important for soil health.

These statistics make going green in the great outdoors a very satisfying decision. Even the tiniest quantities of chemicals and other pollutants around your house (think lawn fertilizers, car-washing compounds, and the like) get picked up by rain and snow and are then carried through the storm drains to surface waters. Such small events go unnoticed, yet they can result in polluted drinking water, beach closings, and endangered wildlife.

I remember the day I put down my bug and weed killer with the sudden conviction that I no longer wanted to care for my lawn in ways that were unhealthy for my family and the environment. "Why," I wondered, "would I put this stuff on the grass and then encourage my children, my dog, my cat, and my bunnies to play, run, and even roll all over it?"

Sometimes we do things that are antigreen simply out of habit. That's why I feel it is so important to raise my children so that their lifestyle habits are naturally green. I have now adopted greener lawn-care strategies and feel the satisfaction of caring for my small plot of earth in ways that cultivate green grass while also respecting the earth it comes from.

Sustainable Lawn Care

There are many ways we can all make changes to reduce our abuse of the earth while caring for our lawns. Here are some suggestions to get you started:

- Choose locally adapted grass. This will give you grass suited for your climate, rainfall, and soil quality.

- Keep grass length slightly long (2.5 to 3.5 inches). A short cut exposes surface roots, dries out the soil, and reduces surface aeration.

- Water deeply. Thorough watering encourages deep root systems, making the lawn hardier and more drought resistant. Although lawn watering in general is a major source of "unnecessary" water consumption, doing it right can actually save total usage. Experts suggest that you let the lawn dry out between waterings (wait until the color begins to dull and footprints are visible for more than a few seconds before resuming the watering). Also, you should water in the early morning when less water is lost to evaporation.[3]

- Use a push mower. New reel mowers are lightweight, efficient, and pollution free.

- Leave grass clipping on the lawn. This provides nutrients equivalent to one application of fertilizer.

- Use corn gluten as a natural weed killer. This nontoxic by-product of corn processing kills weed seedlings and adds nitrogen to the soil.

- Spot-treat weeds with common full-strength vinegar on a sunny day. Boiling water will also kill individual weeds growing in sidewalks and other paving.

For additional organic gardening tips, visit the Web site of the National Wildlife Federation: *www.nwf.org/backyard/organic.cfm.*

Each time you treat your lawn with care and respect, you teach a valuable lesson to your children. Their exploration of nature and their sense of environmental awareness begin in your own backyard.

Green Parent Report

Baby-Friendly Lawn Alternatives

❖ Baby's tears (*Soleirolia soleirolii*). Small, dainty creeping leaves form clean, lush green mats with tiny white flowers in summer. Prefers shade and moderate moisture. In colder regions, the plant dies back during winter, but it returns with lush growth as the temperature increases.

❖ Irish moss (*Sagina subulata*). Dense tufts of slender stems grow together to form a velvety soft green carpet. Small star-shaped white flowers cover completely in spring.

❖ Blue star creeper (*Isotoma*). Forms a flat green ground cover and blooms with pale blue flowers from spring to frost. Easy to grow and maintain.

Check out *www.stepables.com* for ground cover ideas suitable for your needs and climate zone. You can search from 130 varieties of ground covers and lawn substitutes according to plant height, water requirements, flower color, and whether you can walk on it.

Rethinking the Lawn

If you're uneasy about the water, time, money, and chemicals that have been necessary to maintain your lush green grass lawn, then maybe it's time to think about substitutes and alternatives.

One convincing alternative to traditional turf is a lawn of buffalo grass (*Buchloe dactyloides*). This prairie grass is a true native that grows wild from central Montana south to Arizona and could be just the ticket for those who can't quite give up the idea of having some kind of lawn around the house. Buffalo grass is soft enough for going barefoot, yet is tough enough for team sports. It requires just a fraction of the water used for conventional grass lawns, grows to about four inches, and needs only occasional mowing. Buffalo grass grows best in full sun and clay soils.

Conventional sod can be also replaced with low-growing ground covers or creeping fescues that require far fewer resources to sustain and much less effort to maintain. Find species that are native to your area and you will have the fewest problems. If you're unable to locate native varieties, consider a product called Eco-Lawn—a seed mix developed by a Canadian company called Wildflower Farm. Eco-Lawn is a blend of seven fescues that forms a dense turf in many growing conditions. It can be mowed on a monthly basis, or if left in a natural state, takes on the look of a soft, green undulating meadow. Once established, this deep-rooted turf requires little water and no fertilizer or pesticides. Find it at *www.wildflower farm.com*.

Many ground cover advocates recommend combining several varieties both for healthy biodiversity and for the look of a flowering lawn. This idea borrows a bit from the traditional "herb lawns" still found in England, where flowering herbs such as thyme, catmint, and chamomile create a fragrant surface to walk on.

With these kinds of alternatives, some people believe that the best thing you can do for a conventional lawn is get rid of it!

How to Grow an Organic Garden

CHOOSING ORGANIC VERSUS CONVENTIONAL gardening practices to build healthy soil and control pests and weeds has profound consequences both for your own family's health and well-being and for the environment.

For example, organic home gardening eliminates the use of conventional pesticides. It's amazing that on average, homeowners use proportionately three to six times more pesticides in their yards than farmers do on their crops. Most wildlife pest poisonings and most surface-water contamination from pesticides come from single-family homes.[4] Yes, we need to change agribusiness, but starting in our own backyard is at least as important.

Here are some important elements to grow your own healthy garden.

Building Healthy Soil

Working compost (broken-down organic material) into the soil improves soil structure, texture, and aeration, and increases the soil's water retention capacity. It also promotes soil fertility and stimulates healthy root development. You can buy compost in ready-to-use bags at the local garden supply store or, better yet, have fun making it yourself by recycling garden and kitchen debris at home rather than sending it to the trash or landfill.

Buying Green

Nontoxic Garden Care

IF YOU MUST USE pest control products, avoid synthetic pesticides that release toxic compounds that remain in the environment without breaking down. Instead go for organic products.

❖ Garden's Alive! (*www.gardensalive.com*) offers environmentally responsible products. One such exclusive product is "Weed-Aside Weed Killer," an herbicidal soap that contains a blend of naturally occurring fatty acids. This product kills weeds, then decomposes in the soil.

❖ Clean Air Gardening (*www.cleanairgardening.com*) offers organic pest control products, such as the Orange Guard Organic Insect Killer. This product is made from orange peel extract and naturally kills insects by destroying the wax coating of the insect's respiratory system.

❖ Extremely Green (*www.extremelygreen.com*) has a wide assortment of organic gardening products, such as organic fertilizers made from fish and seaweed. These products are known to build sugar in plants to make them more colorful and strong.

A pile of leaves, branches, old roots and weeds, and lawn clippings will eventually decompose slowly as in nature without any special intervention and become fluffy natural compost, the best fertilizer in the world, and without any nasty poisons. You can also speed up this process by layering fresh green plant material, including leafy kitchen waste, with dried organic matter and soil, and then keeping it aerated by turning it periodically. It's also necessary to keep the composting material sufficiently moist.

To improve the soil in our own garden, my family has enjoyed using a rotating compost bin, which can be found at *www.compostumbler.com*. We've also had fun raising worms in the back yard with an innovative device called a Can-O-Worms. Find it at *www.magicworms.com* and many other online retailers.

Controlling Pests and Diseases

The best defense against destructive pests is biodiversity. Growing many different kinds of plants encourages a variety of beneficial insects to take up residence in your yard, where they can eat the harmful insects and create a balanced ecosystem. If you choose this natural method of controlling lawn and garden pests, you will single-handedly make a significant green impact and protect the health of your children.

You will, furthermore, delight your baby with a close-up look at such beneficial insects as the beautiful ladybug, which eats destructive insects that plague gardens. For more solutions, and a list of nontoxic pesticides you can make at home, see "Natural Pest Control" at *www.eartheasy.com*.

Green Weed Control

Mulching is the best recommendation we can make for reducing the weeds in your garden. Whereas compost is at least partially decomposed and ready to be worked into the soil, mulch is a three-inch layer of organic material—leaves, clippings, even vegetable scraps from the kitchen—that you spread on *top* of the soil around your plants in spring or fall. Mulch stabilizes soil temperature, prevents weeds, feeds the soil for healthier plants, and helps conserve water.

Of course you can also get down and pull some weeds yourself too. Great exercise!

Dispose of Toxic Chemicals Safely

If you've decided to go organic in the garden, you need to get rid of those nasty chemical pesticides and fertilizers lurking in the garage, the tool shed, and other hiding places. You don't want to toss this stuff into the trash and the dump, where it can continue to contaminate the environment. Most municipalities now offer toxic waste drop-off sites. To locate your nearest facility, go to *www.earth911.org*. For community-specific information, just enter your ZIP Code, and you'll be taken to information about services in your area. Click on the first menu item on the left side of the page, which will be "Household Hazardous Waste," and from there you can link to sites that will accept your specific kind of toxic waste. If you're pregnant or nursing, take extra care with this task to prevent exposing yourself to toxins. Enlist some help to pack up and transport these chemicals to the toxic waste drop-off site.

Babyproofing the Garden

IF YOU'VE ELIMINATED CHEMICAL fertilizers, pesticides, and weed killers from your gardening supplies, you've taken a giant step toward creating a safe and healthy garden for your baby, your family, and the earth itself. That's wonderful!

Now it's time to survey other potential hazards for babies and children in the garden. These include poisonous plants, bodies of water, play structures, and even the ordinary garden hose.

Poisonous Plants

Indoor and outdoor plants are responsible for a rising number of accidental poisonings, according to the Poison Control Center. Plant ingestion is among the top five causes of accidental poisonings in children younger than five years.

Many common outdoor and houseplants are toxic, and some are deadly. To be safe, you need to identify all the plants in your garden landscape and check them against a poisonous plant reference. If poisonous plants are already in your garden or on your property, consider removing them or fencing them. Make a sketch of the garden, pinpoint the spots of any toxic plants, and write down the correct botanical names. Put the sketch in a safe place where you can easily find it again in case you ever need to quickly identify the name of an ingested leaf or other plant part.

Supervise your baby at all times. When he starts touching and tasting, you need to be sure there is no access to any hazardous plant material. Because babies and small children can't distinguish between safe and toxic plants, you must teach them never to taste any part of a plant without first showing it to you—including the leaves, berries, stems, bark, seeds, flowers, nuts, pods, and bulbs. This is essential if you plan to grow edible plants, simply to avoid confusion over what is OK to eat and what isn't. So the absolute rule should be "Never taste anything in the garden before showing Mommy or Daddy."

Here is a partial list of poisonous outdoor plants:

Mushrooms. Ingesting any part of any mushroom can be dangerous.

Bulbs. The bulbs and leaves of most ornamental bulbs are poisonous, including daffodil (*Narcissus*), lily (*Lilium*), and tulip (*Tulipa*).

Shrubs

- Daphne (*Daphne*). The bright red or orange berries are deadly, and the bark and leaves are also toxic.
- Angel's trumpet (*Datura*). The flowers, leaves, and seeds are deadly. This plant sheds its large, fragrant flowers continually over a long season, requiring daily removal.
- Holly (*Ilex*). The tempting berries are toxic.
- Oleander. All parts are deadly; even the smoke of a burning oleander plant is highly toxic.

Flowers

- Sweet peas (*Lathyrus*). The seeds are poisonous.
- Morning glory (*Ipomaea violacea*). The seeds are extremely toxic.
- Poisonous parts of otherwise edible plants:
    Rhubarb (*Rheum rhaponticum*). The leaves are toxic.
    Potato (*Solanum*). The green parts, including leaves and immature fruit, are toxic.

Pools and Other Water Hazards

Water features, including pools, spas, ponds, birdbaths, fountains, and waterfalls, are popular additions to gardens, but even a bucket of water can be dangerous for a toddler. Always supervise children around water as a child can drown in as little as two inches of water. Fence in and consider removing water features and water gardens for now. And if you have a natural pond or stream on your property, test the water for contaminants, and teach children not to drink it.

While you're looking around the garden for potential water hazards, make a note of the places water collects. Standing water attracts mosquitoes to your yard, and they may carry the dangerous West Nile Virus. The best green solution is to prevent water from pooling. If you find depres-

Green Parent Alert

In Case of Emergency

IF YOU SUSPECT THAT your child has ingested a poisonous plant, follow these instructions from the Poison Control Center:

1. Remove any remaining plant parts from the mouth.
2. If the victim is choking and cannot breathe, call 911.
3. Otherwise, call the Poison Control Center at 800-222-1222, and you will be routed to your local facility.
4. If you are advised to go to an emergency room for treatment, take the plant or a part of the plant with you. Do not take only a single leaf or a single berry.
5. If you are advised to go to a nursery to get the plant identified, keep in mind that plants are usually not very quickly digested, so there is time to get a correct identification. The correct name can result in the proper treatment to prevent symptoms from occurring if the plant was poisonous. If the plant was not dangerous, knowing the name can prevent needless treatment and worry.

sions that turn into little ponds after a rain, you can try filling them with gravel. Also check for empty pots and other containers that hold water and turn them upside down to prevent them from filling.

Replacing Old Play Structures

It may seem premature to think about backyard play structures while your infant is still a lap baby. But if there's a wooden play structure already standing in your yard, there are some important reasons to pay attention to it now, as soon as your baby is born.

If the structure was built before 2003, it was probably made out of pressure-treated lumber preserved with arsenic-based chemicals, as were most decks, gazebos, picnic tables, and other outdoor wooden structures of that period.

The EPA banned the use of this chemically treated wood for residential use in 2003 because of an increased cancer risk—especially to children—but most of these structures are still standing in backyards throughout the country. You can usually recognize pressure treated wood by its greenish tint, and staple-sized slits in the side of the wood. The greenish tint, however, may fade with time, and not all pressure treated wood has the slits. If these indicators are missing, you can try to contact the manufacturer or you can order an inexpensive test kit from the Environmental Working Group (EWG) online at *www.ewg.org/reports/poisonwoodrivals/orderform.php.*

Children are exposed to arsenic through their skin contact with the wood and from hand-to-mouth activity while playing on these wooden structures. Studies have also shown that arsenic slowly leaches from pressure treated wood onto surrounding soil. As a result, children can be directly exposed to arsenic by coming into contact with the contaminated soil. They can also be exposed by way of a splinter.

For these reasons, I think it's best to remove these play structures and replace them if desired, with new ones made of sustainably harvested naturally rot-resistant cedar or other nontoxic materials such as metal or non-PVC plastics.

Special care must be taken when dismantling and discarding the old structure to avoid unnecessary exposure to arsenic. If you are pregnant or nursing, please step aside and let someone else handle this task. The EPA suggests these precautions:[5]

- Avoid creating sawdust. If sawing is necessary, wear goggles, a dust mask, and gloves.

- Clean up every speck of debris and dust and dispose of the wood at a hazardous waste disposal area to avoid sending this toxic material to a landfill where it can continue to leach chemicals. And never burn pressure-treated wood as the smoke would be highly toxic.

- Wash carefully with soap and water after handling.

- Because preservatives or sawdust may accumulate on clothing, they should be laundered before reuse. Wash the items separately from other household clothing.

You should also test the soil for arsenic in the area where the structure stood. Tainted soil is hazardous to humans and other living creatures, and arsenic is absorbed by plants. Arsenic, which is a metal, doesn't biodegrade, but it does remain close to the soil's surface. If testing reveals arsenic contamination, the most prudent solution is to remove the top two to five inches of soil. Dispose of it according to your local regulations—check with your municipal hazardous waste facility. Then fill with clean, fertile topsoil and replant knowing that you've restored your garden's good health.

Always supervise your baby and toddler around play structures, and consider removing the lower railings to prevent them from trying to climb the structure.

Green Baby Story

Plant a Tree

TREES EAT UP CARBON dioxide and make clean air for us to breathe. So I decided that planting a tree was the kind of positive and very visual step I wanted to share with my kids. Early last spring, I bought two small saplings—one for each of my children to plant in our backyard. We all put on our old clothes, got out our shovels, and spent a wonderful morning together digging in the earth and reverently giving new life to our property. My children are only one and three years old, but already they are enjoying watching "their" trees grow. They and their trees are growing up together in what I hope will be a very green and nurturing world.

We've also made an effort to bring that green power indoors by keeping live plants around the house. They improve the air quality, absorb potentially harmful gases, and are natural indoor air filters.

Edith Spitzer
Phoenix, Arizona

Greener Garden Hoses

Most garden hoses are made of PVC, and it turns out that high levels of lead additives in the PVC and in the brass fittings themselves leach easily into the water flowing through the hose—especially if the hose has been lying in the sun. That means that humans, pets, and plants are exposed to lead—which can cause irreversible brain damage in children—if they come in contact with water from the hose. In a lawsuit settled in 2004, the country's largest garden hose manufacturer agreed to post a warning label reading, "Do not drink water from this hose. Wash hands after use."

You can make a much greener choice by replacing those old hoses with hoses labeled "drinking water safe." These are made of food-grade plastics and, in some cases, with nickel-coated fittings. Here are some good ones:

- Aquamate Ultimate Water Coiled 25–FT Garden Hose, made of FDA-approved "drinking water safe" polyurethane. Find it at *www.amazon.com*.

- Water FLEXEEL, made of ether-based "drinking water safe" polyurethane; will generally last for five to ten years or more. Find it at *www.naturestapestry.com/waterhose*.

The Indoor Garden

IF YOU'RE A CITY dweller, you can still reap the green benefits of live foliage by filling your apartment with indoor plants. Adding living plants to every room in your home is of course a nice decorating touch, but it is also an excellent way to protect the health of your baby while reducing air pollution.

Most people spend up to 80 percent of their day indoors.[6] (It's likely that your baby spends even more of each day breathing indoor air.) In apartment and condo buildings, this fact is especially notable when the building is "climate controlled," meaning that it is closed up airtight, and all

Green Parent Report

Top Ten Air-Filtering Plants

A NASA STUDY FOUND that the following indoor plants were most effective in removing formaldehyde, benzene, and carbon monoxide from the air:[7]

* Bamboo palm (*Chamaedorea seifritzii*)
* Chinese evergreen (*Aglaonema modestmu*)
* English ivy (*Hedera helix*)
* Gerbera daisy (*Gerbera jamesonii*)
* Janet Craig (*Dracaena*)
* Marginata (*Dracaena marginata*)
* Mass cane/corn plant (*Dracaena massangeana*)
* Mother-in-law's tongue (*Sansevieria laurentii*)
* Pot mum (*Chrysantheium morifolium*)
* Peace lily (*Spathiphyllum* "Mauna Loa")

heat and cooling is supplied through a closed-loop ventilation system—no open windows! With so many sources of VOCs all around us, this can cause indoor air to become more polluted than the outdoor air.

One solution? Lots of greenery.

We all know that plants recycle oxygen, so it's logical that they can cleanse indoor air, but their ability to break down pollutants is especially important and even scientifically proven. In one such study by NASA, various plants were exposed to high concentrations of pollutant chemicals inside sealed chambers. The study found that some plants are more efficient in filtering out toxins than others (see the Green Parent's Report box

"Top Ten Air-Filtering Plants"), but those in the top ten were able to remove 90 percent of the formaldehyde, benzene, and trichloroethylene within twenty-four hours.[8] The filtering process by which plants break down indoor air pollutants is quite fascinating. Chemicals are absorbed into the plants through the leaves, and bacteria associated with the roots help break down contaminants, which are taken up as nutrients.[9] Amazing!

In fact, according to one study, one six-inch houseplant per one hundred square feet of living area will do a good job of filtering out pollutants. And it was found that the more vigorous the plant, the more air it can filter—a good incentive to keep those plants pruned and watered![10]

To learn more about how plants purify the air, check out *How to Grow Fresh Air: 50 Houseplants to Purify Your Home or Office*, by B. C. Wolverton (Penguin). This book, based on twenty-five years of research by NASA, describes how common houseplants can combat sick building syndrome and cleanse the home or office of common pollutants.

Growing Healthy Indoor Plants

Indoor plants that are well watered (not too much, not too little) and receive adequate light generally do not need to be fertilized. But if you'd like to provide your plants with a little extra nourishment, be sure to keep it green. Avoid synthetic plant foods and opt instead for organic fertilizers that usually contain fish components and seaweed. They are available in liquid or powder form from any plant nursery.

Indoor Edible Gardening

Indoor decorative plants are beautiful and functional as air filters, but to add to the benefits of your indoor greenery, you might try growing your own indoor organic vegetable garden! This is a terrific way to teach kids about the earth as a provider of nourishment, and it's great for apartment dwellers or for anyone living in a cold-winter climate who craves the great taste of homegrown food.

When planning an indoor vegetable garden, it's best to choose smaller plants that take up a limited amount of space, such as carrots, lettuce, tomatoes, peppers, and radishes. But whatever your chosen crop, here are a few tips to make your garden grow:[11]

To begin, choose a planter that has drainage holes, has at least six to eight inches of soil depth, and will be large enough to hold the fully grown produce. It's best to use a potting soil with a lightweight mix in your large planter to ensure quick water drainage. To further encourage good drainage, you might also place your planter in a tray with an inch of stones lining the bottom. The drained water from the plant will provide a source of constant moisture.

Then choose a location in your home where you'll place your indoor garden. This is an important decision, because the sunlight in this location will determine the types of vegetables you can successfully grow. For example, root and leaf crops such as carrots and lettuce will grow well in partial shade, but fruit crops need direct sunlight for at least five hours each day. Most plants will do well in a window that faces south and gets lots of sun. You can also supplement natural light with fluorescent lighting during the winter months.

The ideal indoor temperature for your produce garden will depend on your crop. Root vegetables do well at temperatures in the 60-degree range, whereas fruit crops tend to prefer higher temperatures close to 80 degrees. To start your garden, plant your seeds in individual cups and then transplant them into your large planter when they are strong enough to be moved (when they reach an inch or so in height).

While growing your indoor garden, remember that the goal is to produce food that is good for your family—in other words, organic. Plants in a composted soil will not need any other fertilizer, but if you do need to give your plants a boost, as mentioned earlier you can use liquid fertilizers that are commonly made from fish processing waste combined with mineral-rich seaweed (often kelp). You'll find these liquid fertilizers as concentrates that you mix with water and apply directly to plants' leaves.

As the green foliage of your crops begins to sprout, it will humidify and purify the air. Then when the crop is ready for harvest, you will experience the true joy of nourishing your family with healthy foods grown right in your own home.

Growing an Indoor Herb Garden

To spice up your homegrown vegetables, you might grow a few herbs in a windowsill garden. These beautiful and fragrant plants are a quick and easy way to watch the miracle of nature in your own home. The simplest way to start is by purchasing potted seedlings from your local plant nursery. Or you can try starting from seeds or cuttings as explained online at *www.organicgardening.com*.[12]

Basil. Start basil from seeds and place the pots in a south-facing window—it likes lots of sun and warmth.

Bay. A perennial that grows well in containers all year long. Place the pot in an east- or west-facing window, but be sure it does not get crowded—bay needs air circulation to remain healthy.

Chervil. Start chervil seeds in late summer. It grows well in low light but needs 65- to 70-degree temperatures to thrive.

Chives. Dig up a clump from your garden at the end of the growing season and pot it up. Leave the pot outside until the leaves die back. In early winter, move the pot to your coolest indoor spot (such as a basement) for a few days, then finally to your brightest window.

Oregano. Your best bet is to start with a tip cutting from an outdoor plant. Place the pot in a south-facing window.

Parsley. You can start this herb from seeds or dig up a clump from your garden at the end of the season. Parsley likes full sun, but will grow slowly in an east- or west-facing window.

Rosemary. Start with a cutting of rosemary and keep it in moist soilless mix until it roots. It grows best in a south-facing window.

Sage. Take a tip cutting from an outdoor plant to start an indoor sage. It tolerates dry indoor air well, but it needs the strong sun it will get in a south-facing window.

Tarragon. A dormant period in late fall or early winter is essential for tarragon to grow indoors. Pot up a mature plant from your outdoor garden and leave it outside until the leaves die back. Bring it to your coolest indoor spot for a few days, then place it in a south-facing window for as much sun as possible. Feed well with an organic liquid fertilizer.

Thyme. You can start thyme indoors either by rooting a soft tip cutting or by digging up and potting an outdoor plant. Thyme likes full sun but will grow in an east- or west-facing window.

Green babies need a green environment, and green plants are the best way to provide it. My family has enjoyed the nutritional and environmental benefits of both indoor plants on our tables and windowsills and an outdoor garden.

Now that we've gone through all the rooms and environments of each part of the house, let's pull back and look at the big picture: the whole house.

THE
Whole House

So far we've focused each chapter on a particular room in your house, but in this chapter we want to take an overview of issues that relate to the entire home, like air quality, water conservation, energy conservation, recycling, household pets, and a few other significant activities that are not room specific like driving the household car.

Air Quality in the Home

YOUR NOSE IS ONE indicator of the air quality in your home—the cleanliness of the air your baby breathes each day. Rule of thumb: if the aroma you smell is from a natural source (such as fresh air, flowers, a sliced lemon, essential oils, or homemade bread), breathe deep and enjoy. But if the aroma is from a manufactured product, whether it's from chemically scented candles or that "new carpet smell," it is likely to contain volatile organic compounds (VOCs).

These VOCs are unavoidable in our modern lives; they are all around us. But knowing where they come from is a good step toward avoiding them in our own common household products, such as these:[1]

- Paints and lacquers
- Paint strippers and other solvents
- Wood preservatives
- Aerosol sprays
- Cleansers and disinfectants
- Pesticides
- Building materials and furnishings
- Office equipment, such as copiers and printers, and correction fluids
- Copy paper

- Graphics and craft/hobby supplies
- Permanent markers
- Photographic solutions
- Moth repellents
- Air fresheners
- Stored fuels and automotive products
- Dry-cleaned clothing

To reduce the extent of indoor air pollution caused by these products, the EPA recommends the following:[2]

- Increase ventilation in your home—open a window.
- Use household products according to manufacturers' recommendations. Potentially hazardous products often have warnings aimed at reducing exposure.
- Safely dispose of partially full containers of old or unneeded chemicals. Because gases can leak even from closed containers, this single step could help lower concentrations of volatile chemicals in your home.
- Buy limited quantities. If you use products only occasionally or seasonally, such as paints, paint strippers, and kerosene for space heaters or gasoline for lawn mowers, buy only as much as you will use right away.

In addition, I would add the suggestion that you replace products known to contain VOCs with green alternatives as specified throughout each chapter of this book.

Home Lighting

How many environmentalists does it take to change a light bulb? We don't know yet—their long-lasting eco-bulbs still don't need to be changed! Just kidding.

How about, how many light bulbs does it take to change the world? Saving the planet, one step at a time, really can be as simple as changing a light bulb. You can now find energy-saving bulbs that are dimmable, three-way, recessed can, or designed for outdoors—just to name a few of the newer options.

save the planet one light bulb at a time

The difference between new energy-efficient bulbs and our standard bulbs is really quite impressive: a compact fluorescent light bulb (CFL) uses 60 percent less energy than a standard incandescent bulb; saves anywhere from one hundred fifty to three hundred pounds of carbon dioxide a year,[3] depending on usage; cuts lighting costs by 75 percent; and lasts at least eight times longer.[4] That's the power of changing just one light bulb.

Incandescent bulbs are indisputably wasteful—95 percent of the power used to light them is wasted as heat.[5] If every family in the United States made the switch, we'd reduce carbon dioxide by more than ninety billion pounds![6] You can purchase CFLs in most hardware stores or online from the Energy Federation at *www.energyfederation.org*.

In addition to using CFLs to conserve light energy, look around your home for opportunities to "harvest" daylight. The easiest yet most energy-efficient green change you can make is to turn off the lights. How often do you have both the ceiling light and the desk or end-table light turned on? Flick the switch on one of them. How often do you switch on the room light even when there's enough daylight to guide the way? How often do you turn on the light and then walk out of the room, forgetting to turn the light off?

When you start paying attention to your use of electricity for lighting, you'll probably find that, like most of us, you have a few bad habits to break.

We can also look for ways to increase our use of natural light. Open the blinds, pull back the curtains, let the light in! (Close those drapes again at night to reduce heat loss.) You can also boost the power of natural light by strategically placing decorative wall mirrors so that they reflect daylight into the room. And if you're remodeling, install larger windows and skylights.

Make the Switch

Here's a fun way to help that is profitable for you and for the planet. The Environmental Defense Fund (*www.environmentaldefense.org*) is making it easy for people to find long-lasting light bulbs for their homes.

Using their online tool, enter what type of bulb you are looking for (dimmable, 3-way, recessed can, outdoor, whatever) and up come the results and where to find them. You can use their calculator to find out how much money you'll save. I've already made bulb changes that will over the long run save $1,167.75 on my energy bill and 5,507 pounds of greenhouse CO_2 released over the expected life of these bulbs. And I have pledged that whenever a bulb in my home does wear out, I'll replace it with a renewable one. At the time I am writing this chapter, people have already pledged to replace 204,451 bulbs that will prevent 220,602,629 pounds of CO_2 over these bulbs' lifetimes.

Vacuum Cleaners

VACUUM CLEANERS ARE NOT very green by nature since they eat up so much electricity; make a terrible racket that can disturb the baby, the cat, and you too; and stir up as much dust that resettles as they are able to suck

Try This Today

Save the Light

❖ Install dimmers on all bulbs to save energy and extend their life.

❖ Install lights with occupancy sensors wherever appropriate in the house. These turn on when people enter the room, and off when they leave. You can get passive infrared switches for as little as $15. Nobody need leave a bathroom light on again.

❖ Put timers on front door and security lights.

❖ Use light sensors to turn on outdoor lights only when they are needed.

❖ Use solar-powered outdoor lights as an energy-free option.

up and take away. You can easily be more energy efficient when cleaning by using a broom or a brush and dustpan, but if you have carpets in your home, vacuuming with a good vacuum is necessary for your baby's health.

Because carpets are often warm and soft, babies spend a lot of time on them—first during infancy, when the floor is a safe spot to take a nap, and later when it's gentle on the knees when crawling and toddling. So if you do choose carpet flooring, be sure to refer to Chapter Three for the latest on green carpet materials, and make sure you have a vacuum that enables you to give those rugs thorough and frequent cleanings.

Clean carpets are especially important for young babies, who are particularly sensitive to air and environmental pollutants. Dust mites (a common asthma trigger) burrow among rug fibers, and many forms of outdoor dirt and pollution (including pesticides, herbicides, and lead dust) get tracked into the house and then hide in that soft pile. So vacuum we must.

But the high dust emission rate during operation of many vacuums makes the task almost futile. When a significant amount of dust escapes during vacuuming, it sets up a cycle in which more frequent vacuuming is required. Most vacuuming puts the dust right back into the room that had just been cleaned. This is a big problem for allergy sufferers, but also for all of us trying to cut back on our use of household energy.

To make your vacuuming time productive and as green as possible, I suggest a bagless brand that uses a HEPA filter. HEPA is an acronym for "high efficiency particulate air." The HEPA filter can trap a large amount of very small particles that other vacuum cleaners would simply recirculate back into the air of your home. Some believe that these types of filters are essential for anyone with airborne allergies and for all those wanting to reduce the sources of common air pollution in the home. Vacuums with HEPA filters are available from such major manufacturers as Bissell, Miele, Eureka Sanitaire, Electrolux, Sebo, and EIO.

Buying Green

Vacuum Cleaners

❖ Miele manufactures several vacuums that are environmentally friendly. The S4210 Carina features a "Super Air Clean Filter" that lasts as long as five dust bags. This vacuum can also be fitted with a rechargeable "Electro Brush" that improves energy efficiency. You can find more information at *www.bestvacuum.com*.

❖ The Dyson DC07 All Floors vacuum offers a lifetime HEPA filtration, which allows for cleaner air. This model is approved by the British Allergy Foundation for allergy sufferers. You can find out more information at *www.dyson.com*.

❖ Bissell's Healthy Home vacuum traps and seals 100 percent of dust mites, ragweed, pollen, and mold spores. It also claims to trap and seal 99.9 percent of pet dander. Their Microban antimicrobial protection guards against the growth of mold, mildew, and odor-causing bacteria inside the vacuum. We enjoy our Bissell. More information can be found at *www.bissell.com*.

The Facts About HEPA

HEPA filters trap particles as tiny as .3 micron with an efficiency rating of 99.97 percent. A true HEPA filter is so efficient that for every ten thousand particles that enter the filter within its filtering range, only three particles get through. HEPA filters become even more efficient the longer they are in use.

Unfortunately, imitation HEPA filters that do not filter as well as true HEPA filters are now on the market going by the name "HEPA-type" filters. They will filter the dust better than other generic filters and are less expensive than true HEPA filters, but if your health requires the specific benefits and efficiency of a HEPA filter, check the packaging to make sure the filter is rated at an efficiency of 99.97 percent for microns in size. If it's a true HEPA filter, it will have this rating clearly marked.

HEPA filters are available for both bagged and bagless vacuums. A bagged vacuum cleaner works in the traditional way of using a bag as a filter to trap dirt while allowing air to flow through the bag. The bags must be replaced when they are full and new bags purchased as replacements. This feature adds to a vacuum's nongreen quality—adding waste to the landfills and requiring the manufacture of disposable products—but some vacuum cleaners do come with reusable dust bags, which you empty and reuse. This is a better choice.

Bagless vacuum cleaners may be even better. These use filters to trap dirt and debris in a dirt cup or chamber that can then be emptied. During vacuuming, this type of cleaner reduces the emission rate by reducing the amount of dust that escapes back into the air while vacuuming, but they can expose you and the air in the room to dust during emptying. They do save you the cost of buying replacement bags, however, and they also reduce your contribution to landfill waste.

Conserving Water

CONTROLLING YOUR FAMILY'S WATER use is a simple way to save this precious resource and to pass on the green philosophy to our kids. Our children need to learn from us that water is not an infinite resource that can be washed

Green Baby Story

My Fabulous Vapor Steam Cleaner

WITH A NEW BABY, a dog, two cats and a parrot, keeping the house clean was a major challenge. I was uneasy about the household spray cleaners we had always used, and this seemed like a perfect time to look at alternatives. So after much online research, we were excited to discover something called a vapor steam cleaner that uses only water. Our house has never been cleaner and the air is fresh and free of fumes.

This amazing machine looks like a canister vacuum and deep cleans everything from countertops to wood floors—even crusty bird cages—using nothing but water. No chemicals or cleansers whatsoever! Just extremely hot vapor. This isn't one of those cheesy steam cleaners you might have seen on an infomercial. This heavy-duty appliance heats the water in its tank to more than 240 degrees, which creates a kind of low-moisture high-temperature vapor that's capable of killing mold and dust mites and getting rid of all kinds of garden variety crud—leaving virtually no dampness behind. You just clip a little terry cloth towel to one of the attachments, pull a trigger on the handle to release the vapor and off you go. When the towel gets grimy you just attach a clean one. When you're done you throw the dirty towels (and boy do they collect a lot of dirt) in the washing machine. And that's it.

These machines aren't inexpensive, starting at around $400 up to more than $1,500. I found mine on the Allergy Buyers Club Web site (*www.allergybuyersclub.com*) and purchased a White Wing, a highly recommended low-end model that has performed very reliably. You can find loads of information on vapor steam cleaning on the Web site, as well as in-depth reviews of a variety of machines, including models by Ladybug and Steamax.

It was very satisfying to throw out all the accumulated cleaners under the kitchen sink, knowing that we'd never have to buy another bottle ever again. By the way—this thing even does windows!

Chris Robbins
Seattle, Washington

down the drain without thought or concern. Be sure to review the water tips in Chapters One, Four, and elsewhere, and keep in mind these facts about your water heater and about your water use in the laundry room.

The Water Heater

Hot water use accounts for 19 percent of home energy consumption, so it is a clear target of our green efforts. Heating our water has a direct impact on the environment: a gas water heater pollutes a home's air with carbon dioxide, sulfur dioxide, nitrogen oxides, and other pollutants. An electric water heater also creates pollution, but the pollutants are emitted at the site of the energy production.[7] The easiest and least expensive way to cut down on the waste produced by a hot water heater is to lower the thermostat setting on the heater. With a new baby in the house, it's a smart idea anyway to lower the household hot water temperature to 120 degrees; you won't have to worry about accidentally scalding the baby, and you won't waste energy heating water to such a high temperature that you have to turn on the cold water to moderate it.

Next, insulate. An insulating blanket on the water heater itself will reduce its energy use by 4 to 9 percent. Insulating the pipes running from the

Going Green

Reducing Water Waste

MAKE YOURSELF A PROMISE to reduce water waste with these three simple steps:[8]

1. Fix faucet drips by replacing the washers. Stopping a drip that's going at a rate of one drop per second saves twenty-five hundred gallons per year.

2. Decrease hot water use. Install low-flow shower heads or cut your time in the shower to save up to 350 pounds of carbon dioxide a year.

3. Switch to a tankless water heater to save three hundred pounds of carbon dioxide and as much as $390 a year.

water heater to the shower and faucets will save another 5 to 10 percent on water heating costs and reduce the amount of water wasted when you run the tap waiting for hot water.[9]

When your water heater needs replacement, choose an Energy Star brand (as discussed in Chapter Four) to conserve energy, save money on energy bills, and provide your family with an efficient appliance. Also consider installing a tankless water heater. A conventional water heater has to work constantly, without ever turning off, to maintain a temperature for the entire tank, whereas tankless heaters turn on only when needed.

The Laundry Room

FOR SUCH A LITTLE person, a baby sure goes through a lot of laundry: diapers, bibs, sleepers, undershirts, blankets, sheets, socks, pants . . . and of course all the items the baby spits up on that also need to be cleaned—often. That's why having a baby in the house turns the mundane washer and dryer into wonder machines of incredible convenience.

This increase in laundry loads is also a good reason for you to focus your green efforts on the laundry room.

The Green Washing Machine

If you're buying a new washer, remember to look for Energy Star models. Traditional top-loading washing machines use about forty gallons of water per load, whereas Energy Star washers use only about twenty-five gallons per load. That's a 40 percent savings in water, which translates into an energy cost savings of almost 50 percent.[10]

Make that new machine a front-loader. Front-loading machines work on a horizontal axis that saves both water and energy. A top-loading machine must be filled with water in order to keep the clothing wet and then an agitator swirls the water around, but a front-loading machine uses less water because the tub does not need to be filled completely; the tub itself rotates, making the clothes tumble in the water. These machines also reduce the energy needed for drying clothes because they spin clothes faster than top-loading machines, which reduces the moisture level before the clothes even enter the dryer.[11] As an extra green bonus, front-loading washers are kinder to your clothing, so your clothes last longer.

In comparison to top-loading washing machines, the front-loaders use 50 percent less energy and a third less water. With those savings, it will pay for itself in six years and should last for ten. In addition, a front-loading Energy Star washer will save enough energy annually to light your entire home for a month and a half, and it saves as much water in a year as the average person drinks in a lifetime.[12] Wow.

Laundry Detergent

While you're looking for ways to go green in the laundry room, don't overlook your detergent. You'll find that it's easy to make the switch to green detergents that are plant based (corn, palm kernel, or coconut oil) and to non-chlorine-bleach products made from sodium percarbonate or sodium perborate. See the Buying Green box "Laundry Detergents" on page 232 for specific product details.

For those laundry tasks that require special attention, think simple and homemade:[13]

- For stains, try soaking fabrics in water mixed with one of the following: borax, lemon juice, hydrogen peroxide, or white vinegar.
- For fabric softening, add a quarter cup of baking soda to the wash cycle.

- For static cling, add a quarter cup of white vinegar to the wash water.

- To soften water, use a soap-based, rather than detergent-based, cleaner.

- Buy laundry products in containers that are recyclable.

- There are very good reasons for making the switch to a green product. Most conventional laundry detergents are made from petroleum— a nonrenewable resource. They don't readily biodegrade, and they threaten wildlife after they go down the drain. Many also contain chemical fragrances and phosphates (which build up in streams and lakes, upset the natural balance, and starve fish of the oxygen they need to survive). They also contain chemicals linked to cancer and reproductive problems. That's just plain bad for the earth and for your family.

Chlorine bleach should also be banned from your laundry room. This popular whitener and disinfectant is highly caustic; when it goes from your drain into the natural world, it can create organochlorines, which are suspected carcinogens as well as reproductive, neurological, and immune-system toxins. They also damage the earth's ozone layer.

Buying Green
Washers and Dryers

❖ Bosch washers and dryers use less energy. Their washers meet and exceed Energy Star guidelines, using 76 percent less water and 72 percent less energy than conventional models. For more information, go to *www.bosch appliances.com* or *www.greenbuildingsupply.com.*

❖ Whirlpool's Cabrio washer exceeds Energy Star standards, using 55 percent less energy and 44 percent less water than a traditional top-load washer. For more information, go to *www.whirlpool.com.*

❖ The Equator EZ 3710CEE is a washer and dryer in one unit and earns the Energy Star symbol of quality by using only 237 kilowatt hours per year. For more information, go to *www.ecowise.com.*

Going Green

Washing and Drying Tips to Try Today

❖ When you have several loads to wash, do them back-to-back so you can use the residual heat in the dryer.

❖ Run the washing machine only when you have a full load.

❖ Wash with cold water to save 80 to 90 percent of the energy costs of washing.

❖ To prevent static cling, add one cup white vinegar to the rinse cycle, using your washing machine's dispenser. Static cling, by the way, is caused by using synthetic fabrics, so you could also switch to cotton. Remove the laundry before it's overdried. The vinegar also kills bacteria and prevents the buildup of detergent residue.

❖ Clean out the dryer's lint trap after every load to improve circulation and reduce energy use.

❖ Air dry whenever possible using indoor racks or an outdoor line. This conserves energy—and your clothes. They will not wear out or fade as quickly. (You'll also save about seven hundred pounds of carbon dioxide over six months of warm weather.[14])

❖ Remove clothing from the dryer before the cycle ends and line dry to finish. This conserves energy and increases the life span of the clothing.

❖ Avoid using dryer sheets to soften fabrics. They often contain harsh chemicals that can irritate sensitive skin.

❖ Soften fabric with baking soda in the wash cycle.

❖ Try a commercial green fabric softener like Natural Choices Home Safe Products' Safe 'n Soft, Ecover's Natural Fabric Softener, or Sun & Earth's Ultra Fabric Softener.

The Green Clothes Dryer

Many clothes dryers have an Energy Guide label that will help you compare the energy use of various models, but the label is not required, so it can sometimes be difficult to choose the most energy-efficient type. As a general guideline, the American Council for an Energy-Efficient Economy says that gas dryers are generally less expensive to operate than electric models.[15]

Buying Green

Laundry Detergents

❖ Naturally Yours (*www.naturallyyoursstore.com*) offers laundry detergent that contains no phosphates, which go down the drain and into the ocean, where they are known to kill aquatic life. All of this company's packaging is eco-responsible.

❖ Seventh Generation sells laundry detergent that is vegetable based. It is also nontoxic and does not contain chlorine, phosphates, and artificial fragrances or dyes. You can find this detergent in many stores or at *www.seventhgeneration.com.* (On a personal note, I particularly like this company's Liquid Laundry Detergent for Baby. It's gentle, fragrance free, and produces excellent results.)

❖ Method also sells a baby laundry detergent that contains no phosphates, is biodegradable, and is not tested on animals. Find Method at larger independent grocery stores, or go to *www.methodhome.com.*

If you use one of these eco-detergents, your washing machine can be a great source of recycled "gray" water for the yard. Just snake a drain hose from the washer through the dryer vent and into a storage barrel. You can fit an adapter for a garden hose at the bottom, and drip water on your flowers. Your plants should enjoy the nutrients, and you'll save hundreds of gallons a year—this is kind to your water bill and to the environment.

A major energy consideration is whether the dryer has a moisture sensor option so that it can turn itself off when the load is dry. Another consideration is how dry the clothes are when they are put into the dryer. Today's resource-efficient clothes washers use higher spin speeds to remove more water from clothes while they are still in the washer. Consider upgrading to a high-efficiency clothes washer to maximize energy savings throughout the laundry cycle.

Energy Conservation

REDUCING OUR PERSONAL ENERGY consumption is a very positive way to teach our children how to respect the earth right in our own homes.

The United States is the world's largest energy consumer. And despite common belief, the excessive consumption is not only a problem of industry. Co-op America says that in 2005, *households* accounted for 31 percent of electricity consumed in the United States.[16] It's also known that on average, each U.S. citizen consumes more than twice the energy of a person in Western Europe and almost ten times that of a person in China.[17]

The good news is that today, over 50 percent of consumers already have the option of purchasing renewable energy for their homes (such as wind or solar power, geothermal, hydropower, or power from various forms of biomass)—often for very little extra money. To find out what is available in your state, it's easy to check with the Green Power Network of the U.S. Department of Energy (*www.eere.energy.gov/greenpower/buying*).

Fortunately, moreover, we don't have to make drastic changes to achieve the goals of both growth and sustainability. You and I can have a positive impact on the environment by breaking a few daily habits and thus personally decreasing the levels of greenhouse gases, especially carbon dioxide, that accumulate in the atmosphere and contribute to global warming.

Conserving at the Plug

Americans spend an astonishing $4 billion every year on standby power, which works out to about one whole month's worth of electricity use each year by the average family on appliances and devices they aren't using— that are turned off, but still plugged in. That's incredible but it's true, according to Alan Meier, a scientist at the Lawrence Berkeley National Lab specializing in energy efficiency.[18]

Standby power is the little bit of electricity appliances use when they're idle. Anything with an external power supply, remote control, or clock display requires standby electricity. Think of your TV, the micro-

Try This Today

Kill a Watt

IF YOU START TRACKING your energy use around the house, you'll be surprised by the many places you can conserve. An easy way to assess your home energy use is to buy a device called a Kill-A-Watt meter, made by P3 International Corp. This device is widely available. (I got mine through Amazon .com.) The handheld gadget plugs into a standard wall outlet. Then you plug various other electrical devices into the meter and see how much power they're consuming. Multiply this kilowatt-hour reading by your local utility's rate to figure out the monthly cost of operating each electrical device in your home. The device can also check the quality of your power by monitoring voltage, line frequency, and power factor. This information will tell you if it's time for a new refrigerator or if that old air conditioner is costing you too much money and too much energy for too little cooling.

Eric Bier of San Diego bought the meter and was surprised by the results. He found, for example, that his new computer and accessories were using 242 kilowatt-hours of electricity a month at a cost of $48.50, because he never turned them off. When he shut them down at night, his usage dropped to 94 kilowatt-hours, and his monthly cost of using the computer and accessories dropped to $18.80.[19]

wave, the cable box—all those little green or red lights that glow in the dark. The actual power draw in standby mode is relatively small, but it's consumed twenty-four hours a day, and the cumulative total of a typical household's appliances adds up to around 5 to 8 percent of the total energy bill.

So turn off *and* unplug everything not being used—starting with the biggest wasters: televisions, set-top boxes, printers, VCRs, and laptop chargers. Then move on to DVD players, stereos, computers, toasters, coffeemakers, hair dryers, and cell phone chargers that are eating up energy in standby mode. Unplugging will save thousands of pounds of carbon dioxide a year.[20]

An easy way to begin conserving energy from these electric and electronic items (which some people call "vampires" for the way they suck energy in the dark of night even when clicked off) is to use a power strip with a surge protector in areas of your home where there are many devices (perhaps an area near computers and home entertainment equipment). Before heading to bed at night, click off the strip switch and save energy and money. (With a baby in the house, be sure to use safety outlet plugs for any unused open outlets.)

Although cable and satellite boxes draw huge amounts of energy, turning them off may cause annoying reboot delays, so you might choose to keep these on and plugged into individual outlets until you're leaving home for a long vacation or an extended period.

Green Energy Certificates and Carbon Offsets

According to the EPA, electricity production is the largest industrial air polluter in the United States. It is a leading cause of global warming. The average individual in the United States consumes 250 kilowatt hours of electricity each month. The average family consumes 750 kilowatt hours. Depending on where you live, the great majority of that probably comes from burning fossil fuel of some kind, contributing to smog, acid rain, respiratory diseases, mercury pollution, and climate change.

A $5 Wind Power Card each month will replace 250 kilowatt hours of energy with a clean, renewable form of energy—this offsets about 348 pounds of carbon dioxide pollution, the same as preventing the burning of 187 pounds of coal or not driving 429 miles or planting four new trees (*www.renewablechoice.com*).

Try This Today

Calculate Your Impact

IF YOUR LIFESTYLE IS like that of most Americans, you generate about fifteen hundred pounds of carbon dioxide each year through your use of personal transportation, home energy, and product consumption. Want to check on your contribution to global warming? Try the online energy calculator at *www.climatecrisis.net/takeaction.*

I have mixed feelings about carbon or energy offset credits. They remind me a little of the old practice of buying indulgences—whereby a person could pay money and get a piece of paper removing the punishment for a sin. And today the money doesn't really eliminate your pollution or waste, it just invests in a wind farm or solar panel or plants trees or the like somewhere else, in an equal amount to the energy you use. If someone buys offsets as a means to offset the low fuel economy of their Hummer, and artificially reduce their conscience, I don't like that much. But if someone is taking little steps every day to conserve, reuse, and recycle, then buying offsets can be a great idea. It invests in the future and raises awareness—perhaps the most important steps to a green tomorrow.

Solar Power Incentives

By installing solar power, you make a visible statement to power companies, to your neighbors, and to your children that you care about the health of the planet and support an emissions-free future.

The cost of this switch to sun power, however, has been prohibitive for many in the past. But in our greener society, the price of solar energy is becoming more competitive with electricity generated from coal. And there are financial incentives as well. The federal government and some states are offering cash incentives for the installation of a full system. And solar's ability to lower energy costs also adds value. A study recently found that for every utility bill dollar saved annually because of an improvement, you gain $10 to $20 in property value. So if you can cancel out a $1,000 annual electricity bill by installing solar power, you'll get back $10,000 to $20,000 in home value.[21] For a detailed guide to going solar, see "The Promise of the Future" at *www.coopamerica.org/PDF/CAQ66.pdf.*

Making Recycling a Family Habit

Look through your home for ways to model green living for your children. One family habit that can make the most immediate impression on the very young is an organized system for recycling family waste. Children who grow up knowing that aluminum cans, glass, plastics, newspapers, magazines, and office paper do not go into the garbage can, but instead are reserved for recycling, will surely continue the practice in their own lives as adults. The Web site for Al Gore's movie *An Inconvenient Truth* tells us that we each can save twenty-four hundred pounds of carbon dioxide per year by recycling just half of our household waste.[22]

To find out more about recycling in your neighborhood, go to the Web site of Earth 911 (*www.earth911.org*) and type in your ZIP Code for information about your city's recycling program. You'll also find information about how and where to recycle car parts, oil, unwanted fuels, vehicles, tires, batteries, electronics, construction materials, and so on.

Home Heating and Cooling

The average American family spends $1,900 a year on energy bills, much of which goes to heating and cooling the home. The EPA says that we can each save as much as 20 percent annually on total energy costs—and reduce our environmental impact—by following four simple recommendations from its Energy Star program that will help you "'H.E.A.T.' smartly":[23]

> **Home sealing.** Seal air leaks and add insulation—paying special attention to your attic and basement, where the biggest gaps and cracks are often found. Much of our conventional insulation is not made from things you want near the air you breathe. Thankfully, there are a variety of new, green insulation materials to choose from, including recycled denim, icynene, and aerogels (these last have the advantage of

letting in daylight, but not transferring heat). These new options will keep warm or cool air inside where it belongs and help your equipment perform more efficiently. (*www.inhabitat.com*).

Equipment maintenance. Dirt and neglect are the primary causes of system failure. Get a checkup of your heating system to make sure it's performing efficiently and safely. Clean or replace your system's air filter to help lower energy bills and maintain better indoor air quality.

Ask for Energy Star. Look for the Energy Star label when purchasing products. If just one in ten households bought Energy Star qualified heating and cooling products, the change would keep eighteen billion pounds of greenhouse gas emissions out of our air.

Green Baby Story

Is Our Energy Clean?

I GREW UP ASSUMING that when something was plugged into an electric outlet, whether it was a car or a computer, it was getting clean power. I've since learned most of the energy in homes in the United States comes from coal-burning power plants, and a lot comes from other nonrenewable energy sources such as petroleum. We now have a map in our home that my son adapted from a chart posted online by the Energy Information Administration. His map shows us, state-by-state, where most of the home electric energy comes from. That map makes us all think twice about leaving the lights on.

Cheryl Greene
Danville, California

Try This Today

Getting an Energy Audit

MANY HOMEOWNERS HAVE NO idea how energy efficient their homes are, so local utility companies often offer a free home energy audit. If you'd like to save 30 percent on your energy bill and reduce your impact on the environment by making your home more energy efficient, go to the government's Energy Star site at *www.energystar.gov* to find an energy specialist in your area.

Or try the online energy audit sponsored by the U.S. Department of Energy and developed by the Lawrence Berkeley National Laboratory (*http://hes.lbl.gov*). With this powerful home energy saver tool, all you do is answer a few quick questions about your home, and within minutes the site calculates which upgrades are likely to make the biggest difference for you, reducing your energy bill, reducing your energy footprint, and reducing greenhouse gases.

Thermostat use. Install a programmable thermostat to save energy during times when you're home or away. When properly used, a programmable thermostat can save as much as $150 a year in energy costs.

Weatherizing

You can also conserve energy in your home by weatherizing it.[24]

- Caulk and weather-strip your doorways and windows. This reduction of heating and cooling use can save seventeen hundred pounds of greenhouse carbon dioxide and $274 per year.

- If your walls and ceilings are insulated, you can save two thousand pounds of carbon dioxide and $245 each year.

- When it's time to replace windows, make them double paned. They keep more heat inside your home, so you'll need less energy to pull heat from the furnace. These windows can save ten thousand pounds of carbon dioxide and $436 per year.

Conserving Power in the Home Office

Many of us have home offices, particularly when there's a new baby in the house and we want to stay close by. These home offices also provide more opportunities to conserve power. Here are a few eco-friendly ways to cut your electricity bill, conserve energy and resources, be a good role model for your children, and protect the planet:

- **Use Energy Star equipment.** Using an Energy Star computer, monitor, printer, and fax can conserve enough electrical power to light your entire home for more than four years.[25]

- **Power down.** Turn off your office equipment when you're not working there. Set your computer for "sleep" mode when not in use for ten minutes. Activating sleep settings on just one computer can prevent about three hundred pounds of carbon dioxide emissions each year. Using power management on your desktop computer could save nine hundred kilowatt-hours per year. That amounts to fifteen hundred pounds of carbon dioxide emissions, the equivalent of driving a medium-sized car from New York to Salt Lake City![26]

- **Buy recycled supplies.** Copy paper, envelopes, calendars, planners, and stationery are all available in paper made from 100 percent post-consumer recycled content; remanufactured ink and laser toner for printers and fax machines are also available.

- **Reduce your use.** There are many ways to cut back on paper use: keep only electronic files of notes and memos; print double sided; use the back of draft copies for scrap paper; change the margin settings to get more text per page; edit on screen rather than on hard copy.

- **Reuse.** Many incoming envelopes and boxes can be used again for outgoing mail.

- **Close the loop.** Place a recycling bin next to your office waste basket and recycle all scrap paper. Every half-pound of office paper you recycle saves the equivalent of one pound of greenhouse gas emissions, plus the equivalent weight in trees.[27] Also turn in your old toner and ink cartridges for recycling. Large office supply stores like Staples and OfficeMax accept cartridges. (My youngest son's school raised funds, and awareness, through their cartridge recycling program. A lot better than selling candy!)

Buying Green

Green Office Supplies

❖ **Recycled paper.** Always look for recycled paper products that are made from PCW (post-consumer waste) paper. Sometimes recycled paper products are actually composed mainly of wood chips and mill scraps. You can find 100 percent recycled paper products that are processed without chlorine by going to *www.greenlinepaper.com*. This company also reuses shipping cartons and packs them with recyclable paper or biodegradable peanuts, rather than foam peanuts and plastics.

❖ **Envelopes.** Look for envelopes made of PCW paper and processed without chlorine. You can find a wide selection of environmentally friendly envelopes by visiting *www.ecoenvelopes.com*. They offer 100 percent PCW envelopes in plain and colored stock; these envelopes can be reused.

❖ **Remanufactured ink and toner cartridges.** Look for remanufactured ink and toner cartridges that have been refilled. You can find recycled ink and toner cartridges from the major manufacturers. Such brands as Nukote and Jetfill also provide recycled cartridges that are compatible with the major-brand printers. You can find these products at *www.therealearth.com*.

❖ **Desk calendars.** Look for calendars printed on PCW paper. You can find a variety of calendars that are made from 100 percent PCW paper and printed with soy inks by going to *www.greenearthofficesupply.com*.

❖ **Organizers.** You can find a large variety of different organizing supplies at *www.greenearthofficesupply.com*. This company's letter and legal trays are made from PCW recycled plastics, and its file separators are made from PCW recycled steel.

Keeping Pets and Kids Green

WHEN LOOKING FOR AREAS in your home that can easily be turned green, don't overlook the family pet. The flea and tick shampoos, powders, sprays, and dips that are used on dogs and cats are intended to kill insects—and they do because the products contain potent and dangerous insecticides.

Babies' newborn bodies make them more vulnerable to many chemicals, but when it comes our infants having contact with the family pet who inevitably has ticks and fleas, you have a good reason to find an alternative pest management method knowing that this is one more way you can keep your children away from toxic chemicals. After all, your children are the ones who spend much time hugging and petting the pet and in the areas where the brush-off from pet products accumulate (such as in the rug and floor dust). They also are likely to put their fingers in their mouths after playing with the pet. Your kids will gain an immediate benefit when you ditch the insecticide products—never mind the benefit to your pet!

The Natural Resources Defense Council recommends the following:

- Pet owners should avoid toxic pet products. Check the product's active ingredients label and if it contains any of these seven common organophosphates (OPs), don't use it: chlorpyrifos, dichlorvos, phosmet, naled, tetrachlorvinphos, diazinon, and malathion. Also avoid products containing carbamates. The two chemical names to watch out for and avoid are carbaryl and propoxur.

- Begin using safer products that include alternatives such as insect growth regulators, or IGRs, which are not pesticides, but rather chemicals that arrest the growth and development of young fleas before they turn into biting adults.

- For killing fleas already on your pet, you can try a natural flea powder based on an ingredient called diatomaceous earth that is safe for use on dogs and cats as well as around the home. It kills fleas within twenty-four to seventy-two hours by dehydrating them—which is not only nontoxic to pets, humans, and the environment, but fleas can't develop an immunity to it as they may to other pesticides over time. There are different varieties of diatomaceous earth available. Some types are toxic if ingested so check the label and make sure to use a food-grade variety. That way your pets can clean themselves all they want and it won't hurt them—or your children when they snuggle up to play. Suggested use is approximately one teaspoon per ten pounds of body weight.

- A flea comb can help spread the fine powder throughout your pet's coat. You can also sprinkle it on furniture, carpeting, wood floors, baseboards, and pet bedding to safely get rid of adult fleas throughout your home. Take care to avoid breathing in the dustlike powder when applying it as it can irritate the mucous membranes in the nose and mouth. Once the powder has settled, though, it won't bother you.

- Safer products can be combined with simple physical measures such as brushing pets regularly with a flea comb while inspecting for fleas, mowing frequently in areas where pets spend the most time outdoors (to remove a flea- and tick-friendly environment), frequent washing and combing of the pet, and vacuuming carpets and furniture (be sure to dispose of the vacuum cleaner bags immediately afterward if you find evidence of fleas).

- Pregnant women and families with children should cease using OP-based products immediately.

- Children should never apply flea shampoos, dusts, dips, and so on containing OPs to their pets. The EPA has overlooked and underestimated the particular risks to children when evaluating the safety of these products for home use (Natural Resources Defense Council).

Feeding Your Pets Organic

For many of us, our pets are kids too! And we want to provide these furry family members with food that is as nutritious and wholesome as what we eat ourselves.

In *How Dog Food Saved the Earth*, Pet Promise founder Anthony Zolezzi outlines how our pet food choices extend throughout our agricultural system. By purchasing pet food made with organic ingredients, you know that your dollars are going to support organic farming methods. You'll also avoid some of the nastier ingredients commonly found in conventionally processed pet foods, such as parts from "4-D" animals—which are dead, dying, diseased, or disabled—and other animal and plant by-products, antibiotics, steroids, hormones, artificial colors, dyes, flavors, and preservatives. None of the pet foods on the market now can be certified 100 percent organic, but good choices are becoming available.

Good pet foods include Karma Organic for dogs by Natura Pet Products (*www.naturapet.com*), Pet Promise (*www.petpromise.org*), Newman's Own Organics (*www.newmansownorganics.com*), and Organix, by Castor & Pollux Pet Works (*www.castorpolluxpet.com*).

The Automobile

THE AUTOMOBILE HAS BEEN a target of environmental concern since the term "greenhouse gases" was first introduced to our common language. Fortunately, this attention has pushed car manufacturers to make some (but not enough) positive changes and caused green-conscious citizens to be more aware of their driving habits.

The 2007 North American International Auto Show in Detroit unveiled an interesting array of concept cars:[28]

GM presented its Chevy Volt—a four-seat electric vehicle that is a plug-in hybrid, which when charged from a wall socket should be able to travel forty miles in all-electric mode.

Ford touted its Airstream van, a plug-in fuel cell vehicle (using hydrogen instead of an internal-combustion engine to recharge the batteries in-flight).

German manufacturers displayed their Bluetec diesel powertrains (diesels typically get about 30 percent better fuel economy than comparable gas-powered vehicles) and direct injection systems.

Toyota showed off its aerospace-inspired hybrid-electric sports car, the FT-HS.

These cars are only protypes, not yet available, and may never be. But with these major auto manufacturers beginning to realize there's a market for energy-efficient, more environmentally friendly automobiles, we can hope to see a lot more choices for Americans and other car buyers throughout the world. This move toward eco-friendly transportation is already gaining momentum in the hybrid market.

The Hybrid

The biggest news in auto emissions control is, of course, the hybrid electric vehicle (HEV). In the United States, HEV sales reached 212,000 in 2005 compared to about 9,500 in 2000 (I've still got my 2000 Prius hybrid), and are predicted to account for as much as 6 percent of all car sales globally by 2013.[29]

This popularity is due in part to the fact that HEVs have been a huge hit with environmentally conscious celebrities. To show their support for environmental consciousness at the 2006 Oscar®, several actors left the limo at home and arrived at the ceremony in a hybrid Toyota Prius instead. Those participating in this campaign included Morgan Freeman, Leonardo DiCaprio, Salma Hayek, Charlize Theron, Scarlett Johansson, Orlando Bloom, and Gwyneth Paltrow.

On the Hybrid Center Web site, articles written by members of the Union of Concerned Scientists explain that the HEV combines an internal-combustion engine and an electric motor powered by batteries, merging the best features of today's combustion-engine cars and electric vehicles: "The combination allows the electric motor and batteries to help the conventional engine operate more efficiently, cutting down on fuel use. Meanwhile, the gasoline-fueled combustion engine overcomes the limited driving range of an electric vehicle. In the end, this hybridization gives you the ability to drive 500 miles or more using less fuel and never having to plug in for recharging. Gasoline-fueled HEVs are among a select few vehicle technologies that can provide dramatically increased fuel economy and extremely low levels of smog-forming and cancer-causing emissions."[30]

The Automobile Association of America explains four reasons to go hybrid:[31]

1. Hybrid vehicles run cleaner.

2. Hybrid cars are environmentally friendlier than conventional cars and have lower emissions.

3. Tax deductions or credits may be available, depending on where you live.

4. You will gain the greatest benefit if most of your driving is in stop-and-go traffic at low speeds.

The Department of Energy (*www.fueleconomy.gov*) suggests that for the average person, switching to a car that is just three miles per gallon more efficient, can cut three thousand pounds of emissions a year. (This applies to conventional vehicles as well, not just hybrids.) If you're thinking of purchasing a hybrid, remember that they are not all equally green. Models range from "mild" to "full," with levels in between. As is true of all major purchases, the best advice is to become an informed consumer. The Hybrid Center Web site (*www.hybridcenter.org*) is a great place to start.

The Electric Car Is on Its Way

Zap (which stands for Zero Air Pollution) offers Americans electric cars, fuel cell cars, hybrid cars, electric bicycles, electric scooters, and seascooters. The company entered the automotive market in 2006 with its imported European "Smart Car." Manufactured by Mercedes Benz, these cars have been popular in Europe for years, and their 60 mpg fuel efficiency is now catching the American eye. Zap is now launching Xebra, which is believed to be the first 100 percent production electric vehicle not designated as a "low speed vehicle"; it has a top speed of up to 40 mph.[32] There are also individuals and new local services devoted to converting hybrids to plug-ins that use only electricity. (Keep in mind that an electric car is only as green as the power source—if you plug in your car, but you get electricity from coal-powered plants, you essentially have the inefficiency and pollution of a coal-powered car. You just can't see it.)

Overall, the green car market is on the threshold of a huge expansion. Open the newspaper almost any day, and you'll find reports of new eco-friendly cars, new technologies, and new and innovative plans to reduce auto emissions. You can easily go green the next time you're in the market for a new car.

In the meantime, be sure to check out the Web site of EV World (*www.evworld.com*) for the latest information on sustainable transportation.

Leaving the Car at Home

Whether you drive a hybrid or an SUV, car use is often a lifestyle decision that can be green or not. Show your children through example that there are other, healthier ways to travel. Whenever possible, walk or cycle to your destination. Use public transportation, carpool, and consolidate your errands into one trip. Let your child grow up knowing that although the automobile is a convenient form of transportation, it's not the only or most desirable one.

That New Car Smell

Of course our cars contribute to air pollution; car emissions are a primary source of carbon dioxide. But that "new car smell" is also an air pollutant to consider when gently strapping your infant into her car seat.

An Ecology Center study found that the PBDE flame retardants and phthalates in seat covers and carpeting are toxic chemicals associated with serious health problems and air pollution found in a new car's interior.[33] The study also found that the sun's heat and UV light increase toxicity inside vehicles. The study authors suggest that car owners reduce the release and breakdown of these chemicals by

- Using solar reflectors in the windshield or rear window

- Ventilating car interiors by driving with the windows open

- Parking away from direct sunlight whenever possible

Infant Car Seats

Many parents think that their babies in car seats are the most protected passengers in the car. Not necessarily so. In independent crash testing, some seats have been found to be safer than others.

To secure your baby safely,

- Install the car seat snugly and correctly in the center rear seat, using vehicle safety belts.
- When selecting a car seat, be careful about whom you trust. Many parents have relied on the National Highway Traffic Safety Administration (*nhtsa.gov*), the Consumer Product Safety Commission (*cpsc.gov*), or the Juvenile Products Manufacturers Association (*jpma.org*). *Instead*, I recommend consulting Consumers Union (*consumerreports.org*) until the other organizations use stricter standards. Consumers Union uses higher speeds and tests both front and side collisions. Your baby deserves the best.

- The National Highway Traffic Safety Administration offers an online service to help you find a free local car-seat inspection station. Check out *www.nhtsa.gov*.
- Send in your car seat warranty card so that you will be contacted in the event of a recall.

I recommend the two car seats that performed the best on Consumers Union safety tests: the Baby Trend Flex-Loc and the Graco SnugRide with EPS. The February 2007 crash-test results were withdrawn because they appear to have been performed at significantly higher speeds than intended. Nevertheless, these two car seats passed with flying colors, even at top-speed collisions.

How to Drive Green

- Inflate your car tires. Improperly inflated tires can waste as much as 250 pounds of carbon dioxide a year and $840 in gas money.[34]
- Change the air filter to save eight hundred pounds of carbon dioxide and $130 a year.[35]
- Park in the shade. It lowers the temperature of gas tanks by four to seven degrees, which curbs emissions.
- Avoid ten miles of driving each week. This will save five hundred pounds of carbon dioxide per year.[36]
- Fill your tank in the evening. This decreases evaporation during pumping, so anything that escapes won't be cooked into the ozone. If you have to get gas during the day, go to a station where there's a capture device on the pump that keeps fumes from escaping.
- Drive a warm car. A warm engine pollutes up to five times less than one that's been sitting, so try to run your errands all at once.
- Share a ride just two days a week and reduce carbon dioxide emissions. Check out *www.ERideShare.com* to find other commuters who want to share a ride.[37]
- Share a car! Through the Zipcar or Flexcar program, you can reserve a car online, pick it up at a nearby lot, and return it when you're done. Find out if these programs are in your area by going to *www.zipcar .com* or *www.flexcar.com*.[38]

Where Do We Go from Here?

I HOPE THE INFORMATION and ideas we've presented have inspired you to make positive choices to keep your baby green and sustain a green, healthy, eco-friendly environment.

Because this is the first book of its kind, we also want to hear back from you regarding how these choices, suggestions, and other information have worked for you and what you think should be added for our next edition.

We're thinking of the long-term utility of this book and consider it only the first attempt to be helpful in a constantly changing and really improving green baby movement.

So please write us at my Web site (DrGreene.com) so we can keep working together for a safer, better world for our children, our families, and the earth itself.

Epilogue

FROM THE GROUND UP

As this manuscript was nearing completion, I had the opportunity to give an address at Eco-Farm, the annual gathering of California-based Ecological Farming Association. These are the people on the front lines, nurturing our land, protecting our water, and growing our food. They come together to learn, to celebrate, and to share the latest on sustainable farming.

These people get so excited about soil—improving soil, rich soil, soil teeming with life; they won't stop talking about it! To them, healthy soil is the key to luscious, nutritious crops. In contrast, conventional farmers I know talk about their chemical inputs and boosting yields.

Something struck me as I watched and listened to these frontline farming people. And that is in many ways, we are the soil in which our children grow. This is true literally before they are born, and continues to be true at least as long as they are in our home. It's not so important what gadgets or products we buy; it's how our children grew up and who we are that counts. The latest fads, even the latest green trends, will come and go; it's something deeper that counts. What we must give our children is a heartfelt appreciation and respect for the balance of life and for the enduring health of our planet. And we had best tend to our planet. Our world— its people, its animals, its plants, its minerals, its air, and its water—is the soil in which we continue to grow as adults. And which will nurture our children and their children after us.

So, it was a delight to have farmer and physician come together around how healthy soil produces healthy plants, which eventually produce healthy people. As the celebration was winding down, one of the farmers invited my family to visit the new home he had built.

We followed his truck through emerald green farmland to a big comfortable house surrounded by fields of crops. As John took us through his home he showed us how a simple decision made before the house was built had powerful, lasting impact. The house was situated with lots and lots of windows along the southern face and angled so that during the winter, the sun warms rocks and cement slabs built into the design. But during the summer months, trellises and decks shade those same windows, keeping the heat out. Throughout the year, skylights brighten the rooms with natural light all day long. In addition to planning these active solar panels as part of the original design, our farm friends get water from their own well and grow their own food. They could live there for years with no outside supplies, if need be.

This wonderful home wasn't much more difficult to build than a conventional home. The payoff is huge and enduring (their power bill for their large home is $0), and the home is a delight to be in. The view from the hot tub in the master bathroom is gorgeous. I'd love a house like this! All it took was some learning, planning, choosing the right materials, and angling everything the right way.

That's what *Raising Baby Green* is all about. Setting the angles, the emphases, the building blocks all from the beginning—what a thrilling opportunity!

Don't worry too much about the details. Learn what you can. Think ahead. Choose quality. And get caught up in the joy of the journey. You're reading this book because of something far more important than a new building. You're getting into a brand-new life, from the ground up.

Notes

INTRODUCTION: WHY RAISE BABY GREEN

1. Natural Resources Defense Council. *Shop Smart, Save Forests. A Shopper's Guide to Home Tissue Products.* New York, Author, Sept. 2006.

CHAPTER ONE: THE WOMB

1. Tsiaras, A. *From Conception to Birth.* New York: Doubleday, 2002.
2. "Body Burden—The Pollution in Newborns: A Benchmark Investigation of Industrial Chemicals, Pollutants, and Pesticides in Human Umbilical Cord Blood." *Environmental Working Group,* 2005. www .ewg.org /reports/bodyburden2.
3. Ege, M., and others. "Prenatal Farm Exposure Is Related to the Expression of Receptors of the Innate Immunity and to Atopic Sensitization in School-Age Children." *Journal of Allergy and Clinical Immunology,* 2006, *117,* pp. 817–823.
4. Mennella, J. M. "Prenatal and Postnatal Flavor Learning by Human Infants." *Pediatrics,* 2001, *107,* e88.
5. Breen, F. M., Plomin, R., and Wardle, J. "Heritability of Food Preferences in Children." *Physiology and Behavior,* 2006, *88,* pp. 443–447.
6. Benbrook, C. M., Greene, A., Landrigan, P., and Lu, C. "Successes and Lost Opportunities to Reduce Children's Exposure to Pesticides Since the Mid-1990s." Critical Issue Report 2006.1. The Organic Center. http://organic.insightd.net/science.pest.php?action=view&report_id =55. Aug. 2006.
7. Pimental, D. *Impacts of Organic Farming on the Efficiency of Energy Use in Agriculture. An Organic Center State of Science Review.* http:// organic.insightd.net/reportfiles/ENERGY_SSR.pdf. Aug. 2006.
8. USDA Economic Research Service. *U.S. Certified Organic Farmland Acreage, Livestock Numbers and Farm Operation, 1992–2005.* Dec. 15, 2006.

9. U.S. Department of Agriculture. "NOP Regulations (Standards) & Guidelines." National Organic Program. www.ams.usda.gov/nop /indexIE.htm. Mar. 2007.

10. *United Egg Producers Animal Husbandry Guidelines for U.S. Egg Laying Flocks* (2nd ed.), 2005, and National Agricultural Statistics Service (NASS), U.S. Department of Agriculture. Chicken and Eggs. Jan. 24, 2005.

11. Pew Initiative on Food and Biotechnology. *Public Sentiment About Genetically Modified Food.* Dec. 2006.

12. The Organic Center. "E. Coli O157:H7 Frequently Asked Questions." Critical Issue Report 2006.3. http://organic.insightd.net/reportfiles/ e_coli_final.pdf. 2006.

13. Gilliom, R. J., and others. *Pesticides in the Nation's Streams and Ground Water, 1992–2001.* USGS Circular 1291. U.S. Geological Survey. http://pubs.usgs.gov/circ/2005/1291. Mar. 2006.

14. Swan, S. H., Liu, F., Overstreet, J. W., Brazil, C., and Skakkebæk, N. E. "Semen Quality of Fertile U.S. Males in Relation to Their Mothers' Beef Consumption During Pregnancy." *Human Reproduction.* Fast Track Article. Mar. 28, 2007, pp. 1–6.

15. Weibel, F. P., Bickel, R., Leuthold, S., and Alfoldi, T. "Are Organically Grown Apples Tastier and Healthier? A Comparative Field Study Using Conventional and Alternative Methods to Measure Fruit Quality." *Acta Horticulturae*, 2000, *517*, pp. 417–426.

16. Rauh, V. A., Garfinkel, R., Perera, F. P., Andrews, H. F., Hoepner, L., Barr, D. B., Whitehead, R., Tang, D., and Whyatt, R. W. "Impact of Prenatal Chlorpyrifos Exposure on Neurodevelopment in the First 3 Years of Life Among Inner-City Children." *Pediatrics*, 2006, *118*(6), pp. e1845–e1859.

17. Meeker, J. D., et al. "Exposure to Nonpersistent Insecticides and Male Reproductive Hormones." *Epidemiology*, 2006, *17*(1), pp. 61–68.

18. Soto and Sonnenschein, cited in Davis, D. L., and Bradlow, H. L. "Can Environmental Estrogens Cause Breast Cancer?" *Scientific American*, Oct. 1995, pp. 166–172.

19. Clement, B. *Living Foods for Optimum Health.* Rocklin, Calif.: Prima, 1996.

20. "Bisphenol A: Toxic Plastics Chemical in Canned Food." Environmental Working Group. Mar. 2007.

21. Lu, C., and others. "Organic Diets Significantly Lower Children's Dietary Exposure to Organophosphorus Pesticides." *Environmental Health Perspectives*, 2006, *114*(2), pp. 260–263.

22. Hibbeln, J. R., Davis, J. M., Steer, C., Emmett, P., Rogers, I., Williams, C., and Golding, J. "Maternal Seafood Consumption in Pregnancy and Neurodevelopmental Outcomes in Childhood (ALSPAC Study): An Observational Cohort Study." *Lancet*, Feb. 17, 2007, *369*, pp. 531–614.

23. Pianin, E. "Toxins Cited in Farmed Salmon: Cancer Risk Is Lower in Wild Fish, Study Reports." *Washington Post*, Jan. 9, 2004. www .washingtonpost.com/ac2/wp-dyn/A733-2004Jan8.

24. "Is the Government Too Lax in Advice on Tuna Consumption?" *Consumer Reports*, July 2004. www.consumerreports.org/cro/food/fish-safety-704-fish-tuna-mercury/overview/index.htm?resultPageIndex= 1&resultIndex=1&searchTerm="tuna%20safety".

25. Mahaffey, K., and the Environmental Protection Agency. "Methylmercury: Epidemiology Update." Fish Forum, San Diego, 2004. www.ewg .org/issues_content/mercury/pdf/Fish_Forum_2004.pdf.

26. Myers, R. A., and Worm, B. "Rapid Worldwide Depletion of Predatory Fish Communities." *Nature*, 2003, *423*, pp. 280–283.

27. Dean, C. "Study Sees 'Global Collapse' of Fish Species." *New York Times*, Nov. 3, 2006, p. A21.

28. "Bottled Water Basics." EPA, Sept. 2005. Water Health Series. www.epa .gov/safewater/faq/pdfs/fs_healthseries_bottledwater.pdf.

29. Schonfelder, G., Wittfoht, W., Hopp, H., and others. "Parent Bisphenol A Accumulation in the Maternal-Fetal-Placental Unit." *Environmental Health Perspectives*, 2004, *110*, pp. A703–A707.

    Ikezuki, Y., Tsutsumi, O., Takai, Y., and others. "Determination of Bisphenol A Concentrations in Human Biological Fluids Reveals Significant Early Prenatal Exposure." *Human Reproduction*, 2002, *17*, pp. 2839–2841.

30. "Smart Plastics Guide: Healthier Food Uses of Plastics for Parents and Children." *Institute for Agriculture and Trade Policy.* Oct. 2005.

31. March of Dimes. "Caffeine in Pregnancy." Quick Reference and Fact Sheets. www.ota.com/organic_and_you/coffee_collaboration.html. 2006.

32. Barinaga, M. "A New Clue to How Alcohol Damages Brains." *Science*, Feb. 11, 2000, pp. 54–55.

33. "Facts Help Calm Concerns Brewing over Kids and Caffeine." USDA/ARS Children's Nutrition Research Center at Baylor College of Medicine. www.kidsnutrition.org/consumer/archives/dull-appetite .htm. 2004.

34. Bung, P. R., and others. "Exercise in Gestational Diabetes: An Optional Therapeutic Approach?" *Diabetes*, 1991, *40*, pp. 182–185.

35. Dempsey, J. C., and others. "No Need for a Pregnant Pause: Physical Activity May Reduce the Occurrence of Gestational Diabetes Mellitus and Preeclampsia." *Sport Sciences Reviews*, 2005, *33*, pp. 141–149.

36. Saul, S. "States, Bridling at Insulin's Cost, Push for Generics." *The New York Times.* Jan. 11, 2007.

37. Sorenson, T. K., and others. "Recreational Physical Activity During Pregnancy and Risk of Preeclampsia." *Hypertension*, 2003, *41*, pp. 1273–1280.

38. Narendran, S., and others. "Efficacy of Yoga on Pregnancy Outcome." *Journal of Alternative and Complementary Medicine*, 2005, *11*, pp. 237–244.

39. Narendran, S., and others. "Efficacy of Yoga in Pregnant Women with Abnormal Doppler Study of Umbilical and Uterine Arteries." *Journal of the Indian Medical Association*, 2005, *103*, pp. 12–17.

40. American College of Obstetrics and Gynecology Committee on Obstetric Practice. "ACOG Committee Opinion #267: Exercise During Pregnancy and the Postpartum Period." *Obstetrics and Gynecology*, 2002, *99*, pp. 171–173. (reaffirmed 2005)

41. Gago-Dominguez, M., and others. "Use of Permanent Hair Dyes and Bladder-Cancer Risk." *International Journal of Cancer*, 2001, *91*, pp. 575–579.

Gago-Dominguez, M., and others. "Permanent Hair Dyes and Bladder Cancer: Risk Modification by Cytochrome P4501A2 and N-acetyl-transferases 1 and 2." *Carcinogenesis*, 2003, *24*, pp. 483–489.

Bluhm, E., and others. "Personal Hair Dye Use and Risks of Glioma, Meningioma, and Acoustic Neuroma Among Adults." *American Journal of Epidemiology*, 2007, *165*(1), pp. 63–71.

Petro-Nustas, W., Norton, M. E., and al-Masarweh, I. "Risk Factors for Breast Cancer in Jordanian Women." *Journal of Nursing Scholarship*, 2002, *34*, pp. 19–25.

Takkouche, B., Etminan, M., and Montes-Martinez, A. "Personal Use of Hair Dyes and Risk of Cancer: A Meta-Analysis." *Journal of the American Medical Association*, 2005, *293*, pp. 2516–2525.

Ahlbom, A., and others. "Nonoccupational Risk Indicators for Astrocytomas in Adults." *American Journal of Epidemiology*, 1986, *124*, pp. 334–337.

Burch, J. D., and others. "An Exploratory Case-Control Study of Brain Tumors in Adults." *Journal of the National Cancer Institute*, 1987, *78*, pp. 601–609.

Zahm, S. H., and others. "Use of Hair Coloring Products and the Risk of Lymphoma, Multiple Myeloma, and Chronic Lymphocytic Leukemia." *American Journal of Public Health*, 1992, *82*, pp. 990–997.

Cantor, K. P., and others. "Hair Dye Use and Risk of Leukemia and Lymphoma." *American Journal of Public Health*, 1988, *78*, pp. 570–571.

Zhang, Y., and others. "Hair-Coloring Product Use and Risk of Non-Hodgkin's Lymphoma: A Population-Based Case-Control Study in Connecticut." *American Journal of Epidemiology*, 2004, *159*, pp. 148–154.

42. Gago-Dominguez, M., and others, 2003.

43. U.S. Environmental Protection Agency. *Supplemental Guidance for Assessing Susceptibility from Early-Life Exposures to Carcinogens*. EPA Risk Assessment Forum. EPA/630/R-03/003F. www.epa.gov/iris/children032505.pdf. Mar. 2005.

44. Carlson, B. M. *Human Embryology and Developmental Biology*. St. Louis, Mo.: Mosby-Year Book, 1994.

    Tsiaras, 2002.

45. Mennella, 2001.

46. Lindblad, A., Marsal, K., and Andersson, K. E. "Effect of Nicotine on Human Fetal Blood Flow." *Obstetrics and Gynecology*, 1988, *72*, pp. 371–382.

47. Braun, J. M., Kahn, R. S., Froehlich, T., Auinger, P., and Lanphear, B. P. "Exposures to Environmental Toxicants and Attention Deficit Hyperactivity Disorder in U.S. Children." *Environmental Health Perspectives*, 2006, *114*, pp. 1904–1909.

CHAPTER TWO: THE LABOR AND DELIVERY ROOM

1. March of Dimes. "Choosing a Prenatal Care Provider." Pregnancy and Newborn Health Education Center. www.marchofdimes.com/pnhec /159_830.asp. 2007.

2. Scott, K. D., Berkowitz, G., and Klaus, M. "A Comparison of Intermittent and Continuous Support During Labor: A Meta-Analysis." *American Journal of Obstetrics and Gynecology,* May 1999, *180,* pp. 1054–1059.

   Klaus, M. H., Kennell, J. H., and Klaus, P. H. *The Doula Book: How a Trained Labor Companion Can Help You Have a Shorter, Easier, and Healthier Birth.* (2nd ed.) New York: Perseus Books Group, 2002.

3. Martin, J., and others. "Births: Final Data for 2004." *National Vital Statistics Report,* 2006, *55*(12). Centers for Disease Control and Prevention. http://.cdc.gov/nchs/data/nvsr/nvsr55/nvsr55_01.pdf.

4. Martin and others, 2006.

5. Environment Science Center. *Greener Hospitals: Improving Environmental Performance.* Augsburg, Germany. www.bms.com/static/ehs /sideba/data/greenh.pdf.

6. Martin and others, 2006.

7. McCartney, M. "A Birth Center Provider Explains." Birth Center FAQ's. American Association of Birth Centers. www.birthcenters.org /faq/bcdiff.php.

8. Anderson, R. E., and Anderson, D. A. "The Cost-Effectiveness of Home Birth." *Journal of Nurse Midwifery,* 1999, *44,* pp. 30–35.

9. Johnson, K. C., and Daviss, B. A. "Outcomes of Planned Home Births with Certified Professional Midwives: Large Prospective Study in North America." *British Medical Journal,* 2005, *330*(7505), p. 1416.

10. American College of Obstetrics and Gynecology (Wisconsin Section). *Position Paper on Midwifery Licensure,* 2007. www.acog.org/acog _sections/dist_notice.cfm?recno=17&bulletin=1713.

11. Johnson and Daviss, 2005.

12. Albani, A., and others. "The Effect on Breastfeeding Rate of Regional Anesthesia Technique for Cesarean and Vaginal Childbirth." *Minerva Anesthesiology,* 1999, *65*(9), pp. 625–630.

   Leiberman, E., and O'Donoghue, C. "Unintended Effects of Epidural Analgesia During Labor: A Systematic Review." *Journal of Obstetric Gynecology,* 2002, *186*(5), Suppl. pp. S31–S68.

Leighton, B. L., and Halpern, S. H. "The Effects of Epidural Analgesia on Labor, Maternal, and Neonatal Outcomes: A Systematic Review." *American Journal of Obstetrics and Gynecology*, 2002, *186*(5), Suppl. pp. S69–S77.

Crowell, M. "Relationship Between Obstetric Analgesia and Time of Effective Breast Feeding." *Journal of Nurse Midwifery*, 1994, *39*(3), pp. 150–156.

13. Crystle, C. D., and others. "The Leboyer Method of Delivery: An Assessment of Risk." *Journal of Reproductive Medicine*, 1980, *5*, pp. 267–271.

14. Lavender, T., Hofmeyr, G. J., Neilson, J. P., Kingdon, C., and Gyte, G.M.L. "Caesarean Section for Non-Medical Reasons at Term." (Extract and summary.) *Cochrane Database of Systematic Reviews*, 2007, iss. 1. www.cochrane.org/reviews/en/ab004660.html: Apr. 24, 2006.

15. Hamilton, B. E., and others. "Births: Preliminary Data for 2004." *National Vital Statistics Report*, 2005, *54*(8). Centers for Disease Control and Prevention. www.cdc.gov/nchs/data/nvsr/nvsr54/nvsr54 _08.pdf.

16. Glicksman, M., and DiGeronimo, T. F. *Complete Idiots Guide to Pregnancy and Childbirth.* New York: Alpha Books, 2004.

17. Laubereau, B., and others. "Caesarean Section and Gastrointestinal Symptoms, Atopic Dermatitis, and Sensitization During the First Year of Life." *Child: Care, Health and Development*, 2005, *31*(1), pp. 124–125.

CHAPTER THREE: THE NURSERY

1. U.S. Environmental Protection Agency. *Protect Your Family from Lead in Your Home.* www.epa.gov/lead/pubs/leadpdfe.pdf.

2. U.S. Environmental Protection Agency. "Organic Gases." www.epa .gov/iaq/voc.html. Sept. 11, 2006.

3. Lundquist, P., and Ikramuddin, A. "PVC: The Most Toxic Plastic." Children's Health Environmental Coalition. www.checnet.org /healthehouse/education/articles-detail.asp?Main_ID=185. Sept. 2001.

4. "Recycled Wood Flooring." ToolBase Services. www.toolbase.org /Technology-Inventory/Interior-Partitions-Ceilings/recycled-wood-flooring. 2006.

5. "Cork Flooring." Build It Green. www.builditgreen.org/resource/index .cfm?fuseaction=factsheet_detail&rowid=8.

6. *A Memorandum of Understanding for Carpet Stewardship.* http://eerc .ra.utk.edu/ccpct/pdfs/mou-CarpetStewardship.pdf. Jan. 2002.

   "Frequently Asked Questions." Carpet America Recovery Effort. www .carpetrecovery.org/faqs.php#8.

7. "Carpet." Build It Green. www.builditgreen.org/resource/index.cfm ?fuseaction=factsheet_detail&rowid=6.

8. "Carpet."

9. "FSC Certified Wood." Build It Green. www.builditgreen.org /resource/index.cfm?fuseaction=factsheet_detail&rowid=12.

10. Co-op America. "Green Consumer Tip." *National Green Pages.* Wash- ington, D.C.: Co-op America, 2005.

11. Lundquist, P. "Toxic Toys? No Thank You!" Children's Health Environ- mental Coalition. www.checnet.org/healthehouse/education/articles- detail.asp?Main_ID=138. Jan. 14, 2005.

12. U.S. Environmental Protection Agency. "An Introduction to Indoor Air Quality." www.epa.gov/iaq/formalde.html. Sept. 25, 2006.

13. Chik, B. "Five Problems with Baby Mattresses." Healthy Child. www .healthychild.com/toxic-chemicals-baby-mattress.htm.

14. Reeves, M. "PAN Promotes Organic Cotton Around the World." *Global Pesticide Campaigner,* 1998, *8*(1). www.panna.org/resources/pestis /PESTIS980522.8.html.

15. "Your Baby's Bottom Line." OrganicAuthority.com. www.organic authority.com/index2.php?option=com_content&do_pdf=1&id=50. 2005.

16. "Diapers." *Green Guide.* www.thegreenguide.com/reports/product .mhtml?id=45. June 6, 2006.

   Seventh Generation. www.seventhgeneration.com/making_difference/ newsletter_article.php?issue=48&article=324.

17. "Cloth Diapers." Eartheasy. www.eartheasy.com/live_clothdiapers .htm. 2007.

18. Seventh Generation. "Diaper Daze." *Non-Toxic Times Newsletter,* June 2003, *4*(8).

19. Environment Agency. "Disposable Nappies or Reusables—Does It Make Any Difference to Our Environment?" www.environment-agency .gov.uk/yourenv/857406/1072214.

20. "Air Fresheners Can Make Mothers and Babies Ill." ALSPAC press release. www.alspac.bris.ac.uk/press/air_fresheners.shtml. Oct. 19, 2004.

21. Critchell, S. "Babies Go Green." AP, Aug. 29, 2006. https://allerair.com /air-quality-library/story.php/ret/1159.

22. Lundquist, 2005.

23. Greenpeace USA. "Toxic Toy Story." www.greenpeace.org/raw/content /usa/press/reports/toxic-toy-story.html. Nov. 8, 2003.

24. Greenpeace USA, 2003.

25. Greenpeace USA. "Go PVC-Free." www.greenpeace.org/usa/campaigns /toxics/go-pvc-free. Nov. 30, 2005.

26. Lundquist, 2005.

27. Roosevelt, M. "What's Toxic in Toyland." *Time*, Dec. 11, 2006, p. 78.

CHAPTER FOUR: THE KITCHEN

1. "American Academy of Pediatrics Work Group on Breastfeeding." *Pediatrics*, 1997, *100*, pp. 1035–1039.

2. Michels, D. "A Quick Look at Breastfeeding's Most Revolutionary Year Yet." *Leaven*, 1998, *34*(6), pp. 115–118.

3. Uvnas-Moberg, K. "Oxytocin May Mediate the Benefits of Positive Social Interaction and Emotions." *Psychoneuroendocrinology*, 1998, *23*, pp. 819–835.

   De Wied, D., Diamant, M., and Fodor, M. "Central Nervous System Effects of the Neurohypophyseal Hormones and Related Peptides." *Frontiers in Neuroendocrinology*, 1993, *14*, pp. 251–302.

4. Mezzacappa, E. S. "Breastfeeding and Maternal Stress Response and Health." *Nutrition Review*, July 2004, *62*, pp. 261–268.

5. Radford, A. "Breastmilk: A World Resource." World Alliance for Breastfeeding Action. www.parentingweb.com/lounge/WABA_enviro .htm. 2006.

6. Gordon, S., and editors of *Consumer Reports*. *Consumer Reports Best Baby Products*. (8th ed.) Yonkers, N.Y.: Consumers Union, 2004.

7. U.S. Department of Health and Human Services. "Benefits of Breast-feeding." National Woman's Health Information Center. www .4woman.gov/Breastfeeding/index.cfm?page=227. Oct. 2005.

8. "Bisphenol A: Toxic Plastics Chemical in Canned Food." *Environmental Working Group*. Mar. 2007.

9. Fox, M. K., Reidy, K., Novak, T., and Zieglar, P. "Sources of Energy and Nutrients in the Diets of Infants and Toddlers." *Journal of the American Dietetic Association*, 2006, *106*, pp. 28–42.

10. Nagabhushan, M. [Research presented at the International Scientific Conference on Childhood Leukaemia, sponsored by Children with Leukaemia, www.leukaemia.org], London, Sept. 6–10, 2004.

11. Asai, A., Nakagawa, K., and Miyazawa, T. "Antioxidative Effects of Turmeric, Rosemary and Capsicum Extracts on Membrane Phospholipid Peroxidation and Liver Lipid Metabolism in Mice." *Bioscience, Biotechnology, and Biochemistry*, 1999, *63*, pp. 2118–2122.

    Yetukuri, L., and others. "Bioinformatics Strategies for Lipidomics Analysis: Characterization of Obesity Related Hepatic Steatosis." *BMC Systems Biology*, 2007, *1*, pp. 1–12.

12. Jacobson, M. F. *Six Arguments for a Greener Diet*. Washington, D.C.: Center for Science in the Public Interest, 2006, p. 11.

13. Ash, M., Livezey, J., and Dohlman, E. *Soybean Backgrounder*. Outlook Report No. OCS-200601. U.S. Department of Agriculture, Economic Research Service. www.ers.usda.gov/publications/OCS/apr06/OCS 200601. Apr. 2006.

14. U.S. Department of Agriculture, Economic Research Service. Briefing Rooms: Soybeans and Oil Crops: Background. www.ers.usda.gov /Briefing/SoybeansOilcrops/background.htm. Mar. 13, 2007.

15. U.S. Department of Agriculture, Pesticide Data Program. *Annual Summary Calendar Year 2005*. www.ams.usda.gov/Science/pdp /Summary2005.pdf. Nov. 2006. (This summary reports that 14.5 percent of soybeans had residues of chlorpyrifos.)

    U.S. Department of Agriculture, Pesticide Data Program. *Annual Summary Calendar Year 2004*. www.ams.usda.gov/Science/pdp /Summary2004.pdf. Feb. 2006. (This summary reports that 28.9 percent of soybeans were contaminated with chlorpyrifos.)

16. U.S. Department of Agriculture, Economic Research Service. "Adoption of Genetically Engineered Crops in the U.S.: Soybeans." [Table.] www.ers.usda.gov/Data/biotechcrops/ExtentofAdoptionTable3.htm. July 14, 2006.

    U.S. Department of Agriculture, Economic Research Service. "Adoption of Genetically Engineered Crops in the U.S." www.ers.usda.gov /Data/biotechcrops. July 14, 2006.

    Fernandez-Cornejo, J., and Caswell, M. *The First Decade of Genetically Engineered Crops in the United States*. USDA Economic Information Bulletin No. 11. www.ers.usda.gov/publications/EIB11. Apr. 2006.

17. Fernandez-Cornejo and Caswell, 2006.

18. Mendoza, T. C. "Evaluating the Benefits of Organic Farming in Rice Agroecosystems in Philippines." *Journal of Sustainable Agriculture,* 2004, *24*(2), pp. 93–115.

19. Davis, D., Epp, M., and Riordan, H. "Changes in USDA Food Composition Data for 43 Garden Crops, 1950 to 1999." *Journal of the American College of Nutrition,* 2004, *23*(6), pp. 669–682.

20. Benbrook, C. M. *Elevating Antioxidant Levels in Food Through Organic Farming and Food Processing.* An Organic Center State of Science Review. http://organic.insightd.net/reportfiles/Antioxidant_SSR.pdf. Jan. 2005.

21. Plazier, J. C. "Feeding Forage to Prevent Rumen Acidosis in Cattle." University of Manitoba, Faculty of Agricultural and Food Sciences. www.umanitoba.ca/afs/fiw/020704.html. July 4, 2002.

22. Diez-Gonzalez, F., and others. "Grain Feeding and the Dissemination of Acid-Resistant Escherichia Coli from Cattle." *Science,* 1998, *281*, pp. 1666–1668.

   Russell, J. B., Diez-Gonzalez, F., and Jarvis, G. N. "Potential Effects of Cattle Diets on the Transmission of Pathogenic Escherichia Coli to Humans." *Microbes and Infection,* 2000, *2*, pp. 45–53.

   Benbrook, C. M. "Published Research on the Sources and Spread of E. Coli O157." Organic Center. www.organic-center.org/science.hot .php?action=view&report_id=61. Sept. 2006.

23. Rule, D. C., and others. "Comparison of Muscle Fatty Acid Profiles and Cholesterol Concentrations of Bison, Beef Cattle, Elk, and Chicken." *Journal of Animal Science,* 2002, *80*, pp. 1202–1211.

24. U.S. Department of Agriculture, Economic Research Service. Briefing Rooms: Corn. www.ers.usda.gov/Briefing/Corn. Apr. 20, 2006.

25. U.S. Department of Agriculture, Economic Research Service, 2007.

   U.S. Department of Agriculture, Economic Research Service. "U.S. Consumption of Plant Nutrients." [Table.] www.ers.usda.gov/Data /FertilizerUse/Tables/Table1.xls. (Table indicates that total U.S. 2005 fertilizer use was 22,146,200 tons, or 44.3 billion pounds.)

26. U.S. Department of Agriculture, Economic Research Service. "Adoption of Genetically Engineered Crops in the U.S.: Corn Varieties." [Table.] www.ers.usda.gov/Data/biotechcrops/ExtentofAdoptionTable 1.htm. July 14, 2006.

U.S. Department of Agriculture, Economic Research Service. "Adoption of Genetically Engineered Crops in the U.S." www.ers.usda.gov/Data/biotechcrops. July 14, 2006.

Fernandez-Cornejo and Caswell, 2006.

27. "Hypoxia in the Gulf of Mexico: A Growing Problem." Institute for Agriculture and Trade Policy, Minneapolis, MN, 2002. http://www.iatp.org/iatp/factsheets.cfm?accountID=258&refiD=36133.

"Hypoxia, the Gulf of Mexico's Summertime Foe." *Watermarks, Louisiana Coastal Wetlands Planning, Protection, and Restoration News,* Sept. 2004, pp. 3–5. www.lacoast.gov/watermarks/2004-09/watermarks-2004-10.pdf.

Berman, J. R., Arrigo, K. R., and Matson, P. A. "Agricultural Runoff Fuels Large Phytoplankton Blooms in Vulnerable Areas of the Ocean." *Nature,* 2005, *434,* pp. 211–214.

28. Ahmad, K. "United Nations Calls for Tighter Control on Pesticide Use in Poor Nations." *Lancet,* 2002, *360*(9345), p. 1574.

29. "Frequently Asked Questions." National Cotton Council. www.cotton.org/edu/faq/index.cfm. Oct. 2002.

30. U.S. Department of Agriculture, Economic Research Service. Briefing Rooms: Cotton. www.ers.usda.gov/Briefing/Cotton. Sept. 22, 2006.

31. Jacobson, M., and Center for Science in the Public Interest. *Six Arguments for a Greener Diet: How a Plant-Based Diet Could Save Your Health and the Environment.* Washington, D.C.: Center for Science in the Public Interest, 2006.

32. Committee on Nutrition. "The Use and Misuse of Fruit Juice in Pediatrics." *Pediatrics,* 2001, *107*(5), pp. 1210–1213.

33. Water Quality Association. "Well Water Concerns and Contaminants." *Water Review,* 1992. www.wqa.org/pdf/consumer%20briefs/cwellh2o.pdf.

34. U.S. Environmental Protection Agency. "Frequently Asked Questions." Ground Water & Drinking Water. www.epa.gov/safewater/faq/faq.html. Feb. 20, 2007.

35. Environmental Working Group. *A National Assessment of Tap Water Quality.* National Tap Water Quality Database. www.ewg.org/tapwater/findings.php. Dec. 20, 2005.

36. Harris Interactive. "Three-Quarters of U.S. Adults Agree Environmental Standards Cannot Be Too High and Continuing Improvements

Must Be Made Regardless of Cost." Harris Poll no. 77. www.harris interactive.com/harris_poll/index.asp?PID=607. Oct. 13, 2005.

37. U.S. Environmental Protection Agency. "Private Drinking Water Wells." www.epa.gov/safewater/privatewells/index2.html. Feb. 21, 2006.

38. Water Quality Association, 1992.

39. U.S. Department of Energy, U.S. Environmental Protection Agency, cited in "Good, Green Livin'." *Wired*, Oct. 2006, p. 62.

40. Energy Star. "Useful Facts & Figures." www.energystar.gov/index.cfm ?c=energy_awareness.bus_energy_use#homeappliance.

41. U.S. Environmental Protection Agency. "Keep Some Money in Your Wallet This Winter." EPA Newsroom. http://yosemite.epa.gov/opa /admpress.nsf/a8f952395381d3968525701c005e65b5/6f2717b2150d9 1ae8525721a004c74f8!OpenDocument. Nov. 2, 2006.

42. Energy Star, "Useful Facts & Figures."

43. DeBare, I. "Ridding the World of Plastic Forks." *San Francisco Chronicle*, Jan. 7, 2007. www.sfgate.com/cgi-bin/article.cgi?file=/c/a/2007/01 /07/BUG8KNE27Q1.DTL.

44. U.S. Department of Energy," Good, Green Livin'."

45. Union of Concerned Scientists. "Three Home Energy Hogs." *Earthwise*, 2006, *8*(4). www.ucsusa.org/publications/earthwise/three-home-energy-hogs.html.

46. "Kitchen Energy Savers." Eartheasy. www.eartheasy.com/eat_kitchen _enersave.htm.

47. Traber, A. "Elements of a Green Kitchen." GreenHomeGuide. www .greenhomeguide.com/index.php/knowhow/entry/645/C222. June 12, 2005.

CHAPTER FIVE: THE BATHROOM

1. Janjua, N. R., and others. "Systemic Absorption of the Sunscreens Benzophenone-3, Octyl-Methoxycinnamate, and 3-(4-Methyl-Benzylidene) Camphor After Whole-Body Topical Application and Reproductive Hormone Levels in Human." *Journal of Investigative Dermatology*, 2004, *123*, pp. 57–61.

2. U.S. Food and Drug Administration, Center for Food Safety and Applied Nutrition. *Cosmetic Handbook*. www.cfsan.fda.gov/~dms /cos-hdb1.html. 1992.

3. Code of Federal Regulations, Title 21, sec. 701.3, rev. Apr. 1, 2002.

4. Swan, S. H., and others. "Decrease in Anogenital Distance Among Male Infants with Prenatal Phthalate Exposure." *Environmental Health Perspectives*, 2005, *113*, pp. 1056–1061.

5. "Nail Polishes to Become a Little Safer." Campaign for Safe Cosmetics. www.safecosmetics.org/newsroom/press.cfm?pressReleaseID=19. Aug. 30, 2006.

6. Smital, T., and others. "Emerging Contaminants—Pesticides, PPCPs, Microbial Degradation Products and Natural Substances as Inhibitors of Multixenobiotic Defense in Aquatic Organisms." *Mutation Research*, 2004, *552*, pp. 101–117.

7. De Sutter, A.I.M., Lemiengre, M., and Campbell, H. "Antihistamines for the Common Cold." (Extract and summary.) *Cochrane Database of Systematic Reviews*, 2007, iss. 1. www.cochrane.org/reviews/en/ab001 267.html. May 28, 2003.

8. American College of Chest Physicians. "Guidelines for Evaluating Cough in Pediatrics." *Chest*, 2006, *129*, Suppl. pp. 260S–283S.

9. American Academy of Pediatrics Subcommittee on Management of Acute Otitis Media. "Diagnosis and Management of Acute Otitis Media." *Pediatrics*, 2004, *113*, pp. 1451–1465.

10. "Air Fresheners Can Make Mothers and Babies Ill." ALSPAC press release. www.alspac.bris.ac.uk/press/air_fresheners.shtml. Oct. 19, 2004.

CHAPTER SIX: THE GARDEN

1. "Natural Lawn Care." Eartheasy. www.eartheasy.com/grow_lawn _care.htm.

2. Environmental Control Corporation. [From the entry on Zerofootprint's Web page "Green Organizations: Your Guide to the World of Green Commerce."] www.zerofootprint.net/organizations/1940.

3. "Natural Lawn Care."

4. "Natural Garden Pest Control." Eartheasy. www.eartheasy.com/grow _nat_pest_cntrl.htm.

5. Environmental Protection Agency. www.epa.gov/oppad001/reregis tration/cca/cca_consumer_safety.htm.

6. "Plants and Indoor Air Quality." Ecospecifier. www.ecospecifier.org /knowledge_base/technical_guides/plants_indoor_air_quality__1.

7. Wolverton, B. C., Johnson, A., and Bounds, K. *Interior Landscape Plants for Indoor Air Pollution Abatement*. National Aeronautics and

Space Administration report, Sept. 1989. (Available from the John C. Stennis Space Center, Stennis Space Center, MS 39529-6000.)

8. Wolverton, Johnson, and Bounds, 1989.

9. "Indoor Plants Combat Pollution." Perfection PlantHire. www.perfectionplanthire.com.au/HealthBenefits.htm.

10. "Plants Provide Health Benefits, Studies Show." *Gannett News Service*, May 1, 2004. www.azcentral.com/home/garden/articles/0501ho10fill01.html.

11. "Kitchen Gardening." HGTV.com. www.hgtv.com/hgtv/gl_containers_other/article/0,1785,HGTV_3560_1379790,00.htm.

12. "Ten Best Herbs for Indoors." *Organic Gardening*, 2007. www.organicgardening.com/feature/0,7518,s1-5-71-378,00.htm.

CHAPTER SEVEN: THE WHOLE HOUSE

1. U.S. Environmental Protection Agency. "An Introduction to Indoor Air Quality." www.epa.gov/iaq/voc.html. 2006.

2. U.S. Environmental Protection Agency, 2006.

3. "Reduce Your Impact at Home," 2006. [Page on the Web site of the film *An Inconvenient Truth*.] www.climatecrisis.net/takeaction/whatyoucando.

4. Smith, R. "Less Power to the People." *Wall Street Journal*, Oct. 16, 2006.

5. Sachs, H. "Cheap and Easy Ways to Cut Energy Bills This Winter." *Write on the Money*, Fall 2006. [Newsletter of Hudson City Savings Bank.]

6. "Reduce Your Impact at Home," 2006.

7. "Making Your Bathroom Healthy, Efficient and Comfortable." GreenHomeGuide. www.greenhomeguide.com/index.php/knowhow/entry/706/C217. Feb. 13, 2007.

8. "Saving Water in the Bathroom." Eartheasy. www.eartheasy.com/article_bathroom_water_save.htm.

"Reduce Your Impact at Home," 2006.

9. "Making Your Bathroom Healthy, Efficient and Comfortable," 2007.

10. Union of Concerned Scientists. "Three Home Energy Hogs." *Earthwise*, 2006, *8*(4). www.ucsusa.org/publications/earthwise/three-home-energy-hogs.html.

11. American Council for an Energy-Efficient Economy. "Frequently Asked Questions." *Consumer Guide to Home Energy Savings: Condensed Online Version*. www.aceee.org/consumerguide/faqs.htm. Mar. 2007.

12. "Energy Bill Burning You?" *Real Simple*, Aug. 27, 2006. www.truthout .org/issues_06/082806EC.shtml.

13. Green Guide. "Good, Clean Fun." Grist. www.grist.org/advice/posses sions/2003/03/18/possessions-cleaning/index.html. Mar. 18, 2003.

14. "Reduce Your Impact at Home," 2006.

15. American Council for an Energy-Efficient Economy, 2007.

16. Borkowski, L., and Tarver-Wahlquist, S. "Tackling the Climate Crisis." *Co-op America Quarterly*, Fall 2006, iss. 70. www.coopamerica.org /PDF/CAQ70.pdf.

17. "Cooling Our Heels." *Scientific American*, Sept. 8, 2006.

18. Lawrence Berkeley National Lab. "Standby Power FAQ." 2002. http: //standby.lbl.gov/faq.html.

19. Smith, 2006.

20. "Reduce Your Impact at Home," 2006.

21. Copeland, M. "Go Green, a Smart Home Improvement." *Business 2.0*, Oct. 31, 2006. http://money.cnn.com/2006/10/24/magazines/business 2/newrules_gogreen.biz2/index.htm.

22. "Reduce Your Impact at Home," 2006.

23. U.S. Environmental Protection Agency. "Keep Some Money in Your Wallet This Winter." EPA Newsroom. http://yosemite.epa.gov/opa /admpress.nsf/a8f952395381d3968525701c005e65b5/6f2717b2150d9 1ae8525721a004c74f8!OpenDocument. Nov. 2, 2006.

24. "Take Action!" Stop Global Warming. www.stopglobalwarming .org/sgw_actionitems.asp.

25. Korfhage, A. "Greening Your Office." Co-op America Business Network. www.coopamerica.org/cabn/resources/greenoffice.cfm.

26. "Energy Bill Burning You?" 2006.

27. Korfhage, "Greening Your Office."

28. Neil, D. "A Mere Tinge of Green." *Los Angeles Times*, Jan. 17, 2007. www.evworld.com/view.cfm?page=news&newsid=14000&url=http:// tinyurl.com/2kl7dh.

29. "Hybrid Cars More Than Just a Fashionable Alternative." *Newwire Today*, Jan. 18, 2007. www.evworld.com/view.cfm?page=news&newsid =13998&url=.

30. Union of Concerned Scientists. "Hybrids Under the Hood." Hybrid Center. www.hybridcenter.org/hybrid-center-how-hybrid-cars-work-under-the-hood.html. 2005.

31. "Pros and Cons of Owning a Hybrid." *Traveler* [AAA North Jersey],

Jan./Feb. 2007, p. 26.

32. *Zap! Newsletter*, 2007. www.zapworld.com.

33. "About That 'New Car Smell'." *Eartheasy*. www.eartheasy.com/article
_new_car_smell.htm.2006.

34. Murphy, C. "Ten Ways to Reduce Emissions and Slow Global Warming." Stop Global Warming. www.stopglobalwarming/sgw_read.asp?id
=516198172006. Aug. 17, 2006.

35. Murphy, 2006.

36. Borkowski and Tarver-Wahlquist, 2006.

37. Borkowski and Tarver-Wahlquist, 2006.

38. Borkowski and Tarver-Wahlquist, 2006.

Green Information

THE WOMB

The following table outlines the various chemicals—including consumer product ingredients, banned industrial chemicals and pesticides, and waste by-products—found in the umbilical cords of ten newborn babies.

Sources and Uses of Chemicals in Newborn Blood	Chemical Family Name	Total Number of Chemicals found in Ten Newborns (Range in Individual Babies)
Common Consumer Product Chemicals (and Their Breakdown Products)		47 (23–38)
Pesticides, actively used in the United States	Organochlorine pesticides (OCs)	7 (2–6)
Stain- and grease-resistant coatings for food wrap, carpet, furniture (Teflon, Scotchgard, Stainmaster, and so on)	Perfluorochemicals (PFCs)	8 (4–8)
Fire retardants in TVs, computers, furniture	Polybrominated diphenyl ethers (PBDEs)	32 (13–29)
Chemicals Banned or Severely Restricted in the United States (and Their Breakdown Products)		212 (111–185)
Pesticides phased out of use in the United States	Organochlorine pesticides (OCs)	14 (7–14)
Stain- and grease-resistant coatings for food wrap, carpet, furniture (pre-2000 Scotchgard)	Perfluorochemicals (PFCs)	1 (1)
Electrical insulators	Polychlorinated biphenyls (PCBs)	147 (65–134)
Broad-use industrial chemicals— flame retardants, pesticides, electrical insulators	Polychlorinated naphthalenes (PCNs)	50 (22–40)

Sources and Uses of Chemicals in Newborn Blood	Chemical Family Name	Total Number of Chemicals found in Ten Newborns (Range in Individual Babies)
Waste By-Products		28 (6–21)
Garbage incineration and plastic production wastes	Polychlorinated and polybrominated dibenzo dioxins and furans (PCDD/F and PBDD/F)	18 (5–13)
Car emissions and other by-products of fossil fuel combustion	Polynuclear aromatic hydro-carbons (PAHs)	10 (1–10)
Power plants (coal burning)	Methylmercury	1 (1)
All Chemicals Found		**287** (154–231)

Source: Environmental Working Group analysis of tests of ten umbilical cord blood samples conducted by AXYS Analytical Services (Sydney, British Columbia) and Flett Research Ltd. (Winnipeg, Manitoba). www.ewg.org/reports/bodyburden2/execsumm.php

THE LABOR AND DELIVERY ROOM

Renewable Delivery

Renewable energy is available in three ways: from your utility company, through the purchase of renewable energy certificates (RECs), or through direct purchase from a renewable energy provider. If you deliver at home, any of these might work. In a hospital, RECs might be the way you can make the biggest impact. Either way, the Green-e Web site (www.green-e .org/base/re_products?cust=r) has a wonderful tool for finding renewable energy that works for you.

The greenhouse gas (GHG) advisory group of the Center for Resource Solutions has developed a Retail GHG Reduction Product Certification Program (www.resource-solutions.org/mv/ghg.html). Carbon offsets are intangible. If they have been certified, you'll know that the GHG reduction you purchased is verified: your purchase has resulted in real, additional, and measurable GHG reductions; the reductions came from the type of program advertised; and they came in the amount you purchased.

Midwife Credentials

According to the Midwives Alliance of North America, the following are the six most common credentials for midwives (www.mana.org/definitions .html):

1. **Certified Midwife (CM)**

   A certified midwife is a practitioner whose education is certified according to the requirements of the American College of Nurse-Midwives. The title Certified Midwife is also used in certain states as a designation of certification by the state and by the midwifery organization.

2. **Certified Nurse-Midwife (CNM)**

   A certified nurse-midwife is a practitioner who has a nursing degree and is a certified midwife according to the requirements of the American College of Nurse-Midwives.

3. **Certified Professional Midwife (CPM)**

   A certified professional midwife is an independent practitioner who has met the standards for certification set by the North American Registry of Midwives (NARM). The CPM is the only international credential that requires knowledge about and experience in out-of-hospital settings.

4. **Direct-Entry Midwife (DEM)**

   A direct-entry midwife is an independent practitioner who is educated in midwifery through self-study, apprenticeship, a midwifery school, or a college- or university-based program distinct from the discipline of nursing. A direct-entry midwife is trained to provide maternity care to healthy women and newborns throughout the childbearing cycle primarily in out-of-hospital settings.

5. **Licensed Midwife (LM)**

   A licensed midwife is a midwife who is licensed to practice in a particular jurisdiction (usually a state or province).

6. **Lay Midwife**

   The term *lay midwife* is used to designate an uncertified or unlicensed midwife who has been educated through informal routes such as self-study or apprenticeship rather than through a formal program. This term does not necessarily mean a low level of education, but rather that the midwife either chose not to become certified or licensed, or there was no certification available for her type of education (as was the case before the Certified Professional Midwife credential was available). Other similar terms to describe uncertified or unlicensed midwives are traditional midwife, traditional birth attendant, granny midwife, and independent midwife.

Types of Natural Childbirth

Natural childbirth is an umbrella term for any of the specific types of planned natural birth. Three popular methods include the following:

1. **Lamaze.** Lamaze emphasizes natural birth and offers a variety of relaxation methods to deal with the pain (although an overview of anesthesia and pain relief is included for women who prefer this). Patterned breathing, visualization, guided imagery, massage, and coaching from a partner are all part of this program, the premise of which is that it is possible to block pain messages to the brain. Find out more from Lamaze International at www.lamaze.org.

2. **The Bradley method.** This method was the first to introduce the idea of husband coaches in the delivery room and emphasizes the teamwork approach to bringing a baby into the world. This method does not try to block out pain, but rather encourages concentrated awareness that teaches the mother to trust her body and work through the pain, emphasizing relaxed abdominal breathing and relaxation exercises. Find out more about the Bradley method at www.bradleybirth.com.

3. **Grantly Dick-Read.** Dr. Dick-Read died in 1959, but his theory of natural childbirth remains the basis of many childbirth classes today, and his book *Childbirth Without Fear* (HarperCollins, 1959) is still widely read. The Grantly Dick-Read method relies on education about the birth process and relaxation exercises during labor to reduce the fear of childbirth and therefore the pain.

Types of Nerve Blocks

Drugs that cause a loss of sensation are called anesthetics. They interrupt the pathway of nerves that carry sensations of pain to the brain, blocking the pain message. (For this reason, they are commonly called nerve blocks.) The effect during childbirth leaves the expectant mom fully awake and aware.

There are various types of blocks you should talk about with your health care provider if this is an option you would like to explore.

- The *pudendal block* is administered through a needle inserted in the vaginal area. The numbness is localized and reduces pain only in that area, so it does not ease the pain of contractions.

- The *spinal block* is administered by inserting a long, fine needle into a space between the vertebra of the lower back. The block affects both sensory and motor nerves, numbing the body from the waist down and causing loss of voluntary leg movement and the ability to use abdominal muscles (thus most often used for cesarean deliveries).

- The *epidural block* is also administered by inserting a long, fine needle into a space between the vertebra of the lower back. It blocks only the sensory nerves to numb a person from the waist down, leaving full muscle movement. This is becoming the most widely used type of nerve block for relief of labor pain.

Breastfeeding Resources

Breastfeeding.com (www.breastfeeding.com)

Breastfeeding Links (http://users.aol.com/kristachan/bflink.htm)

Breastfeeding Support Consultants and Center for Lactation Education (www.bsccenter.org)

Bright Future Lactation Resource Center (www.bflrc.com/bflrc.htm)

Food and Nutrition Information Center of the Department of Agriculture (www.nal.usda.gov/fnic)

International Lactation Consultant Association (www.ilca.org)

[Katherine A. Dettwyler's] Thoughts on Breastfeeding (www.kathy dettwyler.org/dettwyler.html)

La Leche League International (www.lalecheleague.org)

World Alliance for Breastfeeding Action (www.waba.org.my)

Health Care Providers and Facilities

For further information about obstetric health care providers and birth centers, contact the following organizations:

The American College of Obstetricians and Gynecologists
409 12th Street, S.W.
P.O. Box 96920
Washington, D.C. 20090-6920
202-638-5577
www.acog.org

The American Medical Association
515 N. State Street
Chicago, IL 60610
800-621-8335
www.ama-assn.org

American College of Nurse-Midwives
8403 Colesville Road, Suite 1550
Silver Spring, MD 20910
240-485-1800
www.midwife.org

National Women's Health Resource
157 Broad Street, Suite 315
Red Bank, NJ 07701
877-986-9472
www.healthywomen.org

La Leche League International
1400 N. Meacham Road
Schaumburg, IL 60173-4808
847-519-7730
www.lalecheleague.org

American Association of Birth Centers
3123 Gottschall Road
Perkiomenville, PA 18074
215-234-8068
www.birthcenters.org

THE NURSERY

Why Babies Are So Vulnerable

In 1993, in a congressionally mandated study, the National Academy of Sciences listed the primary factors that contribute to children's unique vulnerability to the harmful effects of chemicals:

- Pound for pound, a developing child's chemical exposures are greater than those of adults.

- An immature, porous blood-brain barrier allows greater chemical exposures to the developing brain.

- Children have lower levels of some chemical-binding proteins, allowing more of a chemical to reach "target organs."

- A baby's organs and systems are rapidly developing and thus are often more vulnerable to damage from chemical exposure.

- Systems that detoxify and excrete industrial chemicals are not fully developed.

- The longer future life span of a child compared to an adult allows more time for adverse effects to arise.

THE KITCHEN

More About Water Filtration Systems

Even when the annual drinking water quality report gives a thumbs-up to the safety level of your water, during your pregnancy it might be a good idea to buy a bit of "insurance" to further improve the quality. If you haven't done so already, this is a good time to purchase a home water treatment unit to increase the purity of your tap water.

Choosing the right water filter will depend on the contaminants you're trying to filter out. That's why before laying down your money, you should at the very least examine your annual drinking water quality report and, even better, get the water tested yourself. This will give you a clear picture of what it is you'd like to filter out—not all home treatment systems filter out all contaminants. In fact, they vary widely in complexity, price, and efficiency.

- **Point-of-use devices** are the water treatment systems that treat the water as it comes from the tap. They can be freestanding, plumbed in with a dedicated faucet, or connected to a refrigerator's water and ice dispensing system.

  Filter pitchers are stand-alone models that most often use granular-activated carbon and resins to bond with and trap contaminants.

  Distillers boil the water (killing many microbes) and then collect the purer vapor as filtered water, leaving many contaminants behind in the filter. (Note: distilled water can taste flat because the natural minerals and dissolved oxygen are often removed.)

  Reverse osmosis units force water through a membrane under pressure, leaving contaminants behind. (This is what we have in my home.)

- **Point-of-entry devices** are water filtration systems that are centrally attached to treat all water as it comes into the house.

  Adsorptive media filter water through a solid material (such as a carbon filter) that screens liquids, solids, and dissolved or suspended matter, preventing them from entering the home's water system.

  Aerators force water over air jets. Contaminants that easily turn into gases (such as gasoline components and radon) are removed.

- **Water softeners** exchange hard ions (calcium and magnesium) with softer ions (sodium or potassium). This reduces water hardness while also removing radium and barium.

If you choose a water treatment system with a physical filter, you will want to make sure that it uses a **micron filtration system**. In these systems, the smaller the filter holes, the more contaminants the filter can remove. Most highly recommended is an absolute one micron filter.

Water Filter Certification

So many choices. So many ways to get confused. But there is help out there to guide you to the right filtration system for your home. You can be sure that the claims on a filter's packaging are true if the product is certified by one of these three organizations, which are all accredited by the American

National Standards Institute. These organizations are also sources of more information on home water treatment systems in general.

NSF International
P.O. Box 131040
Ann Arbor, MI 48113
877-NSF-HELP (877-867-3435)
Web: www.nsf.org
E-mail: info@nsf.org

Underwriters Laboratories
333 Pfingsten Road
Northbrook, IN 60062
877-854-3577
Web: www.UL.com/water
E-mail: water@us.ul.com

Water Quality Association
4151 Naperville Road
Lisle, IL 60632
630-505-0160
Web: www.wqa.org
E-mail: info@mail.wqa.org

Be aware that an EPA registration or establishment number on a water filter is *not* an endorsement of the product. This registration means that the filter uses an agent to slow the growth of microbes within the filter. That's all.

Recommended models include the following:

- Culligan model 2300 and Aquasana AQ-4000 are installed under the sink, which provides a larger container through which to filter water and offers the widest range of chemical removal. They were tested extensively by former researchers of the EPA's Office of Drinking Water.

- Kenmore 38460 is recommended by *Consumer Reports* as a Best Buy. This under-sink model is certified to remove small particulates, sediment, and cysts.

- Omni CBF-20 and Omni 2500 are recommended because of their claim to remove these chemicals and additional pesticides.

- For water carafes, *Consumer Reports* recommends Pur Advantage CR-1500R and Brita Classic OB01; both had high ratings for the removal of chloroform and lead.

- GE SmartWater GXFM03C and the Pur Ultimate Horizontal FM-4700l ranked the best for faucet-mounted models. Both had high scores for the removal of chloroform and lead.

  You can buy these filters by going to www.filtersfast.com.

To Locate a Certified Drinking Water Laboratory

For a listing of certified drinking water laboratories for testing your water in your state, contact your state laboratory certification office, or call the EPA's Safe Drinking Water Hotline at 800-426-4791, or log on to its site at www.epa.gov/safewater/faq/sco.html.

For more information on your drinking water you can

- Contact your water supplier.

- Use the EPA question-and-answer database at http://safewater.custhelp.com/cgi-bin/safewater.cfg/php/enduser/std_alp.php.

- Contact your state drinking water program at www.epa.gov/safewater/dwinfo/index.html.

- Order publications from the EPA on various topics from source water protection to home well use at http://yosemite.epa.gov/water/owrc catalog.nsf.

- Read *A National Assessment of Tap Water Quality*, issued by the Environmental Working Group, posted on the National Tap Water Quality Database at www.ewg.org/tapwater/findings.php.

THE BATHROOM

Sites for Alternative Cleaning and Personal Care Product Information

National Institutes of Health—Household Products Database (http://householdproducts.nlm.nih.gov)

Consumers Union Guide to Environmental Labels (www.eco-labels
.org/home.cfm)

Centers for Disease Control and Prevention—Antibacterial Household Products (www.cdc.gov/ncidod/eid/vol7no3_supp/levy.htm)

EPA Fact Sheet—Safe Substitutes at Home (http://es.epa.gov/tech
info/facts/safe-fs.html)

Eco-Friendly Alternatives to Commercial Cleaners and Other Household Products (www.ems.org/household_cleaners/alternatives.html)

Children's Health Environmental Coalition—Recipes for Safer Cleaners (www.checnet.org/healthehouse/education/articles-detail.asp?
Main_ID=564)

To learn more about the safety of personal care products, take a look
at these Web sites:

The Campaign for Safe Cosmetics (www.safecosmetics.org)
This Web site gives you a wealth of information, including an up-to-
date list of the more than four hundred companies that have signed
the Compact for Safe Cosmetics. You will also find scientific reports,
FDA regulations, news, and a wealth of other materials and resources.

Skin Deep (www.cosmeticsdatabase.com)
This is a product guide with in-depth information on over fourteen
thousand personal care products and over seven thousand ingredients. Find out how the brands you use stack up. See alternative brands
that are safer for your baby and the environment. This is a resource
you can't do without.

Household Products Database (http://householdproducts.nlm.nih.gov)
What's in your personal care products? And, for that matter, what's in
your bathroom, under the sink, in your laundry room, in your closet,
in your garage? This government database provided by the National
Library of Medicine lets you look up ingredients found on labels or
look up products by brand name to learn about potential health or environmental effects.

You might also want to explore an in-depth study reported by Health Care
Without Harm, called "Aggregate Exposures to Phthalates in Humans";

you can find it at www.noharm.org/details.cfm?type=document&id=662. And be sure to read about the international campaign regarding phthalates in beauty products at www.nottoopretty.org.

Green Resources

GREEN READING

The Complete Organic Pregnancy; Deirdre Dolan and Alexandria Zissu (HarperCollins, 2006)

Conscious Style Home: Eco-Friendly Living for the 21st Century; Danny Seo (St. Martin's Press, 2001)

Eco Chic: Organic Living; Rebecca Tanqueray (Carlton Books, 2000)

Food not Lawns; H. C. Flores (Chelsea Green, 2006)

Good Green Homes; Jennifer Roberts (Givvings Smith, 2003)

The Green House: New Directions in Sustainable Architecture; Alanna Stang and Christopher Hawthorne (Princeton Architectural Press, 2005)

Green Living: A Practical Guide to Eating, Gardening, Energy Saving and Housekeeping for a Healthy Planet; Sarah Callard and Diane Millis (Carlton Publishing Group, 2002)

Green Remodeling: Changing the World One Room at a Time; David Johnson and Kim Master (New Society Publishers, 2004)

Home Safe Home; Debra Lynn Dadd (Tarcher, 1997)

It's Easy Being Green: A Handbook for Earth-Friendly Living; Crissy Trask (Gibbs Smith, 2006)

The Lazy Environmentalist: Your Guide to Easy, Stylish, Green Living; Josh Dorfman (Stewart, Tabori & Chang, 2007)

Living Green: A Practical Guide to Simple Sustainability; Greg Horn (Freedom Press, 2006)

Natural Remodeling for the Not-So-Green House: Bringing Your Home into Harmony with Nature (Natural Home & Garden); Carol Venolia and Kelly Lerner (Lark Books, 2006)

The Newman's Own Organics Guide to a Good Life: Simple Measures That Benefit You and the Place You Live; Nell Newman and Joseph D'Agnese (Villard, 2003)

The Organic Cook's Bible; Jeff Cox (Wiley, 2006)

Organic Housekeeping; Ellen Sandbeck (Scribners, 2006)

Your Organic Kitchen: The Essential Guide to Selecting and Cooking Organic Foods; Jesse Ziff Cool (Rodale, 2000)

GREEN LINKS: HELPING YOU GO GREEN

The Environmental Working Group

www.ewg.org

Whether you're looking for a guide to personal care products, your local water supply, safe seafood, or which foods have the most pesticides, the Environmental Working Group is a great resource. It is a leading example of using the power of information to create change— on the individual, corporate, and policy level.

Healthy Child Healthy World

www.healthychild.org

This Web site is a wonderful, positive resource for learning about the effects of the environment on kids. I love the "daily tips that will help you reduce exposure to chemicals, toxins, and pollutants—for the benefit of your children's health, the health of your home, and the environment."

The Collaborative on Health and the Environment

www.healthandenvironment.org

A network of thousands of partners who are working collectively to advance knowledge and effective action about the links between human health and environmental factors.

DrGreene.com

At DrGreene.com, I've devoted myself to freely giving real answers to parents' real questions—from questions about those all too common childhood conditions to those that address the rarest childhood illnesses. In my answers, my goal is to combine cutting-edge science, practical wisdom, warm empathy, and a deep respect for parents, children, and the environment. Even more powerful are the many insights parents provide for each other. Come, share, and learn.

The Environmental Media Association

www.ema-online.org

EMA mobilizes the entertainment industry to educate people about green issues and to inspire them to action. Al Gore said of EMA, "No group has had a larger impact on the thinking Americans bring to the environment."

You Bet Your Garden

www.whyy.org/91FM/ybyg/

I listen to or read this weekly radio show/podcast/Web site, which offers great ideas for going green in the yard and garden. Mike McGrath is extremely witty, making it all the more fun.

Stop Global Warming

www.stopglobalwarming.org

Stop Global Warming is a site that shows you how to take action now to help avert the global warming crisis. I especially like the Calculate Your Carbon and Cash Savings! Calculator. They also have a great video library with clips that are sure to inspire.

Local Harvest

www.localharvest.org

Purchasing local, sustainable, organic foods is a powerful way to vote with your checkbook. The Local Harvest Web site provides a database of local farmer's markets, family farms, and other sources of sustainably grown food in your area.

Field to Plate

www.fieldtoplate.com

A beautiful guide to sustainable, local, seasonal food. I use the shopping guide all the time.

Chefs Collaborative

www.chefscollaborative.org

You won't always eat at home. When you eat out, you can choose restaurants that subscribe to these principles:

1. Food is fundamental to life, nourishing us in body and soul. The preparation of food strengthens our connection to nature. And the sharing of food immeasurably enriches our sense of community.

2. Good food begins with unpolluted air, land, and water; environmentally sustainable farming and fishing; and humane animal husbandry.

3. Food choices that emphasize delicious, locally grown, seasonally fresh, and whole or minimally processed ingredients are good for us, for local farming communities, and for the planet.

4. Cultural and biological diversity are essential for the health of the earth and its inhabitants. Preserving and revitalizing sustainable food, fishing, and agricultural traditions strengthen that diversity.

5. By continually educating themselves about sustainable choices, chefs can serve as models to the culinary community and the general public through their purchases of seasonal, sustainable ingredients and their transformation of these ingredients into delicious food.

6. The greater culinary community can be a catalyst for positive change by creating a market for good food and helping preserve local farming and fishing communities.

The Chef's Collaborative helps you locate specific restaurants that embody the principles. Simply click on the "restaurant locator" at the top of the front page to begin the process.

Green Festival

www.greenfestivals.org

If you get a chance to attend a Green Festival, don't miss it. You'll find all kinds of great information, as well as products and tools you can sample. And it's a lot of fun. I often speak at the Green Festival. If you see me there, please introduce yourself.

Consumer Reports

greenerchoices.org
eco-labels.org.

The Consumers Union offers consumer green information on these two Web sites. Search them for information about remodeling, electronics, appliances, home and garden products, autos, and food. These sites also give tips about how to address environmental and health issues when considering product purchases, uses, recycling, and disposal.

SustainLane

www.sustainlane.com

This site brings "green to the mainstream" through three key offerings:

1. *SustainLane Government and U.S. city rankings.* This online knowledge base with more than 275 participating U.S. cities and counties is a clearinghouse for state and local government to share best sustainability practices. SustainLane's ranking of the fifty largest U.S. cities is "the nation's most complete report card on urban sustainability."

2. *The Unsustainables.* This series of animated episodes available on air and online depicts the lives of a blended family in a modern urban environment.

3. *SustainLane Reviews.* This is a place to share reviews on eco-friendly products, services, and local green businesses.

Green for Good

http://greenforgood.com

My friend David Kaufer founded this online community that "brings people together to share and provide the best ideas, information and products that allow them to live a greener lifestyle." Besides being a valuable resource, it is a great example of what a parent with vision can do to make a difference.

Queen of Green

www.dld123.com

Hailed as "the Queen of Green" by the *New York Times,* since 1982 Debra Lynn Dadd has been a leading consumer advocate for products and lifestyle choices that are better for health and the environment. Visit her Web site to sign up for her free e-mail newsletters and to browse links to thousands of nontoxic, natural, and earthwise products.

EcoChoices Natural Living Store

www.ecochoices.com

This site can help you create a home that is beautiful, natural, and safe for you and your family. It offers a wide selection of earth-friendly products.

ORGANIC INFORMATION

The Organic Center

www.organic-center.org

A great place to learn about the science behind the benefits of organic farming and organic foods, for you, your baby, and the environment. Here you'll find the latest news on organics, the hottest science, and links to lots of other resources.

Organic Trade Association

www.theorganicreport.org

Content for this site comes from members of the Organic Trade Association (OTA), the association for the organic industry in North America. The OTA offers *The O'Mama Report,* an online resource for parents who want to make the best possible decisions about organic agriculture and organic products. It is a community in which parents share their experience, ideas, and inspiration.

Organic.org

www.organic.org

This site offer many articles on organic foods, as well as recipes, product reviews, a store finder, newsletter, and information just for kids.

Pesticide Action Network of North America

www.panna.org

PANNA is working to replace toxic pesticides with ecologically sound and socially just alternatives. Their Pesticides Database is a great resource on this issue.

ENVIRONMENTAL LINKS

Earth 911 (www.earth911.org/master.asp)

Environmental Defense (www.environmentaldefense.org/home.cfm)

Environmental Working Group (www.ewg.org)

Natural Resources Defense Council (www.nrdc.org)

Nature Conservancy (www.nature.org/aboutus)

Sierra Club (www.sierraclub.org)

Co-op America (www.coopamerica.org)

Go Organic for Earth Day Campaign (www.organicearthday.org)

RECYCLING ORGANIZATIONS

Bureau of International Recycling

www.bir.org

This site is hosted by the international recycling leader, BIR. Most of the information is for industry insiders, but there are some helpful tips for consumers as well.

Recycler's World

www.recycle.net

Recycle.net is a resource for finding local information and options for recycling. They have a great calendar of recycling events for professionals and consumers. Did you know there was an annual conference that deals with composting and food waste recycling? You can find out when the next conference will be held at recycle.net.

Government Agencies

The Home Energy Saver (http://hes.lbl.gov/) This is a powerful Web-based do-it-yourself energy audit, sponsored by the U.S. Department of Energy (www.energy.gov)

U.S. Department of the Interior (www.doi.gov)

U.S. Environmental Protection Agency (www.epa.gov)

U.S. Food and Drug Administration (www.fda.gov)

NOTABLE EPA AND FDA INFORMATION

U.S. Environmental Protection Agency. *What Is the TSCA Chemical Substance Inventory?* www.epa.gov/oppt/newchems/pubs/inventory .htm. 2005.

U.S. Environmental Protection Agency. *Fact Sheets on New Active Ingredients.* www.epa.gov/opprd001/factsheets. 2005.

U.S. Environmental Protection Agency. *Pesticide Industry Sales and Usage: 1994 and 1995 Market Estimates.* www.epa.gov/oppbead1 /pestsales/95pestsales/market_estimates1995.pdf. 2002.

U.S. Environmental Protection Agency. *Water: Things You Can Do.* www.epa.gov/water/citizen/thingstodo.html. 2006.

U.S. Food and Drug Administration, Cosmetics Compliance Program. *Domestic Cosmetics Program.* www.cfsan.fda.gov/~comm/cp29001 .html. July 31, 2000.

U.S. Food and Drug Administration, Center for Food Safety and Applied Nutrition. *EAFUS: A Food Additive Database.* www.cfsan .fda.gov/~dms/eafus.html. 2005.

PUBLICATIONS

The Green Guide (http://thegreenguide.com)

Kiwi: Growing Families the Natural and Organic Way (www.kiwi magonline.com)

The National Green Pages (www.coopamerica.org/pubs/greenpages)

Sierra (www.sierraclub.org/sierra)

Waste Age (www.wasteage.com)

Waste News (www.wastenews.com/headlines.html)

Links to green publications from J. Ottman Consulting available at www.greenmarketing.com/other_resources/news_letters.html

FOR KIDS

Eco Kids (www.ecokidsonline.com/pub/index.cfm) has great information for kids in an interactive format.

Environmental Kids Club (www.epa.gov/kids/index.htm) is a government site that does a very nice job.

Greentimes (www.greenscreen.org) is a site by kids for kids. It has lots of articles written by high school kids in a voice that other kids can hear and appreciate.

Kids Recycle (www.kidsrecycle.org/index.php) has a great tag line: "Tools for zero waste!" Great tools for kids and teachers.

Niehs Kids' Pages (www.niehs.nih.gov/kids/recycle.htm) is the NIH recycling site for kids.

The Authors

ALAN GREENE, M.D., F.A.A.P., is the founder of the leading pediatric Web site, DrGreene.com. Dr. Greene is a graduate of Princeton University and the University of California at San Francisco, and now teaches at Stanford University School of Medicine. He is an attending pediatrician at Packard Children's Hospital and serves on the board of directors of the Organic Center and the Center for Information Therapy, the advisory board of Healthy Child Healthy World, and as pediatric adviser for the Environmental Working Group. Dr. Greene is also a founding Partner of the Collaborative on Health and the Environment. He is the pediatric expert for WebMD, *Kiwi* magazine, and "The People's Pharmacy," as heard on National Public Radio. He is also the author of *From First Kicks to First Steps.*

Dr. Greene appears frequently on TV, radio, and Web sites, and in newspapers and magazines, including the *Today Show, Fox and Friends,* the *Wall Street Journal, Parenting, Parent, Child, Kiwi, Baby Talk, American Baby, Working Mother, Better Homes and Gardens,* and *Reader's Digest.*

He is the father of four, and always wears green socks.

JEANETTE PAVINI is the ConsumerWatch reporter for CBS TV 5 News in the San Francisco Bay Area, host of "The Real Deal" TV consumer show, and columnist for *Bay Area Parent* magazine. Her work has earned her five Emmy nominations, the Edward R. Murrow Award, and a National Headliner Award, among others. She has completed dozens of stories on how consumers can "shop smart" to help save the environment. Jeanette is also a mother who is committed to doing what it takes to keep her child healthy and the earth a sustainable place to live.

THERESA FOY DIGERONIMO, M.Ed., is the author of fifty books in the fields of parenting, education, and medicine. She is the coauthor of

College of the Overwhelmed and *Launching Our Black Children for Success,* both from Jossey-Bass. She is an adjunct professor of English at the William Paterson University of New Jersey, a high school teacher in her hometown of Hawthorne, New Jersey, and the mother of three children.

Index